ALEX FERGUSON

My Autobiography

ALEX FERGUSON

My Autobiography

HODDER &
STOUGHTON

First published in Great Britain in 2013 by Hodder & Stoughton
An Hachette UK company

12

A CIP catalogue record for this title is available from the British Library

Hardback ISBN 978 0 340 91939 2
Ebook ISBN 978 1 848 94863 1

Typeset in ITC New Baskerville 12/16 pt by Palimpsest Book Production Limited, Falkirk, Stirlingshire

Printed and bound in Great Britain by Clays Ltd, St Ives plc

Hodder & Stoughton policy is to use papers that are natural, renewable and recyclable products and made from wood grown in sustainable forests. The logging and manufacturing processes are expected to conform to the environmental regulations of the country of origin.

Hodder & Stoughton Ltd
338 Euston Road
London NW1 3BH

www.hodder.co.uk

To Bridget,
Cathy's sister, rock and best friend

CONTENTS

ACKNOWLEDGEMENTS

THERE are a number of people I want to thank for their help in putting together this book.

Firstly, I must pay tribute to Roddy Bloomfield, my editor, and his assistant Kate Miles. Roddy's wealth of experience, along with his support, was a godsend throughout. Combined with Kate's diligence, they make a formidable team.

Paul Hayward was remarkably easy to work with and a real professional. He kept me on track and I feel he has done a great job of collecting my thoughts and presenting them in a way that I am more than happy with.

Photographer Sean Pollock captured a number of images over a four year period, and has done a fantastic job. His laidback manner and discretion ensured that he got what he wanted without being intrusive in any way.

Les Dalgarno, my lawyer, gave sound guidance over the

course of producing the content; he is the most trusted and loyal of advisers and a great friend.

Overall, there were a large number of people who put in many hours in order to get to this point. Their efforts have been much appreciated by me and it has been a pleasure to have had such a talented team behind me.

PHOTOGRAPHIC ACKNOWLEDGEMENTS

The author and publisher would like to thank the following for permission to reproduce photographs:

Action Images, Roy Beardsworth/Offside, Simon Bellis/Reuters/ Action Images, Jason Cairnduff/Livepic/Action Images, Chris Coleman/Manchester United/Getty Images, Dave Hodges/ Sporting Pictures/Action Images, Ian Hodgson/Reuters/Action Images, Eddie Keogh/Reuters/Action Images, Mark Leech/ Offside, Alex Livesey/Getty Images, Clive Mason/Getty Images, Mirrorpix, Gerry Penny/AFP/Getty Images, John Peters/ Manchester United/Getty Images, Matthew Peters/Manchester United/Getty Images, Kai Pfaffenbach/Reuters/Action Images, Popperfoto/Getty Images, Nick Potts/Press Association, John Powell/Liverpool FC/Getty Images, Tom Purslow/Manchester United/Getty Images, Ben Radford/Getty Images, Carl Recine/ Livepic/Action Images, Reuters/Action Images, Rex Features, Martin Rickett/Press Association, Matt Roberts/Offside, Neal Simpson/Empics Sport/Press Association, SMG/Press Association, SNS Group, Simon Stacpoole/Offside, Darren Staples/Reuters/ Action Images, Bob Thomas/Getty Images, Glyn Thomas/Offside, John Walton/Empics Sport/Press Association, Kirsty Wrigglesworth/ Press Association.

All other photographs are courtesy of Sean Pollock.

INTRODUCTION

SEVERAL years ago I began gathering my thoughts for this book, making notes in the spare time my job allowed me. It was always my plan to assemble a story that people inside and outside the game would find interesting.

So, although my retirement took the industry by surprise, this autobiography has been in my head for many years. It complements *Managing My Life,* an earlier volume. And therefore, while briefly reflecting on my youth in Glasgow and life-long friends made in Aberdeen, it focuses on my magical years in Manchester. An avid reader myself, I was eager to write a book that explained some of the mysteries in my line of work.

In a lifetime's journey in football, you will have dips, lows, defeats and disappointments. In my early years at Aberdeen and Manchester United, I decided right away that in order to build trust and loyalty with the players, I had to give it to them first. That is the starting point for the bond on which great institutions thrive. I was helped by my ability to observe. Some people walk into a room and don't notice anything. Use your eyes; it's all out there. I used this skill in my assessment of players' training habits, moods and behaviour patterns.

Of course I'll miss the banter of the dressing room and all my opponents in management: those wonderful characters of the old school who were the greats of the game when I came down to United in 1986. Ron Atkinson showed no bitterness after leaving the club and had nothing but praise for us. Jim Smith is a fantastic character and a good friend. His hospitality would keep you there all night. When I did get home, my shirt would be speckled with cigar ash.

Big John Sillett, who managed Coventry City, was another great companion, and I can never forget the late John Lyall, who guided me through my early years and was so generous with his time. My first encounter with Bobby Robson was in 1981 when Aberdeen knocked out Ipswich in the UEFA Cup. Bobby came into our dressing room and shook every player's hand. Sheer class, and his valued friendship was never forgotten. He was a big loss to our lives.

There were others of the old school who were survivors because they had a work ethic you had to admire. If I went to a reserve game, John Rudge and Lennie Lawrence would be there, along with one of the big personalities of the game whose Oldham teams brought a freshness that would never be replaced. I mean big Joe Royle. Oldham gave us some scary moments. Yes, I'll miss all that. Harry Redknapp and Tony Pulis are other great characters of my generation.

I was blessed to have had wonderful, loyal staff at United. Some of them worked for me for over 20 years. My P.A. Lyn Laffin, has followed me into retirement and is still my P.A., in my new office; Les Kershaw, Dave Bushell, Tony Whelan and Paul McGuinness. Kath Phipps on reception, who also ran my after-match lounge at Old Trafford, has worked at United for over 40 years. Jim Ryan, who has now retired, my brother Martin who scouted abroad for 17 years (a very difficult job), and Brian McClair.

Norman Davies: what a man. A loyal friend who passed away a few years ago. His replacement as kit man, Albert Morgan, is also a big personality who never wavered in his loyalty. Our doctor, Steve McNally, our head physio Rob Swire and all his staff, Tony Strudwick and his energetic bunch of sports scientists, our laundry girls, all the kitchen staff; the general office of John Alexander, Anne Wylie and all the girls. Jim Lawlor and all his scouting staff. Eric Steele, goalkeeping coach. Simon Wells and Steve Brown of the video analysis team. Our ground staff, led by Joe Pemberton and Tony Sinclair. Our maintenance team, with Stuart, Graham and Tony: all hard-working men. There are maybe one or two I've missed, but I'm sure they know I respected them all.

Assistants and coaches helped me greatly down the years. Archie Knox, a real ally to me in my early years, Brian Kidd, Nobby Stiles, Eric Harrison, a truly wonderful youth coach. Steve McClaren, a very innovative and energetic coach. Carlos Queiroz and René Meulensteen – two magnificent coaches – and my assistant manager, Mick Phelan, a really shrewd, observant, true football man.

The foundation of my longevity lies with Bobby Charlton and Martin Edwards. Their biggest gift to me was the time to build a football club, rather than a football team. Their support was followed by the great bond I had with David Gill over the last decade.

There was plenty of ground to cover in this book. I hope you enjoy retracing the steps with me.

PREFACE

NEARLY three decades before this moment, I had walked through that tunnel and onto the pitch for my first home game, feeling nervous and exposed. I had waved to the Stretford End and been introduced from the centre circle as Manchester United's new manager. Now, I strode onto the same pitch, full of confidence, to say goodbye.

The control I was able to exert over Manchester United was a privilege few managers will be lucky enough to know. However sure I felt of my abilities on the move south from Aberdeen in the autumn of 1986, there could have been no way of knowing it would turn out this well.

After the farewell in May 2013, the pivotal moments filled my thoughts: winning that FA Cup third-round tie against Nottingham Forest in January 1990, in which a Mark Robins goal sent us on our way to the final when my job was supposedly on the line; going through a whole month without winning a game, which gnawed away at my confidence.

Without the FA Cup victory over Crystal Palace nearly four years after my arrival, grave doubts would have been raised about my suitability for the job. We will never know how close I was to being sacked, because the decision was never forced on the United board. But without that triumph at Wembley, the crowds would have shrivelled. Disaffection might have swept the club.

Bobby Charlton would have opposed any move to dismiss me. He knew the work I was doing, the ground we were making up on the youth development side, the graft I was putting in, the hours I spent reforming the football operation. The chairman Martin Edwards knew it too, and it reflects well on those two men that they had the courage to stick by me in those dark days. Martin would have received plenty of angry letters demanding that I be cast aside.

Winning the 1990 FA Cup allowed us breathing space and deepened my sense that this was a wonderful club with which to win trophies. To win the FA Cup at Wembley made the good times roll. But on the morning after our victory, one newspaper declared: 'OK, you've proved you can win the FA Cup, now go back to Scotland.' I never forgot that.

one

REFLECTIONS

If I needed a result to epitomise what Manchester United were about it came to me in game No. 1,500: my last. West Bromwich Albion 5 Manchester United 5. Crazy. Wonderful. Entertaining. Outrageous.

If you were on your way to watch Manchester United you were in for goals and drama. Your heart was in for a test. I could have no complaints about us throwing away a 5–2 lead against West Brom within nine minutes. I still went through the motions of expressing my annoyance but the players could see right through it. I told them: 'Thanks boys. Bloody great send-off you've given me!'

David Moyes had already been named as my successor; as we sat in the dressing room after the match Ryan Giggs teased: 'David Moyes has just resigned.'

Despite our defensive frailties that day I was proud and relieved to be delivering this fine group of players and staff into David's care. My work was done. My family were there, in the Regis Suite, at West Brom's ground, and a new life stretched out before me.

It was one of those days that unfold like a dream. West Brom handled it with real class and looked after me perfectly. Later they sent me the team-sheets signed by both sets of players. Most of my family were with me: three sons, eight grandchildren and one or two close friends. It was a joy to me to have them there, and for us all to experience this final instalment together. Our family marched out as one.

Descending the steps of the team bus outside West Brom's ground, my intention was to savour every moment. It was not hard for me to let go because I knew the time was right. The night before the game the players let it be known that they wanted to make a presentation to mark my retirement. Their most special gift was a beautiful 1941 Rolex from the year I was born, with the time set at 3.03 p.m., the minute of my emergence into the world, in Glasgow, on 31 December 1941. They also handed me a book of photographs encapsulating my time at United, with the grandchildren and family on the centre-spread. Rio Ferdinand, a watch enthusiast, was behind the main gift idea.

After the book and watch were handed over and a round of applause spread round the room I noticed a particular look on some of the players' faces. It was a moment some weren't sure how to handle because they had always had me with them; some for 20 years. I could see a vacant expression that seemed to say: what's it going to be like now? Some had known no other manager but me.

There was still one game to play and I wanted it to be handled properly. We were three–nil up within half an hour but West Brom were in no mood to give me an easy send-off. John Sivebaek scored the first United goal of my time in charge, on 22 November 1986. The last was registered to Javier Hernández on 19 May 2013. At 5–2 to us it could have finished 20–2 in our favour. At 5–5 we might have lost 20–5. Defensively we were a shambles. West Brom scored three goals in five minutes, with Romelu Lukaku running up a hat-trick.

Despite the late avalanche on our goal, it was all light-hearted in the dressing room. After the final whistle we stayed on the pitch to wave to the United end. Giggsy pushed me forward and all the players held back. I was alone in front of a mosaic of happy faces. Our fans spent the entire day singing and chanting and bouncing. I would love to have won 5–2 but in a way 5–5 was a fitting sign-off. It was the first 5–5 draw in Premier League history and the first of my career: one last slice of history in my final 90 minutes.

Back in Manchester a deluge of post landed in my office. Real Madrid sent a beautiful gift: a solid silver replica of La Plaza de Cibeles, home to the fountain in Madrid where they celebrate league title wins, with a lovely letter from Florentino Pérez, the Real president. Another present arrived from Ajax and one from Edwin van der Sar. Lyn, my P.A., worked her way through heaps of correspondence.

For the home game against Swansea City the previous weekend, my last at Old Trafford, I had no idea what to expect, beyond a guard of honour. By then we were at the end of an intense week of telling family, friends, players and staff that I had chosen to move on to a new phase of my life.

The seeds of my decision to step down had been planted in the winter of 2012. Around Christmas-time the thought became sharp and clear in my head: 'I'm going to retire.'

'Why are you going to do that?' Cathy said.

'Last season, losing the title in the last game, I can't take another one like that,' I told her. 'I just hope we can win the League this time and reach the Champions League or FA Cup final. It would be a great ending.'

Cathy, who had lost her sister Bridget in October, and was struggling to come to terms with that bereavement, soon agreed it was the right course. Her take was that if I wanted to do other things with my life I would still be young enough. Contractually I was obliged to notify the club by 31 March if I was going to stand down that summer.

By coincidence David Gill had called me one Sunday in February and asked if he could come to see me at home. A Sunday afternoon? 'I bet he's resigning as chief executive,' I said. 'Either that or you're getting sacked,' Cathy said. David's news was that he would be standing down as chief executive at the end of the season. 'Bloody hell, David,' I said. And I told him that I had reached the same decision.

In the days that followed, David rang to tell me to expect a call from the Glazers. When it came I assured Joel Glazer that my decision had nothing to do with David relinquishing day-to-day control. My mind had been made up over Christmas, I told him. I explained the reasons. Cathy's sister dying in October had changed our lives. Cathy felt isolated.

Joel understood. We agreed to meet in New York, where he tried to talk me out of retiring. I told him I appreciated the effort he was making and thanked him for his support. He expressed his gratitude for all my work.

With no prospect of a change in my thinking, the discussion turned to who might replace me. There was a unanimous agreement – David Moyes was the man.

David came over to the house to discuss his potential availability. It was important to the Glazers that there was no long period of speculation when my retirement became official. They wanted the new man in place within days.

A lot of Scots have a dourness about them: a strong will. When they leave Scotland it tends to be for one reason only. To be successful. Scots don't leave to escape the past. They move away to better themselves. You see it all over the world, in America and Canada especially. Leaving the homeland creates a certain resolution. It's not a mask; it's a determination to get things done. The Scottish dourness others talk about sometimes applied to me as well.

The Scotsman abroad doesn't lack humour. David Moyes is not short of wit. In their jobs, though, the Scots are serious about their labours, an invaluable quality. People often said to me, 'I never see you smile during a game.' I would reply, 'I'm not there to smile, I'm there to win the match.'

David had some of these traits. I knew his family background. His father was a coach at Drumchapel, where I played as a lad. David Moyes senior. They have a good family feel about them. I'm not saying that's a reason to hire someone but you like to see good foundations in someone appointed to such high office. I left Drumchapel in 1957 when David senior would have been a young boy, so there was no direct crossover, but I knew their story.

The Glazers liked David. Right away they were impressed by him. The first point they will have noticed is that he is a straight-talker. It's a virtue to be straightforward about yourself. And to put one concern to bed, there is no way I would get in David's way. After 27 years as manager, why would I want to involve myself on the football side? This was my time to leave that part of my life behind. Equally David would have no trouble embracing our traditions. He was a fine judge of talent and laid on some marvellous football at Everton when he was allowed to sign a higher class of player.

I told myself I would have no regrets about retiring. That won't change. In your seventies it's easy to go downhill fast, physically and mentally. But I was busy from the moment I stepped aside, taking on projects in America and beyond. There was no risk of me lapsing into idleness. I was looking for new challenges.

One great difficulty, in the days around the announcement, was telling the staff at Carrington, our training ground. I particularly remember mentioning the changes in my life and Cathy's sister dying, and hearing a sympathetic, 'Aaah.' That really broke through my barriers. I felt a real jab of sentiment.

Rumours had begun circulating the day before the official statement. At that point I had still to tell my brother Martin. It was a difficult process to manage, especially from the New York Stock Exchange point of view, so the partial leaking of the news compromised me in relation to some of the people I wanted to confide in.

On the Wednesday morning, 8 May, I had all the football staff in the video analysis room, the main staff in the canteen and the players in their dressing room. The moment I walked into the dressing room to tell the squad we made the announcement via the club website. No mobile phones were allowed. I didn't want anyone communicating the news before I had been given the chance to tell everyone at the training ground. With the rumours, though, they knew something big was coming.

I told the players: 'I hope I haven't let some of you down, because you may have joined thinking I would stay.' We had told Robin van Persie and Shinji Kagawa, for example, that I would not be retiring any time soon, which was correct at the point I said it.

'Things change,' I continued. 'My wife's sister dying was one dramatic change. Also, I want to go out a winner. And I'm going out a winner.'

Shock could be seen in some of their faces. 'Go to the races today and enjoy it,' I said. 'See you on Thursday.' I had already given the players the Wednesday afternoon off to go to Chester. And everyone knew that. It was part of the plan. I didn't want people thinking the players were being heartless by attending Chester races on the day I brought the curtain down, which is why I made a point the week before of confirming they would go.

Then I went upstairs to the football staff and told them. They all applauded. 'Glad to get rid of you,' one or two remarked.

Of the two main groups the players were the more dumbstruck. Immediately in those circumstances questions will have filled their minds: 'Will the new manager like me? Will I still be here next season?' The coaches would be thinking: 'This could be the end for me.' The time was approaching for me to retreat from the scene of all this announcing and explaining and gather my thoughts.

I had decided in advance to go straight home because I knew there would be a seismic reaction in the media. I didn't want to be leaving Carrington through a swarm of press and flashing lights.

At home I locked myself in. Jason, my lawyer and Lyn sent texts simultaneously at the point the announcement was made. Lyn would have been sending texts consecutively for 15 minutes. Apparently 38 newspapers in the world carried the news on the front page, including the *New York Times*. There were 10- and 12-page supplements in the British papers.

The range and depth of that coverage was flattering. I had my run-ins with the written press down the years but I never held grudges. I know journalists are under a lot of pressure. They have to try to beat television, the internet, Facebook, Twitter, many things, and they may have an editor on top of them all the time. It's a hard industry.

The coverage proved also that the media held no grudges against me, despite all our conflicts. They recognised the value of my career and what I had brought to press conferences. They even made a presentation: a cake with a hair-dryer on top and a lovely bottle of wine. It was well received.

For the Swansea game the stadium announcer played Sinatra's 'My Way' and Nat King Cole's 'Unforgettable'. We won it the way we did so many of the 895 matches in which my teams prevailed: with a late goal, in the 87th minute, from Rio Ferdinand.

My speech on the pitch was all off the cuff. I had no script. All I knew was that I was not going to praise any individual. It was not about the directors, the supporters or the players: it was about Manchester United Football Club.

I urged the crowd to get behind the next manager, David Moyes. 'I'd like to remind you that we've had bad times here,' I said over the PA. 'The club stood by me. All my staff stood by me. The players stood by me. So your job now is to stand by our new manager. That is important.'

Had I not mentioned David, people might have asked: 'How about that, I wonder whether Ferguson wanted Moyes?' We needed to show our unconditional support for him. The club has to keep on winning. That was the wish that bound us all. I'm a director of the club. I want the success to go on as much as anyone. Now I can enjoy games the way Bobby Charlton has been able to since he retired. You see Bobby after a victory and his eyes are blazing, he's rubbing his hands. He loves it. I want that. I want to be able to attend European ties and tell people: I'm proud of this team, this is a great club.

In the event I found myself picking out Paul Scholes. I knew he would hate it but I couldn't stop myself. Paul was retiring as well. I also wished Darren Fletcher all the best in his recovery from a colonic illness, which few picked up on.

At an airport a few days later, a guy walked up to me with an envelope, saying: 'I was going to post this to you.' It was an article from an Irish paper arguing that I had left the club the way I had managed it: on my terms. Typical

Ferguson, the author wrote. I enjoyed that piece. That was how I saw my time in charge of United and I was proud to see it described that way.

As I slipped out of the picture, David brought in three of his own staff – Steve Round, Chris Woods and Jimmy Lumsden. He also added Ryan Giggs and Phil Neville, which meant that René Meulensteen, Mick Phelan and Eric Steele lost their jobs. It was David's call. I told him that if he kept my staff I would be delighted, but it was not for me to interfere or prevent him bringing in his own assistants.

Jimmy Lumsden had been with David a long time. I knew him from my Glasgow days. Jimmy was born about a mile from me, in the next district along from Govan. He is a good wee lad and a fine football man. It was just a disappointment that good men lost their jobs, which happens in football. But it was handled well. I told the three of them how sorry I was that they would not be staying. Mick, who was with me for 20 years, told me I had nothing to apologise for, and thanked me for all the great times we had shared together.

As I looked back I focused not only on the triumphs but also the defeats. I lost three FA Cup finals, to Everton, Arsenal and Chelsea. I lost League Cup finals to Sheffield Wednesday, Aston Villa and Liverpool. And two European Cup finals to Barcelona. That is part of the tapestry of Manchester United too: the recovery. I always kept in mind that it was not all victories and open-top parades. When we lost the FA Cup final to Everton in 1995 I said: 'That's it, I'm making changes here.' And we made them. We brought in the young players, the so-called Class of '92. We couldn't hold them back any longer. They were a special group of lads.

Losing football matches at Manchester United resonates with you. Mulling it over for a while and then carrying on in the same old way was never an option for me. When you lose a final it affects you deeply, especially if you have 23 shots on goal and the opposition have two, or you end up losing a penalty shoot-out. My first thought was always: 'Think quickly about what you should be doing.' My mind went straight to the business of improvement and recovery. It was an asset for me to be able to make quick calculations when it would have been easier just to be disheartened.

Sometimes defeats are the best outcomes. To react to adversity is a quality. Even in your lowest periods you are showing strength. There was a great saying: It's just another day in the history of Manchester United. In other words fighting back was part of our existence. If you are lackadaisical about defeats you can be sure there will be more to come. Often we would drop two points in a game by the opposition equalising with the last kick of the ball and then go on a six- or seven-game winning run. It was no coincidence.

For the fan there is a culture of going to work on the Monday assailed by emotion from the weekend's game. A guy wrote to me in January 2010 and said: 'Can you please refund me the £41 I paid for my ticket on Sunday? You promised me entertainment. I did not get entertainment on Sunday. Can I have my £41 back?' That was a fan. My idea was to write back saying: 'Can you please debit the £41 from my profit over the last 24 years?'

You win all these games against Juventus and Real Madrid and someone asks for their money back after a slightly quiet

Sunday. Is there any club in the world that can give you more heart-stopping moments than Manchester United? In any set of programme notes I might have warned the supporters: if we're losing 1–0 with 20 minutes to go, go home, or you might end up being carried out. You could finish up in the Manchester Royal Infirmary.

I hope no one will disagree when I say: nobody was short-changed. It was never dull.

two

GLASGOW ROOTS

T HE motto of the Ferguson clan in Scotland is: '*Dulcius ex asperis*' or, 'Sweeter after difficulties'. That optimism served me well through 39 years in football management. Over that time, from East Stirlingshire for four brief months in 1974, to Manchester United in 2013, I saw beyond adversity to the success on the other side. The act of controlling vast change year after year was sustained by a belief that we would prevail over any challenger.

Years ago, I read an article about me that said: 'Alex Ferguson has done really well in his life despite coming from Govan.' Spot the offending phrase. It's precisely because I started out in the shipbuilding district of Glasgow that I achieved what I did in football. Origins should never be a barrier to success. A modest start in life can be a help more than a hindrance. If you're examining successful people, look at their mother and father, study what they did, for clues about energy and motivation. A working-class background wasn't a barrier for many of my greatest players. On the contrary, often it was part of the reason they excelled.

In my time in the dug-out, I advanced from managing East Stirling players on £6 a week to selling Cristiano Ronaldo to Real Madrid for £80 million. My St Mirren squad were on £15 a week and were left to fend for themselves in the summer because they were part-time. The maximum any Aberdeen first-team player earned in my eight years at Pittodrie was £200 a week, the ceiling set by Dick Donald, my chairman. So the financial journey for the thousands of men I managed in nearly four decades was from £6 a week to £6 million a year.

I have a letter on file from a chap who said that in 1959–60 he worked in the dry docks in Govan and used to visit a particular pub. He remembers a young agitator coming into this establishment with a collecting tin for the apprentices' strike fund and delivering a firebrand speech. The only thing he knew about this boy was that he played for St Johnstone. His letter ended with a question: 'Was that you?'

At first I had no recollection of this visit to the political arena, but the note jogged my memory and eventually I recalled going round the pubs in our area to raise money for the strike. I was not auditioning for a role in politics. To call my shouting a 'speech' would embellish it with oratorical qualities it almost certainly lacked. I remember ranting on like an idiot after being asked to justify my request for money. Everyone would have been nicely lubricated and in the mood to hear the young fundraiser explain the cause he was advancing.

Pubs were a large part of my early experiences. My earliest

business idea was to use my modest income to enter the licensed trade, as security for the future. My first establishment was at the junction of Govan Road and Paisley Road West and was populated by dockers. Pubs taught me about people, their dreams and frustrations, in a way that complemented my efforts to understand the football trade, though I was not to know that at the time.

In one of my pubs, for example, we had a 'Wembley Club', into which customers would pay for two years so they could get to the England v. Scotland match at Wembley. I would double whatever was in the kitty and off they would go to London for four or five days. Or, that was the theory. I would join them on the day of the game itself. My best mate, Billy, would head off to Wembley on the Thursday and come back seven days later. Inevitably, this unscheduled extension of the trip would cause ructions with his family.

One Thursday, after a Saturday game at Wembley, I was at home when the phone rang. It was Anna, Billy's wife. 'Cathy, go and ask Alex where Billy is,' Anna said. I pleaded ignorance. Maybe 40 of our customers would make the trip to the Twin Towers and I had no way of knowing why Billy was absent without leave. But for the working men of my generation, a big football match was a sacred pilgrimage, and they loved the camaraderie as much as the game.

The pub we had on Main Street, Bridgeton was in one of Glasgow's biggest Protestant districts. The Saturday before the Orange walk, big Tam the postman would approach me to say: 'Alex, the boys are asking what time you're opening next Saturday morning. For the walk. We're going down to Ardrossan,' which is on the west coast of Scotland. 'The buses leave at ten o'clock,' says Tam. 'All the pubs are open. You'll need to open.'

I was flummoxed. 'Well, what time should I open?'

Tam says: 'Seven.'

So there I was at 6.15 a.m., with my dad, and my brother Martin, and a wee Italian barman we employed. We're well equipped because Tam has told me: 'Get stocked up, you'll need plenty of drink in.' I open at 7 a.m. The pub is soon full of Orangemen in full voice and the police are walking by, not saying a word.

Between 7 a.m. and half past nine I took four grand. Double vodkas, the lot. My dad sat shaking his head. By 9.30 we were hard at work getting the place ready for the rest of our clientele. Scrubbed the place, we did. But there was four grand in the till.

Running pubs was hard work. By 1978 I was ready to escape the onerous responsibilities that came with running two watering holes. Managing Aberdeen left no time for wrestling with drinkers or staying on top of the books. But what good stories those years left in my memory. You could write a book just about those. They would come in on Saturday morning – the dockers – with their wives, having been paid on the Friday night and deposited the money with me behind the bar in the night safe. On a Friday night you felt like a millionaire. You didn't know whether the cash in the safe or the till was yours or theirs. In the early days Cathy would count it on the carpet. On the Saturday morning the money would be away again when these men came to collect it. The record of these transactions was called the tick book.

A female regular by the name of Nan was especially vigilant in tracking the movements of her husband's money. She had a tongue like a docker. 'Do you think we're all daft?' she would say, fixing me in her sights.

'What?' I said, buying time.

'Do you think we're all daft? That tick book, I want to see it.'

'Oh, you can't see the tick book,' I said, improvising. 'It's sacrosanct. The taxman wouldnae let you do that. The taxman examines it every week. You can't see that.'

Nan turns to her man, subdued now, and says: 'Is that right?'

'Er, I'm not sure,' says her man.

The storm had passed. 'If I find out my man's name's in there I'm never coming back,' Nan says.

These are lasting memories of a young life spent around people of great character and resilience. Tough people, too. Sometimes I would come home with a split head or black eyes. That was pub life. When it became too exuberant or fights broke out, it was necessary to jump in to restore order. You would try to separate the protagonists but often take one on the chin. Yet I look back and think what a great life it was. The characters; the comedy.

I always remember a man called Jimmy Westwater coming in, unable to breathe. Grey, he was. 'Christ, are you all right?' I asked. Jimmy had wrapped himself in Shantung silk to creep out of the docks without being caught. A whole bale of Shantung silk. But he'd wrapped himself so tightly in it, he could hardly draw breath.

Another Jimmy, who I employed, and who kept the place immaculate, turned up one night in a bow tie. One of my regulars was incredulous: 'A bow tie in Govan? You must be joking.' One Friday night I came back to find someone selling bags of birdseed by the bar. In that part of Glasgow, everyone kept pigeons.

'What's this?' I asked.

'Birdseed.' Like it was the most obvious answer in the world.

An Irish lad called Martin Corrigan prided himself on his ability to meet any domestic need. Crockery, a canteen of cutlery, a fridge – anything you like. Another guy walked in and announced: 'Want a pair of binoculars? I'm skint.' Out came a beautiful pair of binoculars, wrapped in greaseproof paper. 'A fiver,' he says.

'One condition,' I said. 'A fiver as long as you drink in here. Don't go over to Baxter's.' He was a nice guy with a speech impediment. So I get the binoculars and he immediately spends £3 across the bar.

When I brought purchases home, Cathy would go crackers. I can remember coming back with a nice Italian vase that Cathy later saw in a shop for £10. The problem was that I had paid £25 for ours over the bar. One day I swaggered in with a new suede jacket that really looked the part.

'How much?' says Cathy.

'Seven quid,' I say, beaming.

So I hang it up. Two weeks later we are going to her sister's for a wee party. On goes the jacket, and I'm standing in front of the mirror admiring the cut. You know how a man gives the two sleeves a tug to get it to sit just right? That's what I did – and the two sleeves came right off in my hands. There I stood with a sleeveless jacket.

Cathy was rolling about while I was shouting: 'I'll kill him!' There wasn't even a lining in the jacket.

On a wall in my snooker room hangs a picture of Bill, my best mate. He was some lad, Billy. Couldn't even make a cup of tea. Back at his house one day, after we had been out for a meal, I told him, 'Get the kettle on.' Off he went. But Billy was gone about 15 minutes. Where the hell was he? He was on the phone to Anna, his wife, asking: 'What do you do with the tea?'

Anna left a steak pie in the oven one night, while Billy watched the movie, *The Towering Inferno*. Anna came back two hours later to find smoke spewing from the kitchen.

'Christ, did you not turn the oven off? Look at the smoke,' she puffed.

'I thought it was coming from the telly,' Billy cried. He'd thought it was a special effect from the burning tower.

Everyone congregated at Billy's house. They were moths to his light. He wasn't known as Billy, though. Everyone called him McKechnie. His two boys, Stephen and Darren, are a credit to him and Anna, and are still very close with my sons. Billy is no longer with us. But I still remember him for all the fun we shared.

I have a hardcore of friends from that time. Duncan Petersen, Tommy Hendry and Jim McMillan were at nursery with me from four years of age. Duncan was a plumber who worked for ICI at Grangemouth and retired very early. He has a nice wee place in Clearwater, Florida, and they like to travel. Tommy, who had some heart trouble, was an engineer, as was Jim. A fourth one, Angus Shaw, is looking after his ill wife. John Grant, who I'm also very close to, moved to South Africa in the 1960s. His wife and daughter run a wholesale business.

When I left Harmony Row as a lad, it created a big division between me and the Govan boys. They thought I was wrong to leave the team and go to Drumchapel Amateurs. Mick McGowan, who ran Harmony Row, never spoke to me again. He was intransigent. Mick 'One-Eyed' McGowan. He was an incredible enthusiast for Harmony Row and just blanked me when I left. But the Govan boys and I would still go dancing up to the age of 19 or 20. We all started with girlfriends around that time.

Then came the separation between us, the drift. I married Cathy and moved up to Simshill. They all married too. The friendships seemed to fall apart. Contact was intermittent. John and Duncan had played with me at Queen's Park, in 1958–60. In management you have little time for anything beyond the demands of the job. At St Mirren I certainly didn't. But our bonds were not completely severed. About two months before I left Aberdeen in 1986, Duncan phoned and said it was his 25th wedding anniversary in October. Would Cathy and I like to come? I told him we would love to. It was a turning point in my life. All the lads were there and it brought us back together. Our families were established; we were mature men. I moved to United the following month and we've remained close ever since.

When you get to that age, around 19 to 20, there is a gentle parting of the ways, but they all kept together. It was only me who had a different type of life. It was not avoidance in any way. It was just the way my life unfolded. I was running two pubs and was manager of St Mirren. Then came the Aberdeen job in 1978.

Those friendships sustained me at Manchester United. They would all come to our house in Cheshire for a buffet and a singsong and we'd put all the old records on. They were all good singers. By the time my turn came, the wine would have infused me with an exaggerated sense of my own crooning abilities. It would be neck and neck between me and Frank Sinatra. There would be no doubt in my mind that I could treat my audience to a fine rendition of 'Moon River'. Two words in, I would open my eyes to find the room empty. 'You come and eat my food and there you are watching telly in the next room while I'm singing,' I would complain.

'We're no listening to that. It's crap,' came the reply. They are good solid people. Most have been married over 40 years. God, they give me stick. They pummel me. They get away with it because they are so like me; they are the same stock. They grew up with me. But they were also supportive. When they came down we tended to win. But if we lost a game they might say, sympathetically, 'That was hard work.' Not, 'That was rubbish', but 'That was hard work.'

My friends in Aberdeen remain close. The thing I learned about Scotland is that the further north you go, the quieter people are. They take longer to forge friendships, but when they do those ties run deep. Gordon Campbell goes on holiday with us, my lawyer Les Dalgarno, Alan McRae, George Ramsay, Gordon Hutcheon.

As I became more entrenched in the job at United, my social life diminished. I stopped going out on a Saturday night. The football was exhausting for me. Getting away from the ground after a 3 p.m. kick-off, I wouldn't return home until quarter to nine. That was the price of success: 76,000 people all going home at the same time. The urge to go out weakened. But I developed some strong friendships: Ahmet Kurcer, the manager of the Alderley Edge Hotel, Sotirios, Mimmo, Marius, Tim, Ron Wood, Peter Done, Pat Murphy and Pete Morgan, Ged Mason, the wonderful Harold Riley, and my staff, of course, who were loyal to me. James Mortimer and Willie Haughey were two old pals from my home town, there was Martin O'Connor and Charlie Stillitano in New York and Eckhard Krautzun in Germany, all good people. When we did summon up the energy, we had good nights out.

In my early years in Manchester I grew friendly with Mel Machin, who was manager of City, and who was fired not long after they beat us 5–1. The reason given, I seem to recall, was that Mel didn't smile enough. I would have been sacked a long time ago had that logic applied at United. John Lyall, the manager of West Ham, was a rock to me in those days. I didn't know all the players in England and wasn't sure of the scouting department at United. I would phone John often and he would send me reports on players to supplement my own. I could trust him and confided in him a lot. As a way of telling me United weren't playing well, he would say: 'I don't see Alex Ferguson in that team.'

Jock Wallace, the fiery former Rangers manager, also said to me in a hotel one night: 'I don't see Alex Ferguson in that team. You'd better get Alex Ferguson back in there.' Those men volunteered their advice, knowing that friendship was at the base of their observations. I call those the best friendships. Bobby Robson was manager of England, so that was a different relationship at first, but we too became close. Lennie Lawrence was another friend from that time, and still is.

Bobby Robson and I re-established close contact at Eusébio's testimonial in Portugal when he was coaching there with Porto and Sporting Lisbon. Eric Cantona made his debut in that game. Bobby came to our hotel and I will always remember him seeking out Steve Bruce to say: 'Steve, I made a mistake with you. I should have given you an England cap and I want to apologise for that.' In front of all the players.

So much of what I knew at the end of my career I learned in those early days, sometimes without realising the lessons were sinking in. I learned about human nature long before I headed south to United.

Other people don't see the game or the world the way you do, and sometimes you have to adjust to that reality. Davie Campbell was a player I had at St Mirren. He could run like a deer but couldn't trap a rabbit. I was into him at half-time when the door opened to reveal his father. 'Davie, you're doing brilliant son, well done!' the dad announced, then disappeared.

We were at Cowdenbeath one day with East Stirling and made the mistake of not checking the weather. The pitch was brick hard. So we went into Cowdenbeath to buy 12 pairs of baseball boots. We had no rubber soles in those days. We were down three-nothing at half-time. In the second half I feel a tap on my shoulder from Billy Renton, a former team-mate of mine. He says: 'Alex, I just want to introduce you to my son.'

I say: 'For God's sake, Billy, we're getting beat three-nothing.'

That same day, Frank Connor, a lovely man with a hellish

temper, watched a decision go against him and threw the bench on the pitch. I said: 'Bloody hell, Frank, you're winning three-nothing.'

'It's a disgrace, that,' Frank fired back. These were the passions swirling all around me.

A story comes back to me of Jock Stein and his battles with Jimmy Johnstone, the brilliant player and legendary carouser. One afternoon, Jock took Jimmy off in a game as punishment for Jimmy not wanting to play in a European away game. As Jimmy came off he said: 'You big one-legged bastard, you,' and took a kick at the dug-out. Jimmy runs up the tunnel and big Jock gets after him. Jimmy locks himself in the dressing room.

'Open that door,' shouts Jock.

'No, you'll hurt me,' replies Jimmy.

'Open that door!' repeats Jock. 'I warn you.'

Jimmy opens the door and jumps straight into the bath, which is red hot.

Jock shouts: 'Come out of there.'

'No, I'm not coming out,' says Jimmy. Outside, on the pitch, the game is still going on.

Football management is a never-ending sequence of challenges. So much of it is a study in the frailty of human beings. There was an occasion when a number of Scotland players, after a night of liquid entertainment, decided to jump in rowing boats. This ended with Jimmy Johnstone, wee Jinky, having the oars taken off him and the tide taking him out, while he was singing away. When the information got back to Celtic Park, Jock Stein was informed that Jinky had been rescued by the coastguard from a rowing boat in the Firth of Clyde. Jock joked: 'Could he not have drowned? We'd have given him a testimonial, we'd have looked after Agnes, and I would still have my hair.'

Jock was hilarious. In our time together with Scotland, I recall us beating England 1–0 at Wembley in May 1985 and then flying out to Reykjavik to face Iceland, where we were feeling pretty pleased with ourselves. On the night of our arrival, the staff sat down to a banquet of prawns, salmon and caviar. Big Jock never drank, but I leaned on him to take one glass of white in celebration of our victory over the English.

In the game against Iceland, we scraped a 1–0 win. The performance was a disaster. And afterwards Big Jock turned to me and said: 'See that? That's you and your white wine.'

Despite having all this experience to draw on, I felt my way in the early years at Manchester United. Having a quick temper helped, because if I lost my rag my personality came through. Ryan Giggs has a temper, but a slow one. Mine was a useful tool. I just weighed right in. It helped me to assert my authority. It told the players and staff I was not to be messed about.

There are always people who want to take you on, defy you. When I started, even in my first days at East Stirling, I had a defining confrontation with the centre-forward, who was the son-in-law of one of the directors, Bob Shaw.

I was informed by one of my players, Jim Meakin, that his whole family went away for a weekend in September. It was a tradition.

'What do you mean?' I said.

'You know, I'll not be playing on Saturday,' Jim says.

'Well, I'll tell you what,' I said, 'don't play on Saturday – and then don't bother coming back.'

So he played, and straight after drove down to join his family in Blackpool.

On the Monday I receive a phone call: 'Boss, I've broken down.' In Carlisle, I think it was. He must have thought I was stupid. Quick as a flash I said, 'I can't hear you very well, give me your number, I'll call you back.'

Silence.

'Don't come back,' I said.

Bob Shaw, the director, was deeply unhappy with me. This went on for weeks and weeks. The chairman was saying. 'Alex, please, get Bob Shaw off my back, get Jim back playing.'

I said: 'No, Willie, he's finished. Are you telling me I can do my job with guys deciding when they're going to go on holiday?'

'I understand the problem, but is three weeks not enough?' he said.

The next week he followed me into the toilets at Forfar, stood beside me, and groaned: 'Please, Alex, if there's any Christian understanding in your body.'

After a pause I said: 'All right.'

And he kissed me. 'What are you doing, you silly old sod,' I said. 'You're kissing me in a public toilet.'

In October 1974, in the next stage of my apprenticeship, I went to work for St Mirren. First day, a photograph in the *Paisley Express*. In the print I noticed the captain making a gesture behind my back. The following Monday I called him in and said: 'You've got a free transfer if you want it. There's no place for you here. You'll not be playing.'

'Why?' he says.

'For a start, doing a V-sign behind a manager doesn't tell

me you're an experienced player, or that you're a mature person. If I'm looking for a captain I'm looking for maturity. That was a childish schoolboy trick. You have to go.'

You have to make your mark. As Big Jock said to me about players: Never fall in love with them, because they'll two-time you.

At Aberdeen I had to deal with all sorts of transgressions. I caught plenty out. Afterwards you kill yourself laughing at their reactions.

'Me?' they would say, with the most brilliantly wounded expression.

'Aye, you.'

'Oh, I went to see a mate.'

'Oh did you? For three hours? And ended up pissed?' Mark McGhee and Joe Harper would test me plenty. Then there was Frank McGarvey, at St Mirren. One Sunday in 1977 we took 15,000 fans to a cup game at Fir Park but lost 2–1. Motherwell kicked us off the park and I was reported to the SFA for saying the referee had not been strong enough.

That Sunday night my home phone rang. My mate John Donachie said down the line: 'I didn't want to tell you before the game because I knew you would go off your head, but I saw McGarvey in the pub, pissed, on Friday night.' I phoned his house. His mother answered. 'Is Frank in?'

'No,' she said, 'he's in town. Is there anything I can help you with?'

'Can you ask him to phone me when he comes in. I'll stay up. I'm not going to bed until I've spoken to him.' At 11.45 p.m. the phone went. Pips sounded, so I knew it was a pay phone. 'In the house,' Frank said. 'But that's pips,' I said.

'Yeah, we've got a pay phone in our house,' says Frank. That much was true, but I didn't believe he was ringing from there.

'Where were you on Friday night?'

'I can't remember,' he says.

'Well, I'll tell you. You were in the Waterloo bar. That's where you were. You're suspended for life. Don't come back. You're out of the Scotland Under-21s. I'm withdrawing you. You'll never kick another ball in your life.' And I put the phone down.

The next morning, his mother rang me. 'My Frank doesn't drink. You've got the wrong man.' I told her: 'I don't think so. I know every mother thinks the sun shines out of their son's backside, but you go back and ask him again.'

For three weeks I had him suspended for life and the players were all muttering about it.

A League decider against Clydebank was approaching and I told my assistant, big Davie Provan: 'I need him back for this one.' The club do was at the town hall in Paisley the week before the Clydebank game. I walked in there with Cathy, and suddenly Frank jumped out from behind one of the pillars, begging: 'Just give me one more chance.' This was a gift from heaven. There was me wondering how I could bring him back into the fold without losing face and he jumps out from behind a pillar. I told Cathy to walk in while I maintained my sternest tone with Frank: 'I told you, you're finished for life.' Tony Fitzpatrick, who had been watching, steps forward: 'Boss, give him another chance, I'll make sure he behaves.'

'Talk to me tomorrow morning,' I barked. 'This is not the right time.' I enter the hall to join Cathy, triumphant. We won the Clydebank game 3–1, and Frank scored two.

With young people you have to try to impart a sense of responsibility. If they can add greater awareness to their energy and their talents they can be rewarded with great careers.

One asset I possessed when I started as a manager was that I could make a decision. I was never afraid of that, even as a schoolboy picking a team. I was instructing players even then: 'You play here, you play there,' I used to tell them then. Willie Cunningham, one of my early managers, would say: 'You know, you're a bloody nuisance.' I would talk tactics at him and ask: 'Are you sure you know what you're doing?'

'Nuisance, that's what you are,' he would answer.

The other players would sit there listening to my interventions and assume I was about to be killed for insubordination. But it was just that I could always make a decision. I don't know where it comes from, but I know that as a boy I was an organiser, an instructor, a picker of teams. My father was an ordinary working man, very intelligent, but not a leader of any description, so I was not copying a parental example.

On the other hand there is a part of me, I know, that is solitary, cut off. At 15, playing for Glasgow schoolboys, I came home after scoring against Edinburgh schoolboys – the greatest day of my life – to be told by my father that a big club wanted to talk to me. My response surprised us both: 'I just want to go out. I want to go to the pictures.'

'What's the matter with you?' he said.

I wanted to separate myself. I don't know why. To this day I don't know why I did that. I had to be on my own. My father had been so proud and delighted and my mother was dancing, saying, 'It's so great, son.' My gran was going off her head. Scoring against Edinburgh schoolboys was a big deal. Yet I had to escape into my own wee vacuum, you know?

From there to here is such a vast distance. When I started at Manchester United in 1986, Willie McFaul was the manager of Newcastle United. Manchester City had Jimmy Frizzell and George Graham was in charge at Arsenal. I like George: good man, great friend. When I was having problems with Martin Edwards over my contract, Sir Roland Smith was the chairman of the Plc. The Plc could cause complications at times. You would have to wait for issues to be addressed. One day Sir Roland suggested that Martin, Maurice Watkins, the club solicitor, and I should go over to the Isle of Man to sort out my new deal. George was on double my salary at Arsenal.

'I'll give you my contract, if you like,' George said.

'Are you sure you don't mind?' I said.

So over to the Isle of Man I went, with George's contract. Martin was a good chairman for me. He was strong. The problem was, he thought every penny was his. He paid you what he wanted to pay you. Not just me – everyone.

When I showed him George's contract, he wouldn't believe it. 'Phone David Dein,' I suggested. So he did, and David Dein, the Arsenal chairman, denied that George was being paid the sum on the contract. It was a farce. George had given me his documentation, signed by David Dein. Had it not been for Maurice and Roland Smith I would have left the job that day. I was close to leaving anyway.

There was a moral there, as in all of my 39 years on the front line. You have to stand up for yourself. There is no other way.

three

RETIREMENT U-TURN

O<small>N</small> the sofa that night of Christmas Day 2001, I had nodded off while watching television. In the kitchen a mutiny was brewing. The traditional assembly room of our family home was the scene for a discussion that would change each of our lives. The chief rebel came in and kicked my foot to wake me. In the frame of the door I could pick out three figures: all my sons, lined up for maximum solidarity.

'We've just had a meeting,' Cathy said. 'We've decided. You're not retiring.' As I weighed this announcement I felt no urge to resist. 'One, your health is good. Two, I'm not having you in the house. And three, you're too young anyway.' Cathy did all the early talking. But our sons were right behind her. The gang was united. 'You're being stupid, Dad,' the boys told me. 'Don't do it. You've got a lot to offer. You can build a new team at Manchester United.' That'll teach me to nod off for five minutes. It ended with me working for 11 more years.

One of the reasons I had decided to stand down in the first place was in reaction to a remark Martin Edwards had made after the 1999 European Cup final in Barcelona. Martin had been asked whether there would be a role for me after I surrendered the manager's job and had replied: 'Well, we don't want a Matt Busby situation.' I wasn't impressed by that answer. The two periods could not be compared. In my era, you needed to factor in the added complications brought on by agents, contracts, the mass media. No sensible person would want to be embroiled in those activities once he had finished serving his time as manager. There was not the slimmest chance I would want to be involved in the games themselves or the complexities of the football trade.

What else made me intend to retire in the first place? There was always a sense after that magical night in Barcelona that I had reached the pinnacle. Previously my teams had fallen short in the European Cup and I had always chased that end of the rainbow. Once you've achieved your life's ambition, you ask yourself whether you can achieve such a high again. When Martin Edwards made his remark about avoiding the Matt Busby syndrome, my first thought was 'Nonsense'. My second was: 'Sixty is a good age to walk away.'

So three factors wormed away in my mind: the disappointment of Martin raising the Matt Busby spectre, the imponderable of whether I could win a second European Cup, and that number, 60, which assumed a haunting quality. I had been a manager from 32 years of age.

Reaching 60 can have a profound effect. You think you're entering another room. At 50, a pivotal moment has arrived. Half a century. But you don't feel 50. At 60, you say: 'Christ, I feel 60. I'm 60!' You come through that. You realise it's a notional change, a numerical alteration. I don't feel that way now about age. But back then, 60 was a psychological barrier in my head. It was an obstacle to me feeling young. It changed my sense of my own fitness, my health. Winning the European Cup enabled me to feel I had completed the set of dreams and could now step away fulfilled. That was the catalyst in my thinking. But when I saw Martin casting me as an annoying ghost on the shoulder of the new manager, I muttered to myself, 'What a joke.'

It was a relief to me, of course, to perform a full U-turn, but I still had to argue the practicalities with Cathy and the boys.

'I don't think I can reverse it. I've told the club.'

Cathy said: 'Well, don't you think they should show you some respect in terms of allowing you to change your mind?'

'They may have given it to someone by now,' I said.

'But with the job you've done – don't you think they should give you the chance to go back on it?' she persisted.

The next day I phoned Maurice Watkins who laughed when I told him about my U-turn. The head-hunters were due to meet a candidate to succeed me the following week. Sven-Göran Eriksson was to be the new United manager, I believe. That was my interpretation, anyway, though Maurice never confirmed it. 'Why Eriksson?' I asked him, later.

'You may be wrong, you may be right,' Maurice said.

I remember asking Paul Scholes one day: 'Scholesy, what's Eriksson got?' but Scholesy could shed no light. Maurice's next move was to make contact with Roland Smith, the then chairman of the Plc, whose response to me when we spoke was: 'I told you. Didn't I tell you how stupid you were? We need to sit down to discuss this.'

Roland was one of those wise old birds. He had lived a rich life, a complete life. All kinds of interesting experiences had passed his way and he could unfurl a marvellous array of stories. Roland told us a tale of Margaret Thatcher being at a dinner with the Queen. Her Majesty wanted the royal plane to be refurbished. Roland came rolling along and noticed the two of them with their backs to one another.

'Roland,' called the Queen, 'will you tell this woman I need some work doing on my plane?'

'Ma'am,' said Roland, 'I'll attend to it right away.'

That's what I needed him to say about my change of heart. I needed him to attend to it right away. My first point to Roland was that I needed a new contract. My existing deal would expire that summer. We needed to move fast.

The moment I made the announcement specifying the date of my departure, I knew I had made an error. Others knew it too. Bobby Robson had always said: 'Don't you dare retire.' Bobby was a wonderful character. We were sitting in the house one afternoon when the phone went.

'Alex, it's Bobby here. Are you busy?'

'Where are you?' I said.

'I'm in Wilmslow.'

'Well come round,' I told him.

'I'm outside your door,' he said.

Bobby was such a refreshing man. Even in his seventies he still wanted the Newcastle job back, after losing it early in the 2004–05 season. It was never in Bobby's nature to embrace idleness, and he refused to accept the Newcastle post had suddenly moved beyond his capabilities. That defiance stayed with him to the end and showed how much he loved this game.

Once I had decided I would be standing down, I stopped planning. The minute I reversed that policy, I started plotting again. I told myself: 'We need a new team.' The energy came back. I started to feel that thrust about myself again. To the scouts I announced, 'Let's get cracking again.' We were mobilising once more and it felt good.

I had no physical ailments or impediments that would have stopped me carrying on. In management you are fragile, sometimes. You wonder whether you are valued. I remember my friend Hugh McIlvanney's *Arena* TV documentary trilogy on Stein, Shankly and Busby. A theme of Hugh's study was that these men were too big for their clubs and each, in his own way, had been cut down to size. I remember big Jock saying to me about club owners and directors: 'Remember, Alex, we are not them. We are not them. They run the club. We are their workers.' Big Jock always felt that. It was us and them, the landowner and the serf.

What they did to Jock Stein at Celtic, apart from being distasteful, was ridiculous. They asked him to run the pools. Twenty-five trophies with Celtic, and they asked him to run the pools. Bill Shankly was never invited to join the Liverpool board and as a consequence a resentment grew in him. He even started to come to Manchester United games, or watch Tranmere Rovers. He appeared at our old training ground, The Cliff, as well as Everton's.

No matter how good your CV, there are moments when you feel vulnerable, exposed; though in my last few years with David Gill, the base in which I operated was first-class. Our relationship was excellent. But there is a fear of failure in a manager the whole time, and you are on your own a lot. Sometimes you would give anything not to be alone with your thoughts. There were days when I would be in my office, in the afternoon, and no one would knock on my door because they assumed I was busy. Sometimes I'd hope for that rap on the door. I would want Mick Phelan or René Meulensteen to come in and say: 'Do you fancy a cup of tea?' I had to go and look for someone to talk to; enter their space. In management you have to face that isolation. You need contact. But they think you're busy with important business and don't want to go near you.

Until around 1 p.m. there would be a constant stream of people coming to see me. The youth academy guys, Ken Ramsden, the secretary, and first-team players, which was always gratifying because it meant they trusted you, often with family problems. I always adopted a positive approach to players confiding in me, even if it was to ask for a day off to deal with fatigue, or to address a contract problem.

If a player asked me for a day off, there had to be a good reason, because who would want to miss a training session at United? I would always say yes. I would trust them. Because if you said, 'No – and why do you want one anyway?' and they answered, 'Because my grandmother has died,' then you were in trouble. If there was a problem I would always want to help to find a solution.

I had people who were 100 per cent Alex Ferguson. Examples would be Les Kershaw, Jim Ryan and Dave Bushell. I brought Les in in 1987. He was one of my best-ever signings. I hired him on the recommendation of Bobby Charlton. Because I didn't know the English scene that well, Bobby's tips were invaluable. Les had worked at Bobby's soccer schools and scouted for Crystal Palace. He had also worked with George Graham and Terry Venables. Bobby's view was that Les would love to work for Manchester United. So I hooked him in. He was effervescent. So enthusiastic. Never stops talking. He would call me at 6.30 p.m. every Sunday night to update me with all the scouting reports. Cathy would come through after an hour to say, 'Are you still on that phone?'

The moment you interrupted Les, he would accelerate. What a worker. He was a professor of chemistry at Manchester University. Dave Bushell was a headmaster who ran English schools Under-15s and I took him when Joe Brown retired. Jim Ryan was there from 1991. Mick Phelan was a player for me and became my valued assistant, apart from the spell when he left us in 1995 and rejoined in 2000 as a coach. Paul McGuinness was with me from when I joined the club. He was the son of former United player and manager Wilf McGuinness, and had been a player himself. I made him an academy coach.

Normally a manager brings an assistant and that assistant stays with him. United are a different proposition because my assistants acquired a high profile and became targets for other clubs. I lost my assistant, Archie Knox, to Rangers, two weeks before the 1991 European Cup Winners' Cup final, and in Archie's absence I took Brian Whitehouse to Rotterdam for the game and made sure all the backroom staff were involved.

Later I went scouting for a No. 2. Nobby Stiles said: 'Why don't you promote Brian Kidd?' Brian knew the club and had transformed the local scouting network, bringing in a lot of his old pals, United men and schoolteachers who knew the local area. That was the best work Brian ever did. It was a terrific success. So I gave Brian the job. He did well in the sense that he became very friendly with the players and put on a good training session. He had been to Italy to watch the Serie A teams and brought a lot of that wisdom home.

When he left to go to Blackburn in 1998, I told him: 'I hope you know what you're doing.' When a coach leaves, they always ask: 'What do you think?' With Archie I couldn't get Martin Edwards to match the Rangers offer. As for Brian, I didn't feel he was suited to management. Steve McClaren: management material, no doubt about that. What I told Steve was: you should make sure you get the right club, the right chairman. Essential. Always. West Ham and Southampton were the ones who wanted him at this stage.

From nowhere, Steve took a call from Steve Gibson, the chairman of Middlesbrough, and my advice was, 'Absolutely no doubt, take it.' Bryan Robson, though he had lost his job there, always spoke highly of Steve Gibson, who was young, fresh, and always willing to put his money in. They had a great training ground. 'That's your job,' I told Steve.

Organised, strong and always looking for new ideas, Steve was made for management. He was effervescent and energetic with a good personality.

Carlos Queiroz, another of my No. 2s, was brilliant. Just brilliant. Outstanding. An intelligent, meticulous man. The recommendation to hire him came from Andy Roxburgh, at a time when we were beginning to look at more southern-hemisphere players and perhaps needed a coach from beyond the northern European nations, and one who could speak another language or two. Andy was quite clear. Carlos was outstanding. He had coached South Africa, so I called in Quinton Fortune one day for his opinion. 'Fantastic,' said Quinton. 'To what level, do you think?' 'Any,' said Quinton. 'Well,' I thought, 'that will do me.'

When Carlos came over to England in 2002 to speak to us, I was waiting for him in my tracksuit. Carlos was immaculately dressed. He has that suaveness about him. He was so impressive that I offered him the job right away. He was the closest you could be to being the Manchester United manager without actually holding the title. He took responsibility for a lot of issues that he didn't have to get involved in.

'I need to talk to you.' Carlos had rung me one day in 2003 as I was holidaying in the south of France. What could it be? Who was after him? 'I just need to talk to you,' he repeated.

So he flew into Nice and I took a taxi to Nice Airport, where we found a quiet corner.

'I've been offered the Real Madrid job,' he said.

'I'm going to say two things to you. One, you can't turn it down. Two, you're leaving a really good club. You may not last more than a year at Real Madrid. You could be at Man United for a lifetime.'

'I know,' Carlos said. 'I just feel it's such a challenge.'

'Carlos, I can't talk you out of that one. Because if I do, and in a year's time Real Madrid are winning the European Cup, you'll be saying – I could have been there. But I'm just telling you, it's a nightmare job.'

Three months later, he was wanting to quit Madrid. I told him he couldn't. I flew out to Spain to meet him at his apartment and we had lunch. My message was: you can't quit, see it through, and rejoin me next year. That season I didn't take an assistant because I was sure Carlos would come back. I co-opted Jim Ryan and Mick Phelan, two good men, but I didn't want to dive in with an appointment, knowing Carlos might be returning. I had interviewed Martin Jol, a week or so before Carlos called to say it wasn't working out in Madrid. Martin had been impressive and I was inclined to give him the job, but then came the call from Carlos, which obliged me to go back to Martin and say: 'Look, I'm going to leave it for the time being.' I couldn't tell him why.

Assistant manager at Manchester United is a high-profile position. It's a platform within the game. When Carlos left the second time in July 2008, his homeland was pulling on his heartstrings, so I could understand him wanting to go back to Portugal. But he was smashing, Carlos. He had most of the qualities to be the next Manchester United manager. He could be an emotional man. But of all the ones who worked alongside me, he was the best, no doubt about that. He was totally straight. He would walk in and tell you directly: I'm not happy with this, or that.

He was good for me. He was a Rottweiler. He'd stride into my office and tell me we needed to get something done. He would sketch things out on the board. 'Right, OK,

Carlos, yeah,' I would say, thinking, 'I'm busy here.' But it's a good quality to have, that urge to get things done.

The structure of the team was strong in the year I decided to rescind my retirement plans, though we had lost Peter Schmeichel and Denis Irwin. Now there was a player, Denis Irwin. We always called him eight out of ten Denis. So quick and nimble: quick-brained. Never let you down. There was never any bad publicity with him. I remember a game at Arsenal, when Denis allowed Dennis Bergkamp to score late in the match, and the press said: 'Well, you'll be disappointed with Denis,' and I replied: 'Aye, well, he's been with me for eight or nine years and he's never made a mistake. I think we can forgive him one.'

The biggest challenge was in the goalkeeping position. From the minute Schmeichel left to join Sporting Lisbon in 1999 – and having missed out on Van der Sar – I was throwing balls in the air, hoping one would land in the right place. Raimond van der Gouw was a terrific, steady goalkeeper, and a very loyal and conscientious trainer, but he wouldn't have been the No. 1 choice. Mark Bosnich was, in my opinion, a terrible professional, which we should have known. Massimo Taibi just didn't work out and he returned to Italy, where he rejuvenated his career. Fabien Barthez was a World Cup-winning goalkeeper, but it's possible that the birth of his child back in France affected his concentration, because he was going back and forth a lot. He was a good lad, a fine shot-stopper and a good fielder of the ball. But when a keeper loses his concentration, he's in trouble.

When the team thought I would be leaving, they slackened off. A constant tactic of mine was always to have my players on the edge, to keep them thinking it was always a matter of life and death. The must-win approach. I took my eye off the ball, thinking too far ahead, and wondering who would replace me. It's human nature, in those circumstances, to relax a bit, and to say: 'I'm not going to be here next year.'

United were so used to me being around it wasn't clear what the next chapter was going to be. And it was a mistake. I knew that by the previous October in 2000. By that stage I was wanting the season to be over with. I couldn't enjoy it. I cursed myself: 'I've been stupid. Why did I even mention it?' There wasn't the same performance level on the pitch. I was starting to have doubts about my own future. Where would I go, what would I do? I knew I would miss the consuming nature of the United job.

The 2001–02 season was a fallow year for us. We finished third in the League and reached the semi-finals of the Champions League, losing to Bayer Leverkusen, but there were to be no trophies in the year of my U-turn. This after a run of three straight Premier League titles.

That summer we spent heavily on Ruud van Nistelrooy and Juan Sebastián Verón. Laurent Blanc came in, too, after I sold Jaap Stam – an error, as I have admitted many times since. My reasoning with Blanc, as I said at the time, was that we needed a player who would talk to and organise the younger players. The early part of that campaign was most memorable for Roy Keane throwing the ball at Alan Shearer (and being sent off) in the 4–3 defeat at Newcastle, and our incredible 5–3 victory at Spurs on 29 September 2001, in which Tottenham scored through Dean Richards, Les

Ferdinand and Christian Ziege before we mounted one of the great comebacks.

It is such a vivid memory. As they traipsed into the dressing room, three goals down, the players were braced for a rollicking. Instead I sat down and said: 'Right, I'll tell you what we're going to do. We're going to score the first goal in this second half and see where it takes us. We get at them right away, and we get the first goal.'

Teddy Sheringham was the Tottenham captain and, as the teams emerged back into the corridor, I saw Teddy stop and say: 'Now don't let them get an early goal.' I'll always remember that. We scored in the first minute.

You could see Spurs deflate while we puffed ourselves up. There were 44 minutes left in the half. On we went and scored four more. Just incredible. Tottenham's standing in the game imbued that victory with more lustre than a five-goal comeback at, say, Wimbledon. To beat a great football club in that manner has historical ramifications. Our dressing room afterwards was some place to be: players rolling their heads, not quite believing what they had done.

Teddy's warning to the Tottenham team that day reflected our success in frightening opponents with well-timed retaliatory goals. There was an assumption (which we encouraged) that scoring against us was a provocative act that would invite terrible retribution. Most teams could never relax in front against us. They were always waiting for the counterpunch.

I tapped my watch in games to spook the other team, not encourage mine. If you want my summary of what it was to be Manchester United manager I would direct you to the last 15 minutes. Sometimes it would be quite uncanny, as if the ball were being sucked into the net. Often the players would seem to know it was going to be hoovered in there. The players would know they were going to get a goal. It didn't always happen, but the team never stopped believing it could. That's a great quality to have.

I always took risks. My plan was: don't panic until the last 15 minutes, keep patient until the last quarter of an hour, then go gung-ho.

Against Wimbledon in the Cup one year, Peter Schmeichel went up to chase a goal and we left Denis Irwin on the halfway line against John Fashanu. Schmeichel was up there for two minutes. Wimbledon were kicking the ball up to Fashanu and wee Denis was nipping in front of him and sending it back into the box. Great entertainment. Schmeichel had a physical prowess. He and Barthez liked to play out. Barthez especially was a good player, though he thought he was better than he was. On tour in Thailand he kept on at me to let him play up front, so I relented for the second half. The other players kept battering the ball into the corners and Barthez would come back with his tongue hanging out after chasing the ball. He was knackered.

No team ever entered Old Trafford thinking United might be persuaded to give in. There was no comfort to be gained from thinking we could be demoralised. Leading 1–0 or 2–1, the opposition manager would know he faced a final 15 minutes in which we would go hell for leather. That fear factor was always there. By going for the throat and shoving bodies into the box, we would pose the question: can you handle it? On top of our own frantic endeavours, we would be testing the character of the defending team. And they knew it. Any flaw would widen into a crack. It didn't always work. But when it did, you got the joy that came with a late conquest. It was always worth the gamble. It was rare for us to be hit on the break while we chased a game. We lost at Liverpool once when Luke Chadwick chased back and got sent off. Everyone else was in the box. Against us, teams would have so many players back defending that it would be hard for them break out.

At half-time at Spurs we had looked buried. But as I said at the end of that season: 'In a crisis you're better just calming people down.' We scored five times to win the game, with Verón and David Beckham scoring the last two. Around that time, however, we were having goalkeeping problems. In October, Fabien Barthez committed two howlers. We also lost 2–1 at home to Bolton and 3–1 at Liverpool, where Fabien came for a punch and missed. At Arsenal on 25 November, our French keeper passed straight to Thierry Henry, who scored, and then raced out for a ball that he failed to gather. Henry again: 3–1.

December 2001 started no better, when we lost 3–0 at home to Chelsea, our fifth League defeat in 14 games. Things improved from there. Ole Gunnar Solskjaer struck up a good relationship with Van Nistelrooy (Andy Cole was to leave for Blackburn in January), and we went top of the table early in the New Year of 2002. In the 2–1 win over Blackburn, Van Nistelrooy scored for the tenth time in a row, and by the end of January we were top of the League by four points.

Then came my announcement, in February 2002. I would not be standing down after all.

Once the retirement issue was cleared up, our form picked up dramatically. We won 13 of 15 games. I was desperate to make it to Glasgow for the 2002 Champions League final. I was so sure we would get there that I had scouted the hotels in the city. I tried to play it down but the urge to lead the team out at Hampden Park obsessed me.

In the semi-final against Bayer Leverkusen, we had three shots cleared off the line in the second game and went out on away goals after drawing the tie 3–3 on aggregate. Michael Ballack and Oliver Neuville had scored at Old Trafford. Also in the Leverkusen side was a young Dimitar Berbatov, who was later to join us from Spurs.

But at least I still had my job. On New Year's Day, for my birthday, we had all been to the Alderley Edge Hotel – the whole family. It was the first time for a while we had all been together. Mark, who was usually in London, was there, along with Darren, Jason and Cathy. All the conspirators round a table.

When the players heard the news I would be staying on after all, I braced myself for the barbed comments that would come my way. I couldn't have made an announcement of that magnitude without paying a high price on the banter front.

Ryan Giggs was the most skilful in his mockery. 'Oh, no, I can't believe this,' Ryan said. 'I've just signed a new contract.'

four

A FRESH START

As the new season dawned in 2002, I was bursting with fresh energy. It felt like day one in a whole new job. All the doubt brought on by my intended retirement had cleared and I was ready to refresh the squad after our first season without a trophy since 1998. Those phases of seismic change excited me. I knew there were solid foundations on which to build a new team of winners.

There had been a golden period, from 1995 to 2001, when we had won the League five times out of six and secured the first of my two Champions League trophies. At the start of that six-year spell, we had promoted our home-grown lads to the first XI. David Beckham, Gary Neville and Paul Scholes became regulars, despite a 3–1 defeat by Aston Villa that prompted Alan Hansen to say on television: 'You can't win anything with kids.'

After that hat-trick of League titles we made an error in

letting Jaap Stam go. I thought £16.5 million was a good price and I believed he had slipped back in his game since his Achilles operation. But it was a mistake on my part. This is my chance to nail once and for all the myth that his contentious autobiography had anything to do with my decision to sell him, even though I called him in about the book right away. It accused us of tapping him up, of approaching him directly without PSV's permission.

'What were you thinking of?' I asked. But it played absolutely no part in my decision. Not long after that, an agent told me that a representative of Roma were trying to make contact. They were offering £12 million for Jaap. Not interested, I said. The next week we received an approach from Lazio. I had no interest until the offer reached £16.5 million. By that time Jaap was 30 and we were concerned about his recovery from the Achilles injury. Anyway, it proved a disastrous episode. Having to tell him in a petrol station was agony, because I knew he was a really decent man who loved playing for the club, and who was adored by the fans. It was one of my senior moments. I had tried to get hold of him at the training ground two days before deadline day. By the time I reached him on his mobile, he was already on his way home. An equidistant point was a petrol station, off the motorway, so that's where our meeting took place.

I knew I could get Laurent Blanc, on a free. I had always admired Laurent Blanc and should have acquired him many years earlier. He was so composed and so good at gliding out from the back with the ball. I thought his experience could help John O'Shea and Wes Brown to develop. It was such a misjudgment on my part to let Jaap go – he ended up playing against us, aged 36, in the semi-finals of the Champions League.

Centre-backs were always a big part of my managerial planning and Rio Ferdinand was the big buy in that summer of 2002, when we really should have reached the Champions League final in my home town of Glasgow. To me that would have been special, playing in my birth place against Real Madrid, the place where I saw my first-ever European final, Real beating Eintracht Frankfurt 7–3. I was in the schoolboy enclosure that day because I played for Queen's Park at the time, which entitled me to walk in the front door and head for that part of the ground. I left three minutes before the end of the game to get a bus home, because I was working in the morning, and of course missed all the celebrations at the end, which were unusual in football around that time. Real performed a big parade with the cup and were dancing about the park. I missed out. The next morning, with the papers laid out, I studied the photographs and thought: 'Damn, I missed seeing all that.'

Hampden Park was packed with 128,000 souls. To beat the huge exodus from big games, we would run miles away from the ground: sprint away from Hampden towards the terminus, and take a bus from there. It was a three- or four-mile run to the station, but at least we were on the bus. The queues at the ground would be miles long. Miles long. Dads would pull up in lorries and you would give them sixpence each and pile onto the wagon. That was another route in and out. But it would have been unforgettable to get to Hampden for that 2002 final, which Real Madrid won 2–1, to send a Manchester United side out onto that sacred turf.

Carlos Queiroz joining as my assistant was another major initiative that year. Arsenal had won the Double the previous season and Roy Keane had been sent home from the 2002 World Cup, so there was plenty to occupy my mind as we set off on another journey. When Roy was sent off after tangling with Jason McAteer at Sunderland, I dispatched him for a hip operation, which removed him from the picture for four months. Soon after we struck a bad run of form, losing at home to Bolton and away at Leeds. We managed only two wins from our first six games and were ninth in the table when I took a minor gamble and sent a number of players away for surgery in the hope that they would return to energise us in the second half of our campaign.

In September 2002, though, the knives were out for me. The nature of the job is that the public will attack you when things seem to be going wrong. Plus, I've never been beholden to the press and couldn't count on them for support. I never socialised much with them, didn't give them stories or mark their cards, with the exception – occasionally – of Bob Cass, of the *Mail on Sunday*. So they had no reason to love me or support me through hard times. Other managers were more skilled at cultivating relationships with the press. It maybe bought them a bit more time, but not indefinitely. Results determine whether the guillotine stays up or falls.

Media pressure is usually where it starts. Whenever there was a bad spell I would see the line: 'Your time's up, Fergie; it's time to go.' The old line about shelf-life. You can laugh at it, but you mustn't get yourself in a tizzy, because hysteria is the nature of the beast. There have been so many favour-able headlines about me over the years, because the press could hardly avoid writing them, given the success we had, but to be called a genius you also need to accept that you are probably also going to be called a fool.

Matt Busby used to say: 'Why read them when you have a bad result? I never did.' And he lived in an era when the press wasn't as pervasive as it is today. Matt would always ride the waves of praise and condemnation without both-ering too much about either.

What we did at all times, in success and adversity, was make sure the training ground was sacrosanct. The work there, the concentration, and the standards we maintained never dropped. Eventually that consistency of effort will show itself on a Saturday. That way, when a United player has a couple of bad results, he will hate it. It becomes intol-erable to him. Even the best players sometimes lose confi-dence. Even Cantona had bouts of self-doubt. But if the culture around the training ground was right, the players knew they could fall back on the group and the expertise of our staff.

The only player I ever coached who was totally unaffected by his mistakes was David Beckham. He could have the worst game possible and still not believe that he had under-performed in any way. He would dismiss you, tell you you were wrong. He was incredibly protective of himself. Whether that was developed by the people around him, I don't know. But he would never concede he'd had a bad game, and never accept he'd made a mistake.

You had to admire that. In a way it was a great quality.

No matter how many mistakes he would make (in my eyes, not his), he would always want the ball. His confidence never suffered. Otherwise, dips of that kind are innate to all footballers, and plenty of managers. Public scrutiny penetrates the body armour, whether from the public, press or fans.

The nadir was reached in November, with the last derby game at Maine Road: a 3–1 victory for City, memorable for a mistake by Gary Neville, who dawdled with the ball and was dispossessed by Shaun Goater for City's second goal. Afterwards I questioned the spirit of my players, a nuclear option I seldom employed. The dressing room is a horrible place to be when you lose a derby. Before the game, Keith Pinner, my old friend and a diehard City fan, had said: 'As it's the last derby game at Maine Road, will you come up for a drink afterwards?'

Amused by the audacity of this request, I said: 'If we win, aye.'

So after we'd lost 3–1, I was getting on the bus when my phone went. Pinner on the line.

'Where are you?' he said. 'Are you not coming up?'

'Go away,' I replied, or words to that effect. 'I never want to see you in my life.'

'Bad loser, are you?' laughed Pinner. Up I went for a drink.

At the end of that season Gary Neville observed: 'That was a big crossroads for us. I thought the fans would turn on us that day.'

Sometimes a manager has to be honest with the supporters, over and beyond the players. They are not stupid. As long as you don't criticise individual players in public, admonishing the team is fine, not a problem. We can all share in the blame: the manager, his staff, the players. Expressed properly, criticism can be an acceptance of collective responsibility.

Under the pressure of bad results, we changed the way we played. We moved the ball forward more and quicker rather than concentrating on possession ratios. With Roy Keane present, keeping the ball was never a problem. I said so from the minute he came to the club: 'He never gives the ball away, this guy,' I told the staff and players. Ball retention is a religion at Man United. But possession without penetration is a waste of time. We were starting to lack that real penetration. With a player like Van Nistelrooy in our forward line we needed to supply him quickly. Early passes, in from wide, or between defenders. That's where the change had to come.

We tried Diego Forlán off the front, but we had been playing a lot with Verón, Scholes and Keane in midfield. Verón was free and Scholesy could go into the box. Beckham wide right, Giggs wide left. We had fantastic talents there. Our goal-scoring weapons were the right ones. Van Nistelrooy was relentless in his goal-scoring. Beckham would always get you around ten; Scholes, above that.

Phil Neville was excelling in central midfield as well. Phil was a dream. He and Nicky Butt were perfect allies for me. All they wanted was to play for Man United. They never wanted to leave. The time to let that type of player go is when you see that you're hurting them more than helping them by using them as substitutes or understudies.

Those players end up trapped between extreme loyalty and a kind of sadness at not being involved more in first-team games. That's hard for any man. Phil played a great role where we needed stabilisation. He had great discipline. He was one of those players to whom you could say: 'Phil, I want you to run up that hill, then come back and cut down that tree.'

And he would say, 'Right, boss, where's the chainsaw?'

I had a few like that. Phil would do anything for the team. He would only think of the team. For the most part, if he were to play a limited part in the successful functioning of the side, he would find a way to be happy with that. In the end, though, Gary came to talk to me, to see how I felt about Phil's diminishing role.

'I don't know what to do, he's such a great lad,' I told Gary.

'That's the problem,' Gary said. 'He doesn't want to come to you.' Phil lacked Gary's directness, you see.

I invited Phil out to the house for a talk. He came with his wife Julie. At first I didn't notice her in the car. 'Cathy, go and bring Julie in,' I said. But when Cathy got out there, Julie began crying. 'We don't want to leave Man United,' she was saying. 'We love being at the club.' Cathy took her a cup of tea, but she wouldn't come into the house. I think she was worried she might break down and embarrass her husband.

My point to Phil was that I was doing him more harm than good with the way I was using him. He agreed. He told me he needed to move on. I left him to work out how he would approach that with his wife.

When they had left, Cathy said: 'You're not going to let him go, are you? You can't let people like that go.'

'Cathy,' I said, 'it's for his own good. Do you not understand? It's killing me more than it's killing him.'

I let him go cheaply, for £3.6 million. He was worth double that, because he could play five positions for you – in either of the full-back positions or all across the midfield. He even played centre-half for Everton, when Phil Jagielka and Joseph Yobo were injured.

Letting Nicky Butt go was similarly traumatic, although Nicky had no problem standing up for himself. Nicky was a cheeky sod. Gorton boy. Great lad. He would fight your shadow, would Nicky.

He would come in and say: 'Why am I not playing?'

That was Nicky. I loved that. And I would say, 'Nicky, you're not playing because I think Scholes and Keane are better than you.' Sometimes, away from home, I would put him in ahead of Scholesy. In the Champions League semi-final at Juventus, for example, I played Butt instead of Scholes. Scholes and Keane were on two bookings and I couldn't afford to risk them both missing the final, though in the event both missed out through suspension. I brought Scholes on for Butt when Nicky picked up an injury – and Paul was booked. In the end I sold Nicky to Bobby Robson at Newcastle for £2 million. What a great buy that was.

The clouds began to clear in 2002 with the 5–3 win over Newcastle at the end of November. Diego Forlán, who had taken 27 games to score his first goal for us – a penalty against Maccabi Haifa – was a factor in our 2–1 win at Liverpool, after Jamie Carragher had headed the ball back to Jerzy Dudek and Forlán had nipped in to score. We then beat Arsenal 2–0 and Chelsea 2–1, with Forlán again scoring the decisive goal. On the training ground that winter, we worked intensively on our defensive shape.

In February 2003 we lost an FA Cup fifth-round tie 2–0 at home to Arsenal. It was the game in which Ryan Giggs missed an open goal, lifting the ball over the bar with his right foot, when the net was undefended. 'Well, Giggsy,' I told him, 'you've scored the best-ever goal in the FA Cup, and now you've added the best-ever miss.' He had all the time in the world. He could have walked the ball into the net.

That game, which sent me into a fury, was to have more serious implications for my relationship with another graduate of the 1992 FA Youth Cup winning side. A butterfly plaster was involved, but it couldn't heal the wound. The boot I kicked in anger just happened to fly straight at David Beckham's eyebrow.

After losing the Carling Cup final to Liverpool, we ran into another major rival from that period. By the end of my time as manager, Leeds United were nowhere to be seen on the list of threats, but in the spring of 2003 they were a menace, although we won that match 2–1. I should say a few words about our rivalry with Leeds, which was disturbingly intense.

When I first arrived in Manchester I knew about the derby games with City and the clashes with United's Merseyside rivals, Everton and Liverpool. I knew nothing of the animosity between United and Leeds. In the old first division, Archie Knox and I went to see Crystal Palace beat Leeds.

It was 0–0 at half-time. The second half was all Leeds. With 20 minutes to go, Leeds had a penalty turned down and the crowd were going crackers. A Leeds fan began shouting at me: 'You, you Manc bastard.'

'What's that all about, Archie?' I said.

'No idea,' Archie replied.

So I looked for a steward. The directors' box at Leeds is small and the fans are all around you. Palace went to the other end and scored. That's when the crowd really lost it. Archie wanted us to leave but I insisted we stay. Palace scored again, and that's when our new friend hit me in the back with a Bovril cup. The abuse was astonishing. 'Let's get out of here,' I said to Archie.

The next day I was speaking to our kit man at the time, Norman Davies. He said: 'I told you about Leeds. It's pure hatred.'

'Where does that come from?'

'The sixties,' Norman said.

Leeds used to have a commissionaire called Jack who would come on the bus as we arrived at Elland Road and announce, like the town crier, 'On behalf of the directors, players and supporters of Leeds United, welcome to Elland Road,' and I would mutter: 'That'll be right.'

Some of the fans would have their kids on their shoulders, radiating the most incredible hatred. In the semi-final of the League Cup at Leeds in 1991, they did give us a bit of a battering in the second half, but Lee Sharpe had broken away, at 0–0, with two minutes to go, to score. It looked 10 yards offside. I was on the pitch, Eric Harrison was in the dug-out. A lot of people think Eric looks like me. One Leeds supporter certainly did, because he whacked Eric. Absolutely panned him. The guy thought he was hitting me. On came the fans. Pandemonium. And yet there was something about the hostile atmosphere at Elland Road that I quite liked.

In the Peter Ridsdale years, when Leeds were 'living the dream', as the chairman later put it, I sensed the club was built on sand. When I heard what kind of wages they were paying, my alarm bells rang. When we sold them Lee Sharpe, I believe they doubled Lee's wages, on a 35,000 crowd.

But they constructed a useful team. Alan Smith, Harry Kewell, David Batty. Back in 1992, they won the League with one of the most average teams ever to win the title, but they were as committed as it's possible to be. And they were superbly managed by Howard Wilkinson. A decade later, we would hear about the boy from Derby joining them, Seth Johnson, and him discussing with his agent what they were going to ask for. The story goes that the sum they came up with was £25,000. Leeds' offer was apparently £35,000 a week, climbing to £40–45,000.

Clubs don't learn these lessons. The emotions of the game trap you.

I remember a local Manchester businessman coming to me and saying: 'I'm thinking of buying Birmingham City, what do you think?'

I said, 'If you've got a hundred million pounds to risk, go ahead.'

'No, no,' he said, 'they're only eleven million in debt.'

'But have you seen the stadium?' I replied. 'You'll need a new stadium, for maybe sixty million, and then forty million to get them into the Premier League.'

People try to apply to football the usual principles of business. But it's not a lathe, it's not a milling machine, it's a collection of human beings. That's the difference.

We faced some seismic fixtures before that season's end. A 4–0 home win over Liverpool – Sami Hyypiä was sent off in the fifth minute for stopping Van Nistelrooy's run on goal – led us into a Champions League tie against Real Madrid. In the first of our games against Madrid, Van Nistelrooy was our only scorer. Luis Figo and Raul, twice, left us facing a 3–1 deficit in the home leg, for which I left Beckham on the bench. This was an epic game, watched, the story goes, by Roman Abramovich, who was inspired by our 4–3 win, and the hat-trick by Brazilian striker Ronaldo, to seek his own involvement in the great global drama by buying Chelsea.

Though we had been nine points off the lead at one stage, we raced eight points clear with a 4–1 win over Charlton in May 2003, in which a Van Nistelrooy hat-trick lifted him to 43 goals for the season. On the penultimate weekend, Arsenal needed to beat Leeds at Highbury to have any chance of catching us, but Mark Viduka helped us out with a late goal for our Yorkshire rivals. In our 2–1 win at Everton, David Beckham scored from a free kick in his last game for us. We were champions again for the eighth time in 11 seasons. The players danced and sang: 'We've got our trophy back.'

We regained the League but said farewell to Beckham.

five

BECKHAM

FROM the moment he first laid boot on ball, David Beckham displayed an unbreakable urge to make the best of himself and his talent. He and I left the main stage in the same summer, with him still prominent in European football and opportunities galore ahead of him. He went out at Paris St-Germain much as I did at United: on his own terms.

Sometimes you have to take something away from someone for them to see how much they loved it. When Beckham moved to America to join LA Galaxy, I believe he began to realise he had surrendered a part of his career. He worked incredibly hard to return to the level he had been at in his prime, and showed more enthusiasm for the hard graft of the game than he did at the end of his time with us.

David didn't have many choices at the point of his transfer from Real Madrid to Major League Soccer in 2007. I imagine he also had his eyes on Hollywood and the impact it would have on the next phase of his career. There was no foot-balling reason for him to go to America. He was giving up top-level club football as well as the international game, although he fought his way back into the England squad. That proves my point about the disappointment at the heart of his career in its later stages. He drew on a huge resilience factor to regain his prominence at the elite level.

Because I saw him grow up, along with Giggs and Scholes, David was more like a son to me. He joined United as a young London lad in July 1991. Within a year he was part of the so-called Class of '92, winning the FA Youth Cup with Nicky Butt, Gary Neville and Ryan Giggs. He made 394 appearances for the first team and scored 85 times, including one from the halfway line, against Wimbledon, the goal that really announced him to the world.

When I left the United dug-out in May 2013, Giggs and Scholes were still with us, but by then it had been ten years since David had left for Spain. On Wednesday 18 June 2003 we told the Stock Exchange he would be joining Real Madrid for a fee of £24.5 million. David was 28. The news flashed around the world. It was one of those global moments for our club.

I hold no rancour towards David at all. I like him. I think he's a wonderful boy. But you should never surrender what you're good at.

David was the only player I managed who chose to be famous, who made it his mission to be known outside the game. Wayne Rooney was on the radar of an industry that would have liked to change him. His profile was established in his teenage years. He had offers that would make your mind boggle. He was making twice outside of football what we were paying him. The corporate world would love to have taken over Giggsy, but that was never his style.

In his final season with us, we were aware that David's work-rate was dropping and we had heard rumours of a flirtation between Real Madrid and David's camp. The main issue was that his application level had dropped from its traditionally stratospheric level.

The confrontation between us that caused so much excitement around the game was an FA Cup fifth-round tie against Arsenal at Old Trafford in February 2003, which we lost 2–0.

David's offence in that particular game was that he neglected to track back for the second Arsenal goal, scored by Sylvain Wiltord. He merely jogged. The boy just kept on running away from him. At the end I got on to him. As usual, with David at that time, he was dismissive of my criticism. It's possible that he was starting to think he no longer needed to track back and chase, which were the very qualities that had made him what he was.

He was around 12 feet from me. Between us on the floor lay a row of boots. David swore. I moved towards him, and as I approached I kicked a boot. It hit him right above the eye. Of course he rose to have a go at me and the players stopped him. 'Sit down,' I said. 'You've let your team down. You can argue as much as you like.'

I called him in the next day to go through the video and he still would not accept his mistake. As he sat listening to me, he didn't say a word. Not a word.

'Do you understand what we're talking about, why we got on to you?' I asked.

He didn't even answer me.

The next day the story was in the press. In public an Alice band highlighted the damage inflicted by the boot. It was in those days that I told the board David had to go. My message would have been familiar to board members who knew me. The minute a Manchester United player thought he was bigger than the manager, he had to go. I used to say, 'The moment the manager loses his authority, you don't have a club. The players will be running it, and then you're in trouble.'

David thought he was bigger than Alex Ferguson. There is no doubt about that in my mind. It doesn't matter whether it's Alex Ferguson or Pete the Plumber. The name of the manager is irrelevant. The authority is what counts. You cannot have a player taking over the dressing room. Many tried. The focus of authority at Manchester United is the manager's office. That was the death knell for him.

Then, of course, after finishing top of our Champions League group, we were drawn against Real Madrid. In Spain, for the first leg, David seemed especially keen to shake hands with Roberto Carlos, the Madrid left-back. The following Saturday, after our 3–1 defeat at the Bernabéu, he withdrew from the game against Newcastle, saying he wasn't fit. I played Solskjaer, who was magnificent in a 6–2 win, and he stayed in the side.

David's form, quite simply, wasn't good enough for me to pull Solskjaer out of a winning team for the Old Trafford leg against Real. During a round of head tennis before the return game, I pulled David aside and told him, 'Look, I'm going to start with Ole.' He huffed and walked away.

There was a terrific hullaboo that night, with David coming on as sub for Verón in the 63rd minute and giving what looked like a farewell to the Old Trafford crowd. He scored from a free kick and struck the winner in the 85th minute. We won 4–3, but Ronaldo's wonderful hat-trick and the defeat in Spain sent us out of the competition.

David was looking for the sympathy vote from the fans. But there is no doubt there had been a direct attack on me. The move to Real Madrid was clearly accelerating. From what we could gather, there had been dialogue between his agent and Real Madrid. The first contact we had was probably in the middle of May, after our season had ended. Our chief executive, Peter Kenyon, called to say: 'Real Madrid have been on the phone.'

'Well,' I said, 'we expected that.' We were looking for £25 million. I went to France on holiday and Peter called my mobile, while I was in a restaurant, having dinner with Jim Sheridan, the film director, who had an apartment over the place where we were eating. I needed a private phone.

'Come up to my apartment, use mine,' said Jim. So that's how it was done. 'He doesn't go unless we get the twenty-five,' I told Peter. I believe it was £18 million down, with add-ons, that we eventually received.

David hadn't disappeared from the team altogether. We won the title with a 4–1 win against Charlton at Old Trafford on 3 May 2003. He scored in that game and again at Everton on 11 May as our season ended with a 2–1 win. A free kick from 20 yards was not a bad way for him to depart on a day when our defence was hounded by a young local talent called Wayne Rooney. David had played his part in our victorious League campaign, so there was no reason to leave him out at Goodison Park.

Maybe he wasn't mature enough at that time to handle everything that was going on in his life. Today, he seems to manage things better. He is more certain of his position in life, more in control. But it was reaching the stage back then when I felt uncomfortable with the celebrity aspect of his life.

An example: arriving at the training ground at 3 p.m. before a trip to Leicester City, I noticed the press lined up on the road into Carrington. There must have been 20 photographers.

'What's going on?' I demanded. I was told, 'Apparently Beckham is revealing his new haircut tomorrow.'

David turned up with a beanie hat on. At dinner that night he was still wearing it. 'David, take your beanie hat off, you're in a restaurant,' I said. He refused. 'Don't be so stupid,' I persisted. 'Take it off.' But he wouldn't.

So I was raging. There was no way I could fine him for it. Plenty of players had worn baseball caps on the way to games and so on, but none had been so defiant about keeping one on during a team meal.

The next day, the players were going out for the pre-match warm-up and David had his beanie hat on. 'David,' I said, 'you're not going out with that beanie hat on. You'll not be playing. I'll take you out of the team right now.'

He went berserk. Took it off. Bald head, completely shaved. I said, 'Is that what this was all about? A shaved head that nobody was to see?' The plan was that he would keep the beanie hat on and take it off just before kick-off. At that time I was starting to despair of him. I could see him being swallowed up by the media or publicity agents.

David was at a great club. He had a fine career. He gave me 12 to 15 goals a season, worked his balls off. That was taken away from him. And with that being taken away from him, he lost the chance to become an absolute top-dog player. For my money, after the change, he never attained the level where you would say: that is an absolute top player.

The process began when he was around 22 or 23. He started to make decisions that rendered it hard for him to develop into a really great footballer. That was the disappointment for me. There was no animosity between us, just disappointment, for me. Dejection. I would look at him and think: 'What are you doing, son?'

When he joined us, he was this wee, starry-eyed kid. Football mad. At 16 he was never out of the gymnasium and couldn't stop practising. He loved the game; he was living the dream. Then he wanted to give it all up for a new career, a new lifestyle, for stardom.

From one perspective it would be churlish of me to say he made the wrong decision, in the sense that he's a very wealthy man. He's become an icon. People react to his style changes. They copy them. But I'm a football man, and I don't think you give up football for anything. You can have hobbies. I have horses; Michael Owen had horses; Scholes had horses. One or two players liked art. I had a lovely painting in my office that Kieran Richardson did. What you don't do is surrender the nuts and bolts of football.

A year prior to leaving us, of course, David had taken part in the 2002 World Cup in Japan and South Korea, weeks after breaking his metatarsal in the Champions League tie at Old Trafford in the spring of 2002. That was quite a drama.

Although David sustained the same metatarsal injury that was to afflict Wayne Rooney four years later, there was a difference in the recovery process. David was a naturally fit type of guy. Wayne needed more work to bring him back to sharpness. So I calculated that David might be fit enough for the World Cup, and said so openly at the time.

In the event, when England arrived in Japan, he might still have been carrying the remnants of his injury. It's hard to tell with some players, because in their desperation to play in a World Cup, they tell you they are fine. From the evidence of the tournament, David couldn't have been all right. The proof that physical frailty was still preying on his mind could be seen when he jumped over a tackle near the touchline in a sequence of play that led to Brazil's equaliser in the quarter-final in Shizuoka.

I was surprised at how physically off the pace he seemed, because he was such a fit boy. So he couldn't have been fit, either physically or mentally. People accused me, because I'm Scottish, of not wanting England to do well. If England played Scotland today, bloody right, I wouldn't want England to do well. But I had more players in my teams who were representing England than any other country, and always wanted them to shine.

When you have a player of Beckham's profile (and I had another later, in Rooney), there is a convergence of medical staff always wanting to interfere. England's medical staff would want to come to the training ground. Often I felt that this was an insult to us. I wondered whether my Scottishness was a factor, a reason not to trust me.

Before the 2006 World Cup, when Rooney joined up late with England's squad in Germany, England were texting us virtually every day, asking how he was, as if we couldn't look after him ourselves. The panic was wild. They were petrified. In 2006 I was 100 per cent correct. Wayne Rooney should not have played in that tournament. He was not ready.

He should never have been called to Baden-Baden where England were based. It was unfair to him, to the rest of the players and to the supporters. Wayne was the great hope of that team, of course, which added to the pressure to over-look reality. With David I was confident he would turn up in good shape because I knew his record and had seen all the statistics. He was easily the fittest player at Old Trafford. In pre-season training, in the bleep tests, he was streets ahead of everyone. We told England we were sure David would be fit in time.

The obsession with David's recovery was predictable. An oxygen tent found its way to Carrington. We had good results from that device on Roy Keane's hamstring injury before a European game. Bones are a different matter. The cure is rest. It's time. A metatarsal is a six- to seven-week injury.

In the 2002 World Cup, England failed to make much of an impact. Against Brazil, they were outplayed by ten men. In the first group game, they played long ball against Sweden, who knew the English game, and so were hardly likely to be caught off-guard by direct play.

It's an indictment of England teams at youth level that so many have fallen back on this outdated tactic. Too many played long ball. On one occasion we made a point of monitoring Tom Cleverley in the U-21s against Greece, and our scouts reported that England played one up, with two wide – Cleverley being one of the wide players – and Tom didn't get a kick. Chris Smalling played and kept launching the ball forward. This is the area where England were always likely to be caught out. Because they don't have enough technical and coaching ability, the years from 9 to 16 are thrown away.

So how do they compensate? The boys compete, physically. Great attitude, they have. Sleeves up. But they don't produce a player. They are never going to win a World Cup with that system, that mentality. Brazil would produce young players who could take the ball in any position, at any angle. They are fluid in their movements. They are football-minded people, because they are accustomed to it from five or six years of age.

David worked extremely hard on the technical side of his game. He was also a wonderful networker. Even when he was left out of the GB Olympic squad in the summer of 2012, it was his camp that released the news, rather than the FA. The quotes were all magnanimous. But I'm sure he was as sick as a pig.

I remember Mel Machin saying to me: 'Giggs and Beckham – they're world-class players, and yet you get them to go from box to box as well. How do you do that?' I could only reply that they were gifted not only with natural talent but the stamina to carry them up and down the pitch. We had something special with those two.

It changed with David because he wanted it to change.

His eye was off the ball. A shame, because he could still have been at Manchester United when I left. He would have been one of the greatest Man United legends. The only thing making him a legend at LA Galaxy and beyond was his iconic status. At some point in his life, he may feel the urge to say: I made a mistake.

But let me also pay tribute to him. His powers of perseverance are amazing, as he showed when joining Paris St-Germain in January 2013. At United he was always the fittest boy in the building. That helped him carry on playing to the age of 37. The stamina he built into himself from childhood survived.

The MLS is not a Mickey Mouse league. It's actually quite an athletic league. I watched Beckham in the final of the MLS Cup and noticed how well he did, tracking back, putting in a shift. Nor did he disgrace himself at Milan during his loan period there. At PSG he played for an hour in the quarter-finals of the European Cup. He wasn't in the game much, but he carried out his duties well. He worked hard and hit a few good passes early in the game.

I asked myself, 'How does he do it?'

Stamina was the first answer. But David also discovered a desire to confound everybody. And he could still hit a fine cross, a good cross-field ball, which are traits he never lost. They were ingrained in what he was as an athlete. To play in the later rounds of the Champions League at nearly 38 was quite an achievement after five years in America. He was back in the mix. You can only praise him for that.

One or two people asked me whether I would take him back after he left LA. With him at 37, there was no point going down that road. There was a publicity element for PSG in signing him on a six-month deal. David, however, ignored that part of it. As far as he was concerned, he was still a great player. Giggs, Scholes and I discussed this one day. As I said, he had this talent for blocking out bad performances. I would give him stick and he would go off in a huff, probably thinking, 'That manager's off his head, I was good today.'

In LA, he probably thought Hollywood was his next step in life. There was a purpose and a plan in him going to Los Angeles, I think. That aside, you have to admire his tenacity. He amazed me and he amazed everyone at Manchester United. Whatever he pursues in life, he just keeps on going.

six

RIO

R IO Ferdinand's eight-month suspension was a shock that reverberated to the core of Manchester United, and my indignation endures to this day. My issue is not with the rules on dope testing, but with how the process unfolded on the day Rio was meant to provide a routine sample at our training ground.

On 23 September 2003, a drug-testing team from UK Sport arrived at Carrington to take random samples from four of our players, whose names were picked out of a hat. What started as a routine training day was to have huge ramifications for Rio, his family, Manchester United and England. Rio, who was one of those selected, left Carrington without providing a sample, and by the time we managed to get hold of him, the drug testers had left for the day. He took the test the following day, 24 September, but was told he was in breach of the 'strict liability' rule on dope tests and would be charged.

The outcome was that Rio was banned from 20 January to 2 September 2004 and fined £50,000. Aside from all the Man United games he missed, it also meant he was ineligible for the 2004 European Championship in Portugal. His removal by the FA from the England squad to play Turkey in October 2003 almost caused a strike by the England players.

On the fateful morning in September, the testers were having a cup of tea and, in my judgment, didn't do their job. They didn't go looking for Rio. My view of it is that the testers should go to the pitch and stand there until the player finishes training, then follow him to the dressing room. Round about that time, testers went to Wrexham Football Club and ended up testing my son Darren and two other players. They stayed on the pitch, escorted them to the changing area and extracted the necessary urine sample. Why did that not happen with Rio at Carrington?

We knew the testers were at our training centre because Mike Stone, the doctor, told us the drug people were on the premises. Mike had a cup of tea with them while the message was sent down to the affected players in the dressing room. Rio was given the message, no doubt about that, but if you think of Rio's laidback nature, it was no surprise that he failed to hook up with people who were nowhere to be seen.

He was not a drug taker. Rio Ferdinand was not a drug taker. We would have known. It shows in their eyes. And he never missed a training session. Drug takers are all over the place. They become inconsistent. Rio would never be a drug taker because his sense of responsibility as to who he is in sport is too big. Rio is an intelligent guy but easy-going. He made a mistake, but so did the drug people. They didn't take the steps that would have averted the crisis that ensued. They should have been on that training field, waiting to take him in for his test.

I was aware that a serious breach of the drug-testing rules had been committed but I still found it hard to believe that Rio would end up with such a brutal punishment. The tendency is to treat players the way you would your children, and not believe them to be guilty of any allegation that originated outside the family.

Maurice Watkins, our solicitor, was quite confident we could win our case, on the grounds that the officials had not physically taken Rio away for the test. In my opinion, an example was often made of Manchester United. Eric Cantona was the first major case when in 1995 he was sentenced to two weeks' imprisonment and banned from playing for nine months for his kung-fu kick at a spectator (his prison sentence was later commuted to 120 hours' community service). Then, in 2008, Patrice Evra was disciplined by the FA after a confrontation with a groundsman at Stamford Bridge. Patrice picked up a four-match ban for a skirmish on the pitch – when everyone had gone home – with a groundsman. People assumed Man United received special treatment. The reverse was often true.

After a lot of legal toing and froing, Rio's hearing was held by an FA disciplinary commission at Bolton's Reebok Stadium in December 2003 and lasted 18 hours. It was 86 days after the missed test. I was among those who gave evidence on Rio's behalf. But the three-man panel found

Rio guilty of misconduct. Maurice Watkins called the sentence 'savage and unprecedented' and David Gill said Rio had been made 'a scapegoat'. Gordon Taylor of the PFA called it 'draconian'.

I spoke to Rio's mother right away because the poor woman was in bits. We could feel devastated by the loss of an important player, but it is the mother who will carry the real weight of such a punishment. Janice was crying down the phone as I told her that our high opinion of Rio would not be affected by the events of the last four months. We knew he was innocent, we knew he had been careless and we knew he had been punished too severely.

At that stage we were considering an appeal, but it was obvious we had no chance of winning. I could never understand that a missed drug test was treated as seriously as a failed one. If you admit to being a drug taker, you are rehabilitated. We felt that the player was telling the truth, whereas the system assumed he was not. Nor did we like the fact that information seemed to be leaking to the press from the FA. In our view the confidentiality principle was being breached.

I told the hearing at Bolton that Rio would be in my team to play Spurs that weekend, regardless of the outcome. He played alongside Mikaël Silvestre in a 2–1 win at White Hart Lane. In his last game for eight months, Rio started in our 1–0 defeat at Wolves on 17 January 2004, but came off injured after 50 minutes. Wes Brown took his place. Kenny Miller scored the only goal of the game.

I felt stricken to have lost him for so long. Our relationship started, in a sense, long before I made him the most expensive signing in English football. I was very friendly with Mel Machin, who called me from Bournemouth in 1997 to say he had a boy on loan from West Ham. 'Go and buy him,' Mel said.

'What's his name?'

'Rio Ferdinand.'

I knew that name from England youth teams. Mel was insistent. Mel, of course, was close to Harry Redknapp, then manager of West Ham, where Rio had been nurtured, so I was sure his judgment was based on solid information. I raised the subject of this young Bournemouth loanee with Martin Edwards. We had him watched at Bournemouth and made a note of his attributes: graceful, balanced, first touch like a centre-forward. Then we checked his background. Martin called the West Ham chairman, Terry Brown, who said: 'Give us a million plus David Beckham.' In other words: he's not for sale.

At that time, Jaap Stam and Ronny Johnsen were ensconced in the heart of our defence and Wes Brown was emerging as a young centre-half of promise. In the event, Rio was transferred to Leeds for £18 million. In his first game for our Yorkshire rivals, he played in a back three against Leicester City and was annihilated. Watching that match I felt a surge of relief, which I laugh about now. Thank God we didn't buy him. He was all over the place. But, needless to say, he developed exceptionally well.

Centre-backs were the foundation of my Manchester United sides. Always centre-backs. I looked for stability and consistency. Take Steve Bruce and Gary Pallister: until I found those two we were without a prayer. Paul McGrath was constantly injured; Kevin Moran always had split heads. He was like a punch-drunk boxer by the time I became his manager. I went to a game in Norway, where Ron Yeats was present in his capacity as chief scout for Liverpool.

'I saw your old player at Blackburn last week. Kevin Moran,' said Ron over a drink. I asked: 'How did he do?'

Answer: 'He lasted about 15 minutes. Got taken off with a split head.'

'Not unusual, that,' I said.

Graeme Hogg, meanwhile, had not reached the standard we required. So I always told my chairmen, 'We need centre-backs who will play every week. They give you the steadiness and consistency and continuity.' That led us to Bruce and Pallister, who played forever and never seemed to be injured. I remember one Friday before we played Liverpool, Bruce hobbling around The Cliff rubbing his hamstring and saying, 'Don't pick your team yet.' He had injured it the previous weekend. I liked to set out my team on the Friday so we could practise set pieces and so on. 'What are you on about?' I said.

'I'll be all right,' says Steve.

'Don't be so stupid,' I say.

So he starts running around The Cliff. He jogs round the pitch twice. 'I'm all right,' he says. He's only facing Ian Rush and John Aldridge for Liverpool. Meanwhile he can't stop rubbing his hamstring. Bruce played right through that game. He and Pally were marvellous. Stam brought us the same toughness and reliability. Look, too, at the partnership between Ferdinand and Vidić. Brilliant, solid, nothing given away. Consider Manchester United teams from that whole era and the centre-backs were always a feature.

So buying Ferdinand in July 2002 conformed to my sacred team-building policy of strength in the middle. We paid a lot, but when you spread that kind of transfer fee for a centre-half over 10 or 12 years, it starts to look like a bargain. You can fritter away plenty of money on contenders who simply aren't good enough. Better to spend more on a single player of unquestionable class.

We paid £3.75 million for Roy Keane, which was a transfer record at the time, but we had 11 years out of Roy. In my time at United I sold a lot of players people might not be familiar with: young reserve players and so on. On a cruise round the west of Scotland at the end of my last season, I worked out that I had spent an average of less than £5 million a season over my time at Man United.

I told Rio straight away when he joined, 'You're a big, casual sod.'

He said: 'I can't help it.'

'You'll need to help it. Because it'll cost you goals, and I'll be on your back,' I said.

And he was casual. Sometimes he would glide along in second or third gear, then take off like a sports car. I had never seen a big lad of 6 feet 2 inches possess such an impressive change of pace. With time his concentration improved, and the expectations he placed on himself rose, along with the degree of responsibility he was willing to take on in the team and around the club. He became the complete footballer.

When you acquire a young player, you don't get the complete package on purchase day. There's work to be done. If Rio was going to switch off in a game it would be against one of the lesser teams that he didn't regard as a major threat. The bigger the game, the more he liked it.

With Gary Neville beginning to pick up injuries, and Vidić and Evra settling in, Rio and Edwin van der Sar became the defensive fulcrum of the team in the second half of that decade. I played Rio once in the centre of midfield, in 2006 against Blackburn Rovers, and he got himself sent off. Robbie Savage was the victim of the tackle that put Rio back in the changing room.

This may surprise some, but Pallister was as good a foot-baller as Rio. Oddly, he was quicker, too, but he was no fan of running. Pally was anti-work, and I say that affectionately. He used to say that the less he did, the better he felt. He was the world's worst trainer. I was always after him. In the first 15 minutes he would stagger out of our penalty area after an opposition attack, gasping for air. I would say to Brian Kidd: 'Look at that Pally – he's dying!' I confess I used to slaughter him.

Picking him up one night for a club dinner, I entered his house to find a giant bottle of Coca-Cola on his fireside table and a big bag of sweets: Crunchies, Rolos, Mars Bars. I said to Mary, his wife, 'What about this?'

'I don't know how many times I tell him, boss, he doesn't listen,' Mary said.

So we hear footsteps on the stairs and Pally descends to see me studying this vast stash of kiddie food. 'Why do you buy all that stuff, Mary?' he says to his wife. So I fire back: 'You big lazy so-and-so, I'm fining you for that!'

Gary was no Adonis but he was a seriously good player with a sweet nature. A lovely lad. Like Rio, he could pass a

I had no idea an Old Trafford stand would be named after me. It was a conspiracy, but one that left me very proud.

Bobby Robson had great charisma. We take turns with the media after a 1981 UEFA Cup tie between my Aberdeen and his Ipswich Town.

Left: My big European breakthrough – Aberdeen beat Real Madrid in the 1983 European Cup Winners' Cup.

Above: In Gothenburg, Willie Miller lifts our European trophy. Aberdeen beat one of the biggest names in football.

was assistant Scotland manager alongside Jock Stein. He was touched by genius and I would bombard him with questions about management.

Above: Martin Edwards, the United chairman, stood by me in the dark days before my first trophy.

Left: Did the 1990 FA Cup final replay win over Crystal Palace save my job as United manager? I reckon I would have survived. On the left is Norman Davies, kit man and close friend, who is sadly no longer with us.

Ryan Giggs was revered by the other United players. Here he floats past Wimbledon's Warren Barton in his boyish early days.

Paul Scholes was better than Paul Gascoigne. 'Too small,' I thought when I first saw him a a lad. Wrong.

The 1992 vintage: coach Eric Harrison with the golden boys who became the heart of a great United team, (left to right) Giggs, Butt, Beckham, Gary Neville, Phil Neville, Scholes and Terry Cooke.

The banter always flowed between Steve Bruce (left) and Gary Pallister. But they were one of the greatest centre-half partnerships.

Eric Cantona could shape games in his own artistic image. His late goal won us the 1996 FA Cup final.

Peter Schmeichel was a mighty goalkeeper. A battering from Wimbledon's Crazy Gang soon after his arrival failed to break him.

Never give in. Three–nil down at Spurs in 2001, we fought back to win 5–3. Here Verón has just scored our fourth goal.

David Beckham's self-confidence never wavered. He was a fit boy and a marvellous striker of the ball.

Champions again, in May 2003. Beckham's last match for us. David deserves great credit for reviving his career.

The Brazilian Ronaldo was given a standing ovation after his Old Trafford hat-trick for Real Madrid in 2003. United fans know what talent is.

The heart was in for a test on big European nights. Tension gnawed away at us in that 2003 Champions League tie against Real Madrid.

Left: Rio Ferdinand was due to face a hearing for missing a drugs test when Roy Keane offered his support as they left the Old Trafford pitch.

Below: A draconian sentence. Rio is banned for eight months. The club would not abandon him.

Roy Keane took parts of my own character on to the pitch. In his later years injuries made it harder for him to gallop from box to box.

ball and was quick when he wanted to be. In his last season with us, he sustained a cut on his eyebrow and was howling, complaining that it was the first time he had been cut in his life. It didn't go with his image. Pally thought he was Cary Grant.

I wasn't consciously looking for a centre-back who could carry the ball out of defence, or send an incisive pass like Franz Beckenbauer. Pace, and the ability to read the game, are non-negotiables at the top in modern football. Rio had both, which is why I signed him. Not only could he defend, but he could bring the ball out. So although defending came first with me, it was encouraging to know my new centre-back could also start moves from the back, which became the norm later, with Barcelona and others.

At points in Rio's career, it was fair to say that his life expanded in more directions than we were happy with. I told him I was fed up with reading about him at dinners and launches. 'You know the thing about football? It catches you. What happens on the football field tells everybody,' I told him. When you start to decline, it happens quickly. At a small club you can get away with it. But at Manchester United there were 76,000 pairs of eyes on us and you could never kid them. I told Rio that if any of these distractions reduced his effectiveness as a footballer, he would not be with us much longer because I would not be picking him.

But he responded well to those warnings. We devised a system in which his agent was obliged to tell us everything he was doing, which gave us greater control. There was a music company, a film, a TV production company and a magazine that took him to America to interview P Diddy.

'Give me a break, Rio,' I said when I heard he was going to meet that star of the American rap scene. 'Is he going to make you a better centre-half?'

Rio was not alone in exploring other outlets. It all stemmed from the celebrity status of the modern footballer. Some look to expand it. Beckham was one, and Rio became another. David's success in that respect was miraculous.

Not all Rio's outside work was celebrity driven. His work for UNICEF in Africa was terrific. You can never dismiss the impact a Rio Ferdinand could make on the life of a black child in Africa. Our message was simply that he had to balance fame with a need to remember what made him successful in the first place. Some won't do that. Some can't.

We also thought Rio was always preparing for his life after football, which was not unreasonable. I did much the same by taking my coaching badges. That took me four years. So I also prepared for the second half of my life, after playing, but not by meeting P Diddy. There is that moment when a player asks himself what he is going to do, because stopping is such a void. One minute you're playing in European finals, FA Cup finals, winning championships, then it all fades to nothing. How to cope with that is a challenge all footballers face. Fame offers no immunity from the emotional comedown. The second half is not as exciting, so how do you re-create it? How do you replace the thrill of sitting in that dressing room ten minutes before the kick-off of a game that is going to determine who wins the League?

By the end of my time, Rio had developed back problems. We picked out the goal we conceded to City's Craig Bellamy in the Manchester derby of 2009 as an example of him working under a physical handicap. Two years previously he would have taken the ball off Bellamy and thrown him aside. Another was the Fernando Torres goal at Liverpool, when Torres beat him for speed and leaned on him one-on-one in the penalty box in front of the Kop.

We analysed that with him in a DVD review. Rio stepped up to play Torres offside and a year previously would have recovered from that error to dispossess him. But in this instance he was fighting to get back to deal with the threat and Torres shouldered him out of the road and blasted it into the net. Nobody did that to Rio. It told you the back injury was not only causing him pain, but also adversely affecting his balance.

Rio always cruised. He never had to fight to run. After the long lay-off that caused him to miss most of the winter, he came back brilliantly in training, and excelled against City in the semi-final second leg in 2009 at Old Trafford after almost three months out.

In his autumn years I had to tell him to change his game to take account of age and what it does to all of us. The years catch up with you. I told him, publicly and privately, that he needed to step back a yard or two to give himself a chance against strikers. Five years previously it had been lollipop stuff. With his change of pace he'd rob a centre-forward just when the striker thought he was in business. He could no longer do that. He needed to be on the scene before the crime could happen.

He was fine with my analysis. He wasn't insulted. I was simply explaining the changes in his body. And he had a great season in 2011–12, marred only, for him, by his omission from the England Euro 2012 squad. When Roy Hodgson asked my opinion about whether Rio could work with John Terry I replied, 'Ask him. Ask Rio about their relationship,' because I couldn't really give him an answer.

Another minor incident with him was when he refused to wear a Kick It Out T-shirt in 2012–13 after I thought we had all agreed to publicly back the campaign. It was a lack of communication. When he decided to boycott the Kick It Out T-shirt, Rio should have come to me, because he knew it was on the cards for us all to wear them. I know he had an issue over Anton, his brother, and John Terry but I didn't anticipate it spilling over in that way. Terry, of course, was punished by the FA for using racially abusive language against Anton in a game between QPR and Chelsea at Loftus Road.

I was in my office when Mark Halsey came in to tell me Rio was not wearing the Kick It Out jersey. I found Albert, our kit man, and instructed him to tell Rio to put the garment on.

The word came back that Rio would not be putting it on.

When I confronted him he said nothing, but after the game came in to explain that he felt the PFA were not doing enough to fight racism. My position was that by not wearing the T-shirt, he wasn't supporting the anti-racism cause. If he had a problem with the PFA he should, I felt, take that up with them. I thought it was divisive not to wear the T-shirt.

My view on racism is that I really don't comprehend how anyone could hate anyone else on the basis of their colour.

seven

LEAN TIMES

A WIND of change was coming. But it was not here yet. From the summer of 2003 to May 2006 was one of my least fertile spells. We won the FA Cup in 2004 and the League Cup two years later, but Arsenal and Chelsea were the League's title-winning outfits in that period.

Before Cristiano Ronaldo and Wayne Rooney could become the core of our 2008 Champions League winning side, there was a rocky road when we attempted to implant experienced players, many of whom failed to make the expected impact. David Beckham had left for Real Madrid and Verón was to leave for Chelsea. Barthez was replaced in goal by Tim Howard, and Kléberson, Eric Djemba-Djemba and David Bellion were among the new faces. Ronaldinho might have been, too, had he not said yes, then no, to our offer.

You can't dodge the truth about those years. We rushed

down the path of buying in proven players – who we thought would match our standards right away. Kléberson, for example, was a World Cup winner with Brazil and was only 24. Verón was an established player with a worldwide reputation. Djemba-Djemba had been playing at a decent level in France. They were easy or obvious signings, a fact that worried me. I don't like easy signings. I like having to fight for a player on the grounds that a battle to extricate him means you're acquiring something valuable. I liked it when the selling club were desperate to hang on to their man. But the players we bought around then were easy to recruit.

It felt as if we were signing every goalkeeper in the country. Mark Bosnich was a prime example. The Bosnich buy stemmed from Peter Schmeichel announcing in the autumn of his final season that he would be retiring, which caught us on the hop. We jumped into decisions.

We met Bosnich in January, despite reports filtering through to us about his conduct off the pitch. I sent someone down to watch him in training. He was doing nothing in the sessions that convinced me he was the right man for Manchester United. So I changed tack and went for Edwin van der Sar instead, spoke to his agent and then to Martin Edwards, who told me, 'Alex, I'm sorry, I've shaken hands with Bosnich.'

That was a blow. Martin had shaken Mark's hand and would not go back on his word, which I respect. But it was a bad piece of business. Bosnich was a problem. His training and fitness levels were below what we needed. We pushed him to a higher tier and felt we did quite well with him. He was terrific in our victory over Palmeiras in the Intercontinental Cup, in which he ought to have been man of the match, ahead of Giggs. Not much later, we played down at Wimbledon in February, and Bosnich was tucking into everything: sandwiches, soups, steaks. He was going through the menu, eating like a horse.

I told him: 'For Christ's sake, Mark, we've got the weight off you, why are you tucking into all that stuff?'

'I'm starving, gaffer,' he said.

We arrived back in Manchester, and Mark was on a mobile phone to a Chinese restaurant to order a takeaway. 'Is there no end to you?' I asked him. 'Think what you're doing.' I just couldn't make an impact on him.

You don't recover easily from losing a Peter Schmeichel. He was the best goalkeeper in the world, and his presence, his personality, were suddenly no longer there. We should have replaced him with Van der Sar. His agent had told me, 'You'll need to be busy, because he's talking to Juventus,' but we missed the boat. I had to return to Edwin's agent and tell him we had already agreed to take someone else and that I would have to withdraw my interest.

I should have taken him as well, as a second purchase. We'd have soon found out about Bosnich and Edwin would have played from the end of the Schmeichel era pretty much to my last years in charge. I wouldn't have needed to spend money on Massimo Taibi or Barthez, who was a good goalkeeper, but had problems back in France.

Later we saw that Van der Sar's qualities were in the same league as those of Schmeichel. There was little between them, talent-wise. Schmeichel pulled off saves he wasn't entitled to make. There were moments of wonder. 'Jesus, how did he do that?' I would ask. He had such spring, such athleticism. With Van der Sar I would point to his composure, his calmness, his use of the ball, his organisational ability. It was a different style of goalkeeping but still invaluable. It affected people around him in a good way.

Schmeichel, by contrast, had a love–hate relationship with Steve Bruce and Gary Pallister. He would come out screaming and bawling at them and Brucey would say, 'Get back in your goal, you big German tart.' Schmeichel hated that. 'I'm not German,' he would hiss. They were great buddies off the field, though. On it, Schmeichel was a volatile individual.

In the dressing room, Van der Sar was very emphatic about performances. He had a strong voice, a Dutch voice. 'No messing about here!' he would bark. Schmeichel would impose his voice on the team as well. I was lucky to have the two best goalkeepers of those three decades. An honourable mention would have to go to Peter Shilton, and to Gianluigi Buffon; but to me, Schmeichel and Van der Sar were the best from 1990–2010.

There is more to the art than the goalkeeping. It's a question of the personality you bring to the job. Not only do keepers have to deal with the business of making saves, they must cope with the process of making errors. You need a big character at Manchester United to handle the aftermath of a high-profile mistake. I had scouted Schmeichel half a dozen times. Alan Hodgkinson, the goalkeeping coach, had told me: 'He's a certainty. Take him.'

At first I was ambivalent about bringing foreign goalkeepers into the English game. One of Schmeichel's early games was against Wimbledon. The 'Crazy Gang' were blitzing him, dropping bombs on top of him and elbowing him. Schmeichel was going crazy, shouting for the officials to help him. 'Referee, referee!'

I watched this scene unfold and thought, 'He's got no chance.' The ref couldn't get back up the pitch and away from the conflict zone quickly enough. In another of his early matches, Peter came out for a cross at the back post and missed it by about two days. Lee Chapman knocked it in. So he did make mistakes while he was adjusting to the game in this country, and people were saying, 'What have we got here?' But he also had an incredible physique, he covered the goal and he was brave. His distribution of the ball was marvellous. All those qualities came to his assistance in those torrid early days.

Van der Sar oversaw a lot of change in our defence. Schmeichel stood behind the same back four just about every week. Parker, Bruce, Pallister, Irwin. They played virtually every game. Van der Sar had to get used to different centre-backs, new full-backs. There was flux. In those circumstances it's a great credit to him that he was able to organise that part of the team so well.

This was a time when Peter Kenyon was our chief executive in charge of transfer dealings. Arsenal's Patrick Vieira was one we liked a lot. I asked Peter to phone Arsenal to inquire about Vieira. He told me he had. One day later I mentioned it to David Dein and he looked at me as if I had horns on my head. There was no recognition of what I was talking about. One of them was playing his cards close to his chest and, to this day, I have no idea which one it was.

Time and again I had agents phoning me to say, 'My man would love to play for Manchester United.' I never doubted the claim. But I also knew they would have loved to play for Arsenal, Real Madrid, Bayern Munich and all the other elite teams. Players obviously like to get to the big clubs. The agent gets more out of it, too. It was in that phase of playing the market that we fixed our gaze on Verón.

The team was altering. It's not an easy thing for a manager to see change coming from a long way down the road. The old back four broke up fastest. When these sudden changes strike, you realise you don't necessarily have the backup. Later I made it my policy to plan much further ahead.

Verón was a superb footballer with immense stamina. I confess I found working with Argentinian footballers quite difficult. There was deep patriotism towards Argentina. They always had the flag round them. I had no problem with that, but the ones I managed didn't try particularly hard to speak English. With Verón it was just, 'Mister.'

But what a good footballer. His intelligence in the game and his engine were first-rate. The problem? We couldn't find a position in which to play him. If we played him in the centre of midfield he would end up at centre-forward, or wide right, or wide left. He just hunted the ball. We found it increasingly hard to fit him, Scholes and Keane into a midfield.

Although he played some terrific games for us, you couldn't see the shape of the team forming. You couldn't see the positional stability that you look for normally. Beckham had left us, Ryan was getting older, as were Roy and Paul, and we were looking for that freshness to give us the impetus to evolve a bit. Although there were spectacular contributions, Verón just couldn't play in our team. He was an individual. He was the sort who, if you played red v. yellow on the training ground, Verón would play for both teams. He just played everywhere. He went wherever he liked. If I managed him for a hundred years I wouldn't know where to play him. He was the wild card, the joker. Somebody once said to me: 'Have you ever thought of playing him in a sitting position, holding, in front of the two centre-backs?' I replied, 'Are you dreaming? I can't get him to stay in any other position, why would he stay in that one?' Apparently he had played there for Lazio and been magnificent. But he was a free bird, flying everywhere.

There were moments when he would take you to the heavens. In one pre-season game he beat a couple of men on the by-line and knocked it in for Van Nistelrooy to score. He hit a pass for Beckham with the outside of his foot, and no back lift, and it bent away round the defence. Beckham ran on to it and lobbed the goalkeeper. In moments he could be sublime. Talent-wise there was absolutely nothing wrong with him. He had two fine feet, he could run, his control was magnificent, his vision was brilliant – he just couldn't fit into the team. The English game was not a barrier to him. He was brave. He always had the balls to play.

There was talk during his time with us of Verón falling out with other players, but I don't think he did, partly because he never spoke to anyone. He was alone in the dressing room. He didn't speak the language. He wasn't antisocial; he just wasn't a communicator.

I'd come in for work: 'Morning, Seba.'

'Morning, mister.' And that was it. You couldn't drag anything from him. I do remember a fall-out with Roy Keane, after a European tie. That became a bit ugly. There was another with Gabriel Heinze at Portsmouth. Heinze was ready to fight him. But no, he was not a disruptive influence.

We were trying to alter the way we played in Europe. Two years after the 1999 European Cup win, we went to play Anderlecht in Belgium and PSV in Eindhoven and we were battered. Only on the counter-attack. We played the traditional United way, 4–4–2, and were thumped. I told the players and staff that if we could not keep the ball better and stay solid in midfield, we were going to suffer more that way because opponents had sussed us out. So we switched to playing three in the centre of the park. Verón was part of that development.

Managing change, which I had to do so often over that decade, I came up against many players I admired. I tried so hard, for example, to get Paolo Di Canio. The deal was all done. We had made an offer that he had accepted, but then he came back saying he wanted more. We couldn't agree to the new demand. But he was the sort of player Manchester United should have: one who can put bums on seats and get people off them, too. I had players like that for the whole time I was there.

Then there was Ronaldinho, another who slipped the hook. I agreed a deal to bring him to Old Trafford. Carlos was there and would vouch for that. The attempt to buy Ronaldinho reflected the fact that United have always sported talismanic players. I was always hunting for that kind of talent. My line of reasoning was, 'We're getting twenty-five million pounds for Beckham, and we're getting Ronaldinho for nineteen million. For God's sake, wake up. It was a steal.'

On the way home from our trip to America, we stopped in Newfoundland to refuel, at a tiny outpost. Only a single hut marked the landscape. As we waited for the refuelling, the cabin crew opened the door to let fresh air in and a small boy was standing at the fence, alone with a United flag. We weren't allowed to disembark. We could stand on the steps but not the tarmac, so all we could do was wave to this little United fan, pressed against a fence in the middle of nowhere.

Returning to Europe, for a stop in Portugal, we sold Verón, who had told Quinton Fortune he would be joining Chelsea. I wouldn't let him go for less than £15 million. Chelsea offered £9 million. I said, 'No way, he's not going for nine million.' But in Portugal, Kenyon told me, 'I've agreed the deal – fifteen million.' Then came the game against Sporting Lisbon and Ronaldo v. John O'Shea. I can still hear myself shouting at John, 'Get close to him, Sheasy.'

'I can't,' came the plaintive reply.

One month later David Gill rang and said, 'What about this, Kenyon is off to Chelsea.' David took over and was fantastic – a big improvement. Peter Kenyon, I felt, tried to take on too much and was consequently unable to deliver on some of the most important tasks. The expertise you need in a chief executive role is a talent for completing missions.

When David Gill moved into the hot seat, I suspect he was uncertain about his function. David was an accountant by trade. My advice was, 'On the back of Peter Kenyon, don't take on too much. Delegate.' Without doubt he was the best administrator or chief executive I ever dealt with. First class. Straight as a die. Very approachable. Kept his feet on the ground and knew the value of the game. Understood it, too. Martin Edwards also had a good knowledge of the game, but there were no complications with David. He might tell you something you didn't like, but he would not shirk from saying it. That was the only way to be.

Although Martin supported me at the most important times, I was always underpaid until David took charge. There is no substitute for being appreciated at work. To be told you are doing a fine job is all very well, as far as it goes, but there has to be monetary recognition.

Dealing with changes in ownership is immensely difficult for club directors. After a takeover the whole picture changes. Do they fancy you? Do they want a new manager, a new chief executive? The Glazer buy-up was the toughest period for David. The media focus was intense. The debt issue was never out of the news. But David's accountancy qualifications gave him an advantage in that respect.

My vision of the club was as a place where young talent could develop. To sustain that aim we needed to preserve the foundation of Giggs, Scholes and Neville. And Roy Keane. We had enough backbone to enable us to shop around for potential. Van der Sar was another foundation player. He was one of my best-ever signings.

The search for the new Bryan Robson had led us to Keane. Eric Djemba-Djemba struck us as potentially another top central midfielder. I went to see him playing in France and he did really well. He understood the game, nipped attacks in the bud very well and was available for 4 million euros. I was at that game to see the Rennes goalkeeper too: Petr Čech, who was 18 or 19. I told myself he was too young for us.

Sometimes you lost one player but gained another of similar merit. We missed out on Paul Gascoigne, for example, but landed Paul Ince. We didn't persuade Alan Shearer to join us but we did sign Eric Cantona.

The balls are always in the air. You have a range of targets and compensate from the list when one gets away. The unifying aim was to develop whichever player we ended up with. Cantona was in his mid-twenties, but our normal target area would be younger than that. Rooney and Ronaldo came as teenagers. After 2006 or so, we redoubled our efforts to avoid falling into the old trap of seeing a team grow old together. We refocused on that. With Andy Cole, Dwight Yorke and Teddy Sheringham, there was either a falling off in performance levels or an advance in years. In those circumstances, the demands on the scouting network intensify. The heat is on the talent-spotters. You are saying to them all the time, 'Come on, what have you seen out there?'

The Kléberson signing came after he had excelled for Brazil at the 2002 World Cup. He was still playing in his homeland when we signed him. But he was an example of the risks associated with making a purchase in a hurry. What we were looking for was someone to take over eventually from Keane, which is how Vieira had entered the picture. He would have been ideal. He was used to the English game, an imposing figure; a leader. One sign of a great player is that the opposing fans sing songs against him. Opposing fans always sang songs against Patrick Vieira. That tells you they feared him. Alan Shearer was another. Always on the wrong end of chants from the opposition.

Kléberson was a talented player. But he exemplifies my point about careful examination of background and character. We acquired him too easily. It made me uncomfortable. When the boy arrived, we discovered he had married a 16-year-old girl. He was 23. She brought all her family over. In pre-season training in Portugal at Vale do Lobo, only the players were meant to come to breakfast before training. Kléberson brought his father-in-law. He seemed to have no authority in that area. Lovely lad, but he lacked the confidence to learn English.

In games he displayed terrific stamina and a high degree of skill but was unable to impose his personality. Perhaps the way Brazil had used him was not the way we wanted to employ him. With his country he sat in front of the back four to help Roberto Carlos and Cafú bomb on from full-back.

When there is a sudden rush to solve problems, mistakes are made. We were at our best when we worked from a plan, over years, and studied players, compiled detailed information. We knew all about Cristiano Ronaldo before we signed him. We tried to get Rooney at 14, and tried again at 16. Finally we cracked it when he was 17. You could plan for Rooney. He was an obvious target for us. That was Manchester United's scouting at its very best. The Veróns and the Klébersons were improvised. Not panic buys, but rushed.

Djemba-Djemba, another smashing lad, was hammered

by the press for not being a signature signing. They always liked the marquee names and took a much dimmer view of players with a lower recognition rating. They loved Verón, at first. They were lukewarm about Kléberson and Djemba-Djemba. David Bellion was young and we felt we could develop him. He was lightning quick, a charming boy, a Christian, but also very shy. He had been at Sunderland and had come on as a sub against us. Tore us apart. We made a move for him when his contract was up. Had we looked into his background more, we'd have known he was diffident. We sold him to Nice for 1 million euros, and he moved from there to Bordeaux, which brought us an additional fee. The Bellion transfer was not one you could classify as an attempt to lay a foundation stone for a new side. He was an add-on who was available at a good price.

The turning point in this whole chapter was capturing Ronaldo and Rooney, which gave us the signature signings we needed: talismanic, match-winning players, in line with our tradition. Patrice Evra and Nemanja Vidić, in January 2006, were to be other stellar acquisitions. The first point in our notes on Vidić was his courage, his determination. He could tackle, head the ball clear. We were looking at a typical English centre-back. Vida hadn't played since the end of the season in Moscow, in November. In his first game for us, against Blackburn, he was breathing out of his backside. He needed a pre-season. That was the gist of it.

At left-back, in Denis Irwin's old position, we had Heinze briefly but then moved on to Evra, who was used as a wing-back at Monaco, where he featured in the Champions League final against Porto.

With full-backs it's like searching for a rare bird. When we first saw Evra, he was playing as a wing-back, but he had the speed and was young enough to switch to full-back in our system. We knew plenty about his attacking capabilities. He was quick, had superb technique and a strong personality. Very strong. Heinze was another matter. Ruthless, would kick his granny. But an absolute winner who could also play centre-back. In both cases we were successful.

As all United fans will remember, Evra's debut came in the Manchester derby at Eastlands and was a total disaster. You could see him thinking, 'Why am I here?' Eventually he settled and developed. Heinze, on the other hand, had a mercenary streak and I always had the sense he was scanning the horizon for his next deal. After one year he wanted to leave. We were playing Villarreal, and stationed in a lovely complex outside Valencia, when his agent came to see me to say he wanted to move.

Things were never the same after that. The following day he injured his cruciate. We did everything possible to accommodate him. He was allowed to pursue his rehabilitation in Spain. He was there for six months and came back for a single game. We did our best. But at the end of December he came back wanting away, wanting new terms, a new contract. When he returned fully from injury, he went to see David Gill with his agent and we agreed we would be better off without him. We agreed to let him go for £9 million. They went straight to Liverpool, who said they would take him.

Gabriel was told, with no ambiguity, that historically Manchester United do not sell players to Liverpool, and vice versa. Heinze's advisers then tried to make a legal issue of it, which led to a meeting in London, in which the Premier League sided with us.

During that process, the chairman of Crystal Palace contacted David Gill to say someone representing Heinze had asked them to buy him so they could later sell him on to Liverpool. We used that information as part of our evidence. The judgment came down in our favour and eventually we offloaded him to Real Madrid. These guys move around. Heinze had been at two Spanish clubs already before he went to PSG, from where he came to us.

Alan Smith was another addition from that time, in May 2004, for £7 million. Leeds were in financial trouble by then and word came through to David Gill that Alan could be bought for around £5 million. I had always liked Alan. He was what I called an attitude player, with a good character. He could play a few positions: wide right, midfield, centre-forward. He was a Mark Hughes-type player: not a great goal-scorer but useful to the team. We later sold him to Newcastle for £6 million. Alan did a fair job for us and put in some smashing performances. His leg-break at Liverpool in 2006 was one of the most horrific I've seen. I'll always remember rushing to see him as he lay on the Liverpool treatment table – Liverpool's doctor was exemplary, I should say – while they injected him to stop the onset of trauma.

His foot was pointing in all sorts of directions. Bobby Charlton, who was with me, winced. And he had been through the Munich air disaster. Alan, on the other hand, was unperturbed. He was sitting there emotionless. It was a horror of an accident. Alan's reaction told me that some men's pain thresholds are higher than others'. Jabs terrify me. I'm hopeless with needles. In my pub-keeping days in Glasgow, during a keg-change one Sunday morning, I was releasing a spear to let the air out when a rat jumped on my shoulder. I leapt back and the spear of the keg sank into my cheek. You can still see the skin graft. I drove the two miles to the hospital, afraid to touch it. The nurse whipped it out and I fainted as soon as they put the needle in me. The nurse said: 'This is the big centre-forward of Rangers Football Club and he's fainting.' I was dying there. Alan was sitting with one of the worst injuries I've ever seen and not a bit of stir in him. That's what Alan was: a supremely brave lad.

He was a good, honest professional, too. What he lacked was the real top quality you need to excel at the biggest clubs. When we were offered the money by Newcastle, we had to let him go.

Our final use of him was as a defensive midfielder. He tackled well but didn't read the game like an authentic holding player. He was a midfield player who could tackle, wherever the ball was. In his centre-forward days, centre-backs seldom had an easy time with Alan. But the whole process of replacing Roy required us to find a player who could sit in good areas of the pitch, the way Owen Hargreaves did for a while. Alan wasn't that type, but he was a good, honest player who loved playing for us. It took me a long time to persuade him that I couldn't guarantee him a game. The team had moved on.

Louis Saha was another major signing, from Fulham in

January 2004, but persistent injuries counted against him, and us. We watched him a couple of times at Metz but the scouting reports gave no indication that he would be a target for the biggest clubs. He turned up at Fulham, and every time he played against us he gave us a 'doing'. In an FA Cup tie at Craven Cottage, he turned Wes Brown on the halfway line, flew at our goal, cut it back and Fulham scored. From then on we watched him all the time, and by January were ready to make our move.

Dealing with Mohammed Fayed, Fulham's owner, was a complicated process. Word came back that a figure had been agreed and we were told: 'This is the best you're going to get.' It was a middle position: £12 million.

Of all the centre-forwards we employed, when you talk about their talents (two-footed, good in the air, spring, speed, power), Saha would be one of the best. He posed a perpetual threat. But then came the injuries. Louis, who lived about 50 yards from me, and was a lovely lad, had to be 150 per cent to play. It was agony for us. And it wasn't a case of him being out for weeks; it tended to be months. The reason for selling him was that no matter how talented he was, I could never plan around him, could never say, 'This is my team for the next two or three years.' Saha was young enough to be viewed in that way, as a cornerstone player, but the uncertainty caused by his constant non-availability rendered it impossible to look far down the line.

It became so vexing to him that he considered retiring. 'You're a young man, you don't give in because of an injury, you've just got to work to get back. This can't last forever,' I told him.

He was assailed by guilt. He thought he was letting us down. He would send me apologetic texts to that effect. I tried to impress on him that he had been unlucky, and that unlucky players could be found throughout footballing history. Viv Anderson was one. When we were assessing Viv's playing record at Arsenal, we noticed that in four years he missed four games. Suspension, every time. Viv came to us and was never fit. We gave him a free transfer to Sheffield Wednesday and he played there for three years and hardly missed a game. I used to give him stick about that. I'd say, 'I don't think you wanted to play for me.' He's a big United fan and was desperate to shine for us, but was halted by persistent knee trouble.

Louis knew his injuries were hampering his form, and that's where the guilt complex began biting away at him. Carlos devised a two-week programme for him to enable him to be fully ready in a fortnight. This was tailored work, which he did on his own. We explained that to him, and he embraced it – shooting, turning, and generally throwing himself into these preparatory exercises. He was flying. Friday, the day before the game, and Saha walks off, saying he had felt something in his hamstring. We were never going to conquer that physical sensitivity, so we reached a deal with Everton in 2008.

Everton copied our approach and tried to raise Louis to a level where he would be confident of playing. It might have helped him to be away from the pressure of Manchester United. He was a fantastic centre-forward, though. In the 2009–10 season, I thought France would be mad not to take him to the World Cup.

A constant in our discussions about young players – in terms of whether they could handle the demands of the Old Trafford crowd and the short patience span of the media – was temperament. Would they grow or shrink in a United shirt? We knew the make-up of every young homegrown player who came into the United starting XI, from the training ground, from reserve team football.

You can't leave your character in the dressing room. It has to come out of that room, down the tunnel and onto that pitch.

In the 2003–04 season we finished third in the League behind the Invincibles of Arsenal, but finished off with a 3–0 win over Millwall in the FA Cup final in Cardiff. Ronaldo was majestic in that match, scoring our first goal with a header before Van Nistelrooy added two more, one from the penalty spot.

The year had been overshadowed by the death of Jimmy Davis in a road accident. Jimmy, 21, was one of those bright, breezy individuals. He had a chance too. He would have had a career in the game. We had loaned him to Watford. On the way to an academy game at our place that Saturday morning, I heard that Watford's game that afternoon had been postponed. There were no details given. Then I was told, at the academy game, of Jimmy's death in a road accident.

He was a tenacious wee lad, very popular. A large number from the club attended his funeral. Two years later, at a wedding, I felt a creeping sense of déjà vu. As the photographs were being taken outside, the minister came over to me and said, 'Would you like to come round and see Jimmy's grave?' I hadn't made the connection, and it chilled me to the core. It was so sad. He would not be forgotten by Manchester United.

eight

RONALDO

CRISTIANO Ronaldo was the most gifted player I managed. He surpassed all the other great ones I coached at United. And I had many. The only ones who could be placed near him would be a couple of the home-produced players, Paul Scholes and Ryan Giggs, because they contributed so prodigiously to Manchester United for two decades. That longevity, consistency and those behaviour patterns were quite exceptional.

We lost our wizard, Cristiano, to Real Madrid, in the end, but we looked back at his time with us with pride and gratitude. In six seasons with us, from 2003 to 2009, he scored 118 times in 292 games and won the Champions League, three Premier League titles, one FA Cup and two League Cups. He scored in the 2008 Champions League final, against Chelsea in Moscow, and kicked a ball for us for the final time 12 months later, in the final against Barcelona in Rome.

In between we watched a special talent bloom on our training pitches at Carrington and in our first XI, which passed through a lean spell in the middle years of the decade. We helped Ronaldo to be the player he was and he helped us recapture the excitement and self-expression of Manchester United teams.

Madrid paid £80 million in cash for him, and do you know why? It was a way for Florentino Pérez, their president, to say to the world, 'We are Real Madrid, we are the biggest of the lot.' It was a clever move by them and a declaration of their intent to chase the game's most famous players.

Ramón Calderón, Pérez's predecessor, had claimed the previous year that Cristiano would one day be a Real Madrid player. I knew full well that if they produced the £80 million, he would have to go. We could not block his fervent wish to return to Iberia and wear the famous white shirt of Di Stefano or Zidane. The reality of managing Ronaldo, as of other talents who came to Manchester United as teenagers, was that you could oversee the early years fairly comfortably, because they were not yet global idols, they were on the way up. At the point they became mega-stars, as Ronaldo did, you asked yourself a question that Carlos Queiroz and I discussed all the time: 'How long are we going to be able to keep Cristiano Ronaldo?'

Carlos was as accurate as it was possible to be. He said: 'Alex, if you get five years out of him, you've struck gold. There's no precedent for a Portuguese player going to another country at seventeen years old and staying five years.' The fact that we had him for six was a bonus. In that period we won a European Cup and three League titles with him. I consider that a pretty good return.

When the possibility of him leaving edged towards being a probability, I reached a gentleman's agreement with him. I went to Carlos's house in Portugal to find the boy expressing an urge to go to Real Madrid, and told him: 'You can't go this year, not after the way Calderón has approached this issue.' I said, 'I know you want to go to Real Madrid. But I'd rather shoot you than sell you to that guy now. If you perform, don't mess us about, and someone comes and offers us a world record fee, then we will let you go.' I had already conveyed that message to his agent Jorge Mendes.

I did well to calm him down. I told him that the reason I was refusing to sell him that year was because of Calderón. I said, 'If I do that, all my honour's gone, everything's gone for me, and I don't care if you have to sit in the stands. I know it won't come to that, but I just have to tell you I will not let you leave this year.'

I reported this conversation to David Gill, who passed it through to the Glazers. I'm sure it found its way back to Real Madrid as well. At that point we were petrified that the details of our agreement might creep out. We warned Cristiano to that effect. I don't believe he would have told Real Madrid. His agent Jorge Mendes is, I should say, the best agent I dealt with, without a doubt. He was responsible, looked after his players to an incredible extent and was very fair with clubs. My feeling was that he was anxious about Cristiano going to Spain for the obvious reason that Real might just swallow him up. Different agents, different people. I think he feared losing him.

What I always thought about Ronaldo was that, even if he was having a dire game, he would always create three chances. Every game. Look at all the matches. In the mountain of video evidence, you could not find one instance where he failed to create at least three chances. He possessed an unbelievable talent. I can place everything on that list: training performances, strength, courage, skill with either foot, heading ability.

In the early days, there is no doubt that he acted a bit. His earliest lessons were in a theatrical footballing culture. Injustice was never far from the judgments formed around him. But he changed. One aspect frequently ignored by his critics was the speed he moved at. You only need to tap a player going that fast and there is a tendency for him to go over. Human balance isn't refined enough to protect the runner from tipping over at an unnaturally fast speed. A wee prod into the side of the leg or an elbow into the body can disturb the equilibrium. The failure to appreciate that speed-to-balance factor was unfair.

In the early days, I accept, he showboated a lot, and Carlos worked hard on that part of his repertoire. He would say to Cristiano all the time, 'You're only a great player when people outside the club start recognising you as such. It's not enough to be a great player to us at Manchester United. When you start delivering the passes, delivering the crosses, at the right time, people won't be able to read you. That's when the great players emerge.'

Opponents knew what to expect of him. They knew he was going to hold on to the ball. If you looked at his goal in the semi-final against Arsenal, you see the transition. We struck on the counter-attack, Ronaldo back-heeled it into Ji-Sung Park and we were up at the other end within nine seconds. It took nine seconds to put the ball in the back of the net.

That was the transformation from the wee show-off who was desperate to convince everyone how good he was. Yes, that's really what it was: the need that so many gifted players have to prove just how blessed they are. And nobody could kick him out of that. No matter how many tackles or fouls he absorbed, his whole being expressed defiance: 'You're not going to kick me out of this game. I'm Ronaldo.' He had that wonderful courage and confidence in his ability. He elevated himself, in my mind, and in those of the other United players, to a point where those around him were in awe of his talent.

The players were good with him in training. They helped him learn. At first when he was tackled at Carrington he would let out a terrible scream. 'Aaggh!' The players would give him pelters. He soon learned not to make that kind of racket. His intelligence helped. He was a very smart boy. Once he realised the players would not be a willing audience for his screaming and amateur dramatics in training, he stopped. Over time it erased itself from his game. In his last season he overreacted a couple of times to earn himself a foul, but no more than anyone else. He was granted a penalty kick against Bolton in 2008 that was never a penalty kick. Equally he hadn't tried to earn that advantage. It was just a bad mistake by the referee. The defender stretched to win the ball, intercepted it cleanly and Ronaldo went over. It was embarrassing, not from Ronaldo's point of view, but for Rob Styles, the match official.

Despite everyone saying they could have signed him (Real Madrid and Arsenal made that claim), we had an alliance with Sporting Lisbon, his first club in Portugal. We were sending coaches over there and they were dispatching them in the opposite direction. When Carlos joined us in 2002, he told me, 'There's a young boy at Sporting and we need to keep an eye on him.'

'Which one?' I asked. Because there were two or three.

'Ronaldo,' he said. We knew all about him. At that stage Cristiano had been playing centre-forward. Carlos said we would need to act because this boy was special, so we sent Jim Ryan to watch Sporting Lisbon train as part of our reciprocal deal. Jim returned and said, 'Wow, I've seen a player. I think he's a winger, but he's been playing centre-forward in the youth team. I wouldn't be waiting too long. At seventeen someone will gamble.'

So we threw the boy wonder's name into a conversation with Sporting. The response was that they wanted to keep him for two more years. I suggested a deal that would keep him at Sporting for that length of time before we took him to England. At this point, though, we had not spoken to the agent or the player. It was purely a club-to-club discussion.

That summer Carlos left, to coach Real Madrid, and we went to America on tour. Peter Kenyon left, Juan Sebastián Verón left. Part of our arrangement was that we would play against Sporting Lisbon in their new stadium, which had been built for the 2004 European Championship.

So over we went. John O'Shea was right-back. People persist in saying Gary Neville was in that unenviable position. But it was John O'Shea. The first pass Ronaldo took prompted me to howl: 'For Christ's sake, John, get tight to him!'

John shrugged his shoulders. A look of pain and bewilderment was creeping across his face. The other players in the dug-out were saying: 'Bloody hell, boss, he's some player, him.'

I said: 'It's all right. I've got him sorted.' As if the deal had been done ten years ago. I told Albert, our kit man: 'Get up to that directors' box and get Kenyon down at half-time.' I told Peter, 'We're not leaving this ground until we've got that boy signed.'

'Is he that good?' Kenyon asked.

'John O'Shea's ended up with migraine!' I said. 'Get him signed.'

Kenyon spoke to the Lisbon people and asked their permission to speak to Cristiano. They warned us that Real Madrid had offered £8 million for him.

'Offer them nine, then,' I said.

Ronaldo was downstairs in a small room, with his agent, where we told him how much we would love to sign him for Manchester United. In front of Jorge Mendes I said, 'You won't play every week, I'm telling you that now, but you'll become a first-team player. There's no doubt in my mind about that. You're seventeen years of age, it'll take time for you to adjust. We'll look after you.'

A private plane was hired for him, his mother, his sister, Jorge Mendes and his lawyer to come over the next day. We needed to get that deal done. Speed of action was paramount. I used to scout myself, on a Saturday morning in Glasgow, and I would always say to the men I employed in that capacity:

'It must be great when you can spot someone you know is going to be the business.'

One night I was watching a movie, *White Fang*, the Jack London book about going down to Klondike in search of gold. That's what it must be like for a scout. You're standing watching a game on a Saturday morning and you see a George Best, a Ryan Giggs or a Bobby Charlton. That's what I felt that day in Lisbon. A revelation.

That was the biggest surge of excitement, of anticipation, I experienced in football management. The next best was from Paul Gascoigne, for a different reason. Newcastle had been fighting relegation and Gascoigne had been out injured. We were at St James' Park on the Easter Monday. I played Norman Whiteside and Remi Moses in the centre of the park. It was hardly a midfield of choirboys. You wouldn't dance round that duo. Well, Gascoigne nutmegged Moses right in front of where I was sitting in the dug-out, and then patted him on the head. I flew out of that dug-out, shouting, 'Get that so-and-so . . .'

Whiteside and Moses tried to impress on Gascoigne that he had just made a serious error of judgment. A little re-education was in order. But Gascoigne just skipped all round them.

We tried our best to sign him that summer. But Newcastle sold him to Tottenham instead. When you have that experience, of seeing this talent right before your eyes, you know you're experiencing one of those moments you search for every hour in management. And that sense of discovery rushed me into trying to tie up a deal for Gascoigne that very day.

With Ronaldo, in contrast, Kenyon did manage to complete the deal. I sensed that Sporting might have been happy not to have sold him to a Spanish club. The deal was concluded quite swiftly, with add-ons that took it up to about £12 million, with the sole condition that, should we ever sell him, Sporting would have the option of taking him back. A couple of days before we sold him to Real Madrid, we had to tell Sporting that they could have him back, but it would cost them £80 million. Not surprisingly, no cheque was forthcoming.

As Cristiano started his new life in Cheshire, his mother and sister came with him. That was good. His mother was very protective, as you would expect, and was a good, straight-talking woman, with no airs or graces. She was highly maternal. I explained to Ronaldo that Lyn and Barry Moorhouse would look after them with things for the house, bank accounts and so on. We got them some dwellings, tucked away, near Alderley Edge, and they settled in quickly.

We had returned from America, after the Sporting Lisbon game, in a plane belonging to the Dallas Cowboys, who had rented it to us for the summer. Ferdinand, Giggs, Scholes and Neville enthused about Ronaldo all the way home: 'Get him signed, get him signed.'

So Ronaldo came into the training ground knowing that our players knew all about him and had a sense of how good he was. I think that helped.

His first appearance was against Bolton at home on 16 August 2003, where he started on the bench. The Bolton defenders ended up in knots. The right-back rattled him straight away in the centre of the park, took the ball off him, but Cristiano got straight back up and demanded another pass. Right away. 'He's got the balls, anyway,' I thought.

The next minute he was pulled down and won a penalty. Van Nistelrooy missed it. Then, of his own volition, Ronaldo moved out to the right-hand side and hit two superb crosses in. One was met by Scholes, who passed to Van Nistelrooy; his shot was parried by the keeper and Giggs tapped the ball in for the second goal. The crowd on that side of the ground responded as if a Messiah had materialised right before their eyes. The Old Trafford crowd build up heroes quickly. They see someone who gets their rears off seats and take to them right away. Ronaldo had the biggest impact on Manchester United fans of any player since Eric Cantona. He could never have matched the idolatry that came with Cantona, because Eric had all this defiant charisma, but his talent was instantly apparent.

The goal Ronaldo scored on the break in the Champions League semi-final at Arsenal in 2009 confirmed his majesty as a counter-attacker. The ball moved from Park to Rooney to Ronaldo with devastating speed. I always said to him: 'When you're going through on goal, lengthen your stride.' By lengthening your stride you slow yourself down and your timing is enhanced. When you're still sprinting, you have less coordination in your body, but when you slow your mechanics down you give the brain a better chance. He did that. You watch him.

In the spring before the 2004 FA Cup final in Cardiff, where we beat Millwall 3–0, Walter Smith, who had joined me as assistant manager in March, asked me about the various talent levels of all our players.

'What about Ronaldo,' he said, 'is he that good?'

I told him: 'Oh yes, unbelievable. Even in the air. He's a magnificent header of the ball.'

Later, Walter said, tentatively: 'You keep telling me this Ronaldo is a magnificent header of the ball. I see him heading the ball in training but never in a game.'

That Saturday, against Birmingham, Ronaldo scored with a superb header. I turned to Walter. 'I know, I know,' he said.

I had watched Millwall beat Sunderland in the semi-final and told my staff: 'That Tim Cahill's not bad, you know.' Good leap for a little lad. No great talent on the ball, but he was a constant nuisance. A pest. You could have bought him then for a million. He would have scored a lot of goals in a good team. Dennis Wise was especially combative in that match. But there have been plenty of nasty little players like him down the years, the sort who prompt you to think: 'I wish to Christ I was still playing.' There will be plenty who would have said that about Dennis Wise. He would never have survived in the old days, I'm certain of that.

If you're cute enough in the modern game, you can get away with a kind of underhand physicality. Wise would be good at leaving his foot in, arriving a fraction late. He played his game well. In the modern game it is hard to pick out genuinely thuggish players: those who step out to cause hurt. It hardly mattered, because Ronaldo destroyed Millwall that day.

The one political drama we had with Ronaldo was, of course, the 2006 World Cup, when he winked at the Portugal bench after Wayne Rooney had stamped on Ricardo Carvalho. This raised the brief possibility that the two men would fall out to such an extent that they would never be able to play together again. What saved the day for Ronaldo was Rooney, who was terrific. On holiday, I texted Rooney and asked him to call me. He suggested the two of them granting an interview together to show there was no bad blood.

The next day I ran it past Mick Phelan, who thought it might look a bit prompted and artificial. I decided he was right. But the generosity of Rooney was what impressed Ronaldo, who thought it might be impossible for him to go back to Manchester. He felt he had burned his boats and that the press would kill him. Rooney called him a couple of times to reassure him. It wasn't the first time two United team-mates had clashed in the international arena. I'll take you back to Scotland v. England in 1965, and Nobby Stiles' first game for his country. Denis Law is standing in the Scotland line and Nobby shuffles over to him and says, 'All the best, Denis.' Nobby idolised Denis, who says, 'Eff off, you English so-and-so, you.' So Nobby is left there, stunned.

Yes, Ronaldo did run to the referee to help get Rooney in trouble, which is common in the modern game. But Ronaldo was thinking only of one thing – winning that game for his country. He wasn't thinking about playing for Man United the following season. That was a World Cup game. And he did regret it. When we visited him it was clear he understood the implications. The wink was misinterpreted. The manager had told him to stay out of trouble, so the wink was not to convey pleasure to the bench at his own role in Rooney's sending-off. I believed him when he told me he was not saying, with that gesture: 'I sorted him out, I got him sent off.'

We met at a villa in Portugal and had lunch. Jorge Mendes was present. Rooney calling him had helped to change Ronaldo's mind and put him at ease. I told Cristiano, 'You're one of the bravest players to come to Manchester United, but walking away isn't courage.' I quoted the Beckham situation in 1998: 'It was exactly the same as this. They were hanging effigies of him outside pubs in London. He was the devil incarnate. But he had the balls to fight it.'

Beckham's first game after that incident had been against West Ham – the worst possible place to go after such a drama with England – and he was terrific. 'You've got to get through it,' I told Ronaldo. The next game in London for Ronaldo was at Charlton on a Wednesday night. To begin with I watched from the directors' box, where there was a local guy screaming unbelievable abuse: 'You Portuguese bastard' was one of the politer epithets. Five minutes before half-time, Ronaldo received the ball, danced round about four players and hit the underside of the bar with a shot. That guy didn't rise from his seat again. It deflated him. Perhaps he thought that his screaming had motivated him.

Ronaldo was fine, had a good start to the season and was getting on well with Rooney. These young lads will have their clashes. Rooney was going to be sent off anyway, but equally Ronaldo's intervention was unhelpful. I was so relieved that the incident passed and we were able to keep him in the side that was to go on and win the 2008 Champions League final in Moscow.

In the summer of 2012, I attended a Q &A hosted by the BBC's Dan Walker, with Peter Schmeichel and Sam Allardyce. A guy asked: 'Who's the better player, Ronaldo or Messi?'

My reply was: 'Well, Ronaldo's got a better physique than Messi, he's better in the air, he's got two feet and he's quicker. Messi has something magical about him when the ball touches his feet. It's as if it's landed on a bed of feathers. His low sense of gravity is devastating.'

Schmeichel thought Ronaldo could play in a bad team while Messi could not. That was a fair point. But Messi would still produce great moments with the ball on his toes. Peter's point was that Messi depended on Xavi and Iniesta directing the ball to him. Ronaldo is much the same in the sense that you need to keep feeding him. In all the times I'm asked I find it impossible to definitely say which is the better player because to relegate either to second place would feel wrong.

Almost as important to me as his brilliant displays in our colours was that we stayed close after he left for Madrid. Our bond survived our parting: a happy outcome in a game of transitory relationships.

nine

KEANE

R OY Keane was a player of energy, of guts and blood, with a fine instinct for the game and its strategies. He was the most influential presence in the dressing room in the time we worked together. Roy took a lot of the onus off me in making sure the dressing room was operating at a high level of motivation. A manager could never be dismissive of that kind of help from a player.

But by the time Roy left United in November 2005, our relationship had broken down. I have strong views about the sequence of events that led to him joining Celtic. But first, I should set out why he was such an immense driving force for our club.

If Roy Keane thought you weren't pulling your weight he would be right on top of you, straight away. Many players faced his wrath for committing that crime and there would be no place to hide from him. I never felt that was a bad aspect of his character. In all my time, the strong personalities have helped shape the team's actions. Bryan Robson, Steve Bruce, Eric Cantona: those players enforced the will of the manager and the club.

In my playing days, managers seldom interrogated players in the adrenaline-drenched moments straight after the match. The initial finger-pointing tended to come from the players, often in the bath. Or there would be confrontations while the water was still running: 'You, you missed that chance, you . . .'

As a player I was always having a go at the goalkeepers and defenders for conceding goals. So I knew that if I missed a chance at the other end, I would be receiving it back with interest from those with the less glamorous jobs whom I had criticised on previous occasions. Those were the risks of being outspoken. These days, managers always have their say after the game. If they want to analyse, criticise or praise, there's an area of managerial involvement right after the final whistle where influence can be brought to bear: 10 to 15 minutes.

With Roy there were episodes of great friction and drama as he tried to impose his will on the team. On one occasion, as I came into the dressing room, Roy and Ruud van Nistelrooy were at it, hammer and tongs. They had to be pulled apart by the players. At least Van Nistelrooy had the courage to stand up to Roy, because not everyone did. He was an intimidating, ferocious individual. His mode when angry was to attack, to lay into people.

I believe – and Carlos Queiroz was at one with me on this – that Roy Keane's behaviour pattern changed when he realised he was no longer the Roy Keane of old. We're certain of that. Acting on a conviction that some of his strengths had been stolen from him by injury and age, we tried to change his job description, for his benefit as much as ours.

We tried to alter his role by discouraging him from charging all over the pitch and making forward runs. Every time a team-mate received the ball, Roy would want it off him. That was an admirable quality. The religion at United was that when one of our players had the ball, we moved, and all the others supported the play. Roy was at an age where he shouldn't have been doing that, but he could not accept the new reality.

I think he could see the truth of what we were saying to him, but to surrender to it was too threatening to his pride. He was a player constructed around his own passions. In the season prior to the fall-out, he was beginning to show physical signs of weakness in terms of getting back to fulfil his defensive duties. He wasn't the same player – but how can you be, after hip operations, and cruciate knee ligament operations, and being on the front line of so many ferocious battles for so long?

The energy Roy expended in games was quite exceptional, but when you enter your thirties it's hard to comprehend where you're going wrong. You can't change the nature that has driven you to so much success. It became transparent to us that we were no longer dealing with the same Roy Keane.

Our solution was to tell him to stay in that same area of central midfield. He could control the game from there.

Deep down, I believe, he knew that better than anyone, but he simply could not bring himself to abandon his old talismanic role.

That was the long-term context to the confrontation that ended with him leaving the club and joining Celtic. He thought he was Peter Pan. Nobody is. Ryan Giggs is the closest you might come to that mythical ageless figure, but Ryan never had any serious injuries. Roy had some bad ones. His hip problem was the one that caused the biggest deterioration in his physical prowess.

The first major fracture in our relationship appeared in pre-season, before the 2005–06 campaign, on our trip to a training camp in Portugal. Carlos Queiroz went out to set it up because it had been his idea, and led us to the most marvellous facility. Vale do Lobo. It was out of this world. Training pitches, a gym and small houses, which were perfect for the players.

I arrived there at the end of my summer holiday in France. All the staff and players were nicely ensconced in their villas. But bad news awaited me. Carlos was having a nightmare with Roy.

I asked what the problem was. Carlos explained that Roy considered the houses at Vale do Lobo to be beneath the required standard and was not willing to stay in his. According to Carlos, Roy had rejected the first house because one of the rooms lacked air conditioning. The second threw up a similar problem. The third, which I saw, was a fantastic house. Roy wouldn't take it. He wanted to stay in the next village, Quinta do Lago, with his family.

That first night, we organised a barbecue on the patio of

the hotel. It was beautifully presented. Roy approached me and said he needed to talk to me.

'Roy, come on, not now. We'll talk in the morning,' I said.

After training I pulled him to one side. 'What's going on, Roy?' I started. 'I've looked at the houses, they're fine.'

Roy erupted, issuing a long list of complaints, which included the air conditioning. Then he started on Carlos. Why were we doing the pre-season here?, and so on. It was all criticism. It placed a strain on his relationship with us. He became quite reclusive, I thought, on that tour. I was disappointed. Carlos had worked his socks off to make the trip right for everyone.

When the visit was over, I resolved to bring Roy up to the office to at least get him to say sorry to Carlos. He was having none of it.

When we were embroiled in an argument once, Roy said to me, 'You've changed.'

I replied, 'Roy, I will have changed, because today is not yesterday. It's a different world we're in now. We have players from twenty different countries in here. You say I've changed? I hope I have. I would never have survived if I hadn't changed.'

He said: 'You're not the same man.'

We had a real set-to. A proper argument. I told him he was out of order. 'You're the captain. You showed no responsibility to the other players. It's not as if we asked you to live in a hovel. They were nice houses. Good places.'

The bad feeling didn't subside. The deterioration in our relationship really started there. Then came the MUTV interview episode, in which Roy let rip at some of the younger members of the squad for supposedly failing in their duties.

We had a rota for MUTV interviews, and on this occasion it was Gary Neville's turn. On the Monday after we played Middlesbrough, I was not particularly interested when a press officer informed me that Roy was taking over the slot from Gary. It didn't strike me as significant.

But apparently Roy had been giving the other players terrible stick about Saturday's game. Cut to 4 p.m. I receive a call at home: 'You need to see this.'

In the interview Roy described Kieran Richardson as a 'lazy defender', doubted why 'people in Scotland rave about Darren Fletcher' and said of Rio Ferdinand, 'Just because you are paid a hundred and twenty thousand pounds a week and play well for twenty minutes against Tottenham, you think you are a superstar.'

The press office had phoned David Gill right away. It was stopped pending a decision from me on what we ought to do with the tape. 'OK, get the video to my office tomorrow morning and I'll have a look at it,' I said.

Jesus. It was unbelievable. He slaughtered everyone. Darren Fletcher got it. Alan Smith. Van der Sar. Roy was taking them all down.

There was no game that week and I was due to go to Dubai to visit our soccer school. That morning Gary Neville called me from the players' dressing room and asked me to come in. Down I went, expecting Roy to have apologised. I took my seat. Gary promptly announced that the players were not happy with the training. I couldn't believe my ears. 'You what?' I said. Roy had a major influence on the dressing room and I believe that he had used that influence to try and turn the situation. Listen, Carlos Queiroz was a great coach, a great trainer. Yes, he could be repetitive with some exercises, but that's what makes footballers: force of habit.

I let them have it. 'You pulled me down here to complain about the training? Don't you start, the pair of you . . . Who are you talking to?' And I walked out.

Later, Roy came up to see me and I told him, 'I know what's happened.' Then I started on the video. 'What you did in that interview was a disgrace, a joke. Criticising your team-mates. And wanting that to go out.'

Roy's suggestion was that we should show the video of the interview to the players and let them decide. I agreed and the whole team came up to see it. David Gill was in the building, but declined my invitation to take a seat for the show. He thought it best to leave it to me. But Carlos and all the staff joined the audience.

Roy asked the players whether they had anything to say about what they had just seen.

Edwin van der Sar said yes. He told Roy he was out of line criticising his team-mates. So Roy attacked Edwin. Who did he think he was, what did Edwin know about Manchester United? Van Nistelrooy, to his credit, piped up to support Van der Sar, so Roy rounded on Ruud. Then he started on Carlos. But he saved the best for me.

'You brought your private life into the club with your argument with Magnier,' he said.

At that point, players started walking out. Scholes, Van Nistelrooy, Fortune.

The hardest part of Roy's body is his tongue. He has the most savage tongue you can imagine. He can debilitate the most confident person in the world in seconds with that tongue. What I noticed about him that day as I was arguing with him was that his eyes started to narrow, almost to wee black beads. It was frightening to watch. And I'm from Glasgow.

After Roy had left, Carlos saw I was quite upset. Never in his life, he said, had he witnessed a scene of that nature. He called it the worst imaginable spectacle in the life of a professional football club. 'He needs to go, Carlos,' I said. 'One hundred per cent,' he said. 'Get rid of him.'

I was away until the following Wednesday, but phoned David Gill from Dubai and told him, 'We need to move Roy out.' His response was that, from the accounts I had given him, there was no choice. He said he would need to speak to the Glazers, who approved the move. I agreed with David Gill that the club would pay Roy's contract up and honour his testimonial. No one could say we had treated Roy unjustly.

When I returned from the Middle East, David instructed me that the Glazers were coming over on the Friday, and that he had phoned Michael Kennedy to say we wanted a meeting with him. We called Michael and Roy into the meeting and set out our decision, with all the details.

Roy said publicly later that he was disappointed I didn't end his Manchester United career on my own. But after the original confrontation, I was finished with him. There was no way I wanted another war with him or even to get involved with him again.

I walked out to the training pitch and told the players, and registered the shock on each face.

I always felt that my best moments as a manager were

when I made quick decisions based on irrefutable fact, on conviction. It was so clear to me what I had to do to stem this crisis. If I had prevaricated, it would have given Roy more strength in the dressing room, more confidence in his own mind that he had been right, more time to convince everyone he was correct in his behaviour. And he was not right. What he did was wrong.

There was so much to look back on, so much to process as Roy Keane became an ex-Manchester United player. High on the list would be the 2002 World Cup, and Roy flying home after a bust-up with Mick McCarthy, the Republic of Ireland manager.

My brother Martin had taken me for a week's holiday for my 60th birthday. At dinner I didn't take my phone along with me, but Martin had taken his, and as we left, it rang. It was Michael Kennedy saying he had been trying to contact me. Michael made it clear there had been an eruption in Saipan, where the Republic of Ireland team had arrived to prepare for the World Cup. 'You need to talk to him. You're the only man he'll listen to,' Michael said. I was baffled. I couldn't imagine what Michael could have been so distressed about. He told me the story of Roy's confrontation with Mick McCarthy. The number Michael gave me was no good so I suggested Roy should ring me instead.

Keane's voice came on the line. 'Roy, what on earth are you thinking about?' Roy unspooled all his anger at McCarthy. I said: 'Calm down. A bit of advice. You cannot afford to make your children go to school every day with this as the background to their lives. Think of your family. It will be horrendous. Forget the World Cup finals. This will be the biggest story all summer.'

He knew I was right. I told him to get back in there with McCarthy, just the two of them, sort it out and tell the manager he would be playing. Roy agreed. But by the time he went back, Mick had already given a press conference to explain what had been going on. There was no way back for Roy.

I defended Roy to the hilt because he had come from Manchester United, with the high standards we had. Going to a substandard training base, with no training kit, is a reasonable issue to get angry about, and as captain he had every reason to complain. The question in life is: how far do you take a grievance?

As bad as the conditions were in Korea, Roy shouldn't have pushed his anger to such levels. But that was Roy. He was a man of extremes.

I always protected my players and Roy was no exception. It was my job. For that reason I can't apologise for the times I stuck up for them when there were sound reasons to lurch the other way. There were times when I thought, 'Christ, what were you thinking about?' Cathy posed that question to me many times. But I couldn't take sides against my players. I had to find solutions other than castigating them in public. Sometimes I had to fine or punish them, of course, but I could never let it out of the dressing room. I would have felt I had betrayed the one constant principle of my time as a manager: to defend. No, not to defend, but to protect them from outside judgments.

In modern football, celebrity status overrides the

manager's power. In my day you wouldn't whisper a word about your manager. You would fear certain death. In my later years, I would hear constantly about players using their power against managers, and the player receiving the support of the public and even the club. The player will always spill his resentments to whoever might care to listen, but the manager will not do that, because he has wider responsibilities.

I think Roy realised he was coming to the end of his playing career and was starting to think he was the manager. He was assuming managerial responsibilities, and, of course, it's not a managerial responsibility to go on Manchester United television and slaughter your team-mates.

By stopping it going out, we saved Roy from losing the respect of everyone in that dressing room. But once the meeting in my room developed such a venomous tone, that was the end of him.

The one thing I could never allow was loss of control, because control was my only saviour. As with David Beckham, I knew the minute a football player started trying to run the club, we would all be finished. The real players like that. They like a manager who's tough. Or can be tough.

They like the manager to be a man. There's a reward. The player will be thinking: '1. Can he make us winners? 2. Can he make me a better footballer? 3. Is he loyal to us?' These are vital considerations, from the player's side. If the answer to all three is yes, they will tolerate murders. I had some terrible mood-storms after games and was never proud of my outbursts. Some nights I would go home assailed by fear of the consequences. Maybe the players wouldn't be talking to me next time I entered the training ground. Perhaps they would be raging or conspiring against me. But on Mondays, they would be more terrified of me than I was of them, because they had seen me lose my temper and were not keen to see it happen again.

Roy's an intelligent guy. I saw him reading some interesting books. He's a good conversationalist and good company when he's in the right mood. The physio would come in and ask, 'What sort of mood is Roy in today?' because that would determine the whole mood of the dressing room. That's how influential he was in our daily lives.

With his contradictions and mood swings he could be wonderful one minute and antagonistic the next. The switch would flick in a moment.

In one deep sense, him leaving was the best thing that could have happened, because a lot of the players were intimidated by him in the dressing room, and those players emerged well from his departure. John O'Shea and Darren Fletcher were certainly beneficiaries. When we went to France to pay Lille in Paris in November 2005, the players were booed on the pitch in the warm-up, partly as a conse-quence of what Roy had said in the MUTV interview. Fletcher and O'Shea took most of the heckling.

I think the dressing room relaxed when Roy left. Relief swept the room. They no longer had to listen to the barrage that some of them had grown to expect. Because he'd been a declining force, the gap he left was not as big as it would have been three years previously. I watched him in a Celtic v. Rangers game and said to Carlos beforehand, 'He'll be the star man today.'

Roy was never in the game. He played a passive role. The dynamic, fist-clenching, demanding Roy Keane wasn't there. He loved it at Celtic Park. I spoke to him about it and he praised the training, the facilities, the Prozone. Things did settle down between us. About two months later I was sitting in my office discussing team business with Carlos, when a member of staff called to say that Roy was here to see me. I was startled.

'I just want to apologise to you for my behaviour,' he said. That's when he began describing the scene at Celtic and telling me how well his work was going. But when I saw him in that Rangers–Celtic game I knew he wouldn't carry on with it.

Changes were already in motion before Roy left, but they weren't yet apparent. There is one abiding truth about Manchester United: we are always capable of producing new players, fresh names, and we had them on tap again as Roy was heading out. Fletcher was acquiring maturity and experience; I brought Ji-Sung Park to the club; Jonny Evans was breaking through.

Often first-team players can't recognise the regeneration going on around them because they can't see beyond themselves. They have no clue what's going on further down the scale. Giggs, Scholes and Neville were exceptions. Maybe Rio and Wes Brown. Others would have no idea. They see their job as playing. But I could see foundations developing. That wasn't a great period for us in terms of trophies. Yet when you're managing change, you have to accept the quieter spells and acknowledge that transformations take longer than a year.

I could never ask for three or four years to achieve change, because at Manchester United you would never have that time, so you try to expedite it, and be bold sometimes: play young players, test them. I was never afraid of that. It was never just a duty, but a part of the job I loved. It's who I am. I did it at St Mirren and Aberdeen and Manchester United. So, when we faced those periods, we always put our trust in younger players.

In terms of recruitment targets, Carlos fancied Anderson strongly. In one day, David Gill travelled to Sporting Lisbon to sign Nani and then drove up the motorway to buy Anderson from Porto. They cost a bit of money, but it showed what we thought, as a club, about young talent. We had a good defensive nucleus of Ferdinand, Vidić and Evra. We were a solid unit at the back. Rooney was developing. We let Louis Saha go because he was always picking up injuries. We had Henrik Larsson for a while, and he was a revelation.

After an initial rapprochement, relations with Roy soured again. I saw a remark he had made in the newspapers to the effect that he had washed Man United out of his life. His claim was that we would all have forgotten him by then. How could anyone forget what he did for the club? The press used to see him as a quasi-manager, because of his winning appetite, and the way he drove the team on. They would ask me all the time: 'Do you think Roy Keane will be a manager?' As his career in coaching developed, it became apparent that he needed to spend money to achieve results. He was always looking to buy players. I didn't feel Roy had the patience to build a team.

In the 2011–12 season, we crossed swords again when Roy was highly critical of our young players after the defeat in Basel, which knocked us out of the Champions League, and I responded by referring to him as a 'TV critic'. If you studied his final days at Sunderland and Ipswich, his beard would get whiter and his eyes blacker. Some might be impressed with his opinions on TV and think: 'Well, he's got the balls to take on Alex Ferguson.' From the minute he became a TV critic, I knew he would focus on United.

As for blaming the young players? He wouldn't have aimed that accusation at Wayne Rooney, who wouldn't have stood for it. The senior players would sort him out. Fletcher and O'Shea are the two he picked on, and they were booed as a result by our fans when we played Lille in Paris. His two spells in management proved one thing: he needs money. He spent at Sunderland and failed. He spent a lot at Ipswich and came up short.

He gave an interview to David Walsh of the *Sunday Times* saying I only looked after myself, and used the John Magnier/Rock of Gibraltar situation as an example. Unbelievable. That day in my office, when we clashed, I saw the anger in him. His eyes blackened. He went on about John Magnier that day as well. I never understood his obsession with the Rock of Gibraltar affair.

In the arrangement we reached on that momentous Friday, it was agreed that no one would ever talk about our fall-out. I would have honoured that agreement, but for the fact that Roy breached it first. When Roy was at Sunderland he accused United of insulting him and lying to him in the build-up to his departure. The club considered legal action against him. Roy said he would not retract the accusation. My feeling was that he was looking for a day in court to impress the fans. He was still a hero to them, after all. So my advice to David Gill was to pull the legal action. I feel we preserved our dignity.

ten

OUTSIDE INTERESTS

T HE football-watching public probably saw me as an obsessive who seldom looked beyond Manchester United for entertainment. But as the demands of the job intensified, I found refuge in numerous interests and hobbies that kept my mind stretched, my book shelves packed and my cellar stocked with good wines.

Apart from my love of horse racing, this other life stayed hidden from view. It was the world I returned to when the day had run its course at Carrington, our training ground, or when the match had been played, commented upon and filed away. Over the final ten years or so, I eased myself into a range of other interests that helped me manage United more effectively. I worked just as hard but used the muscles of the mind in a more varied way. Home was a base for all my fascinations, from biographies of the dictators to documents on the John F. Kennedy assassination and files on my wine collection.

My political convictions have remained largely unchanged from my time as a shop steward in the shipyards of Govan. People's opinions change over time with success and wealth, but in my youth I acquired not so much a range of ideological views as a way of seeing life; a set of values.

I've never been active in the sense of becoming a Labour Party animal who attended every dinner and popped up in every election campaign. But I always supported local Labour MPs. Cathy would say that the minute you extend yourself into politics, they will want you every time. An expectation will develop that you're always ready and willing to give your time. Being a believer in the Labour Party and socialist principles is one thing, but becoming an active member was another. I just didn't have the time as Man United manager to accommodate those demands. I would put my cross on the ballot paper and support them in a visual way. You wouldn't see me sitting beside David Cameron, would you? You would see me alongside a Labour MP. That would be my impact.

I've always been on the left of the party, which explains my high opinion of Gordon Brown's work. John Smith's, too. The late John Smith would have been a fine Labour prime minister. I felt sorry for Neil Kinnock: a good guy with bad luck. I would have loved to see him in Downing Street. He had that fiery nature. I was closer to Brown in principle but accept that Blair's more populist way was the route to get elected. He was correct in his positioning. Plus, he had charisma to go with it and was popular for a long time until the invasion of Iraq undermined the public's view of him.

My friendship with Alastair Campbell developed through that great man, veteran Scottish football reporter and confidant of several Labour prime ministers, Jim Rodger. He called and asked me to do a piece with Alastair, who was with the *Mirror* at the time. Alastair and I got on well and he would send me wee letters and so on. He was a good networker. Then he became Tony's press secretary and we became good friends through his role in the Labour Party. I had dinner with Alastair, Tony and Cherie in the Midland Hotel in Manchester the week before the 1997 election. I told Tony, 'If you can keep your government in one room and lock the door you'll have no problems. The problem with government is that they all fly off on their own, they have their own allies, their own journalistic contacts. Controlling the cabinet is going to be the hard part.'

Tony was receptive to that message. In any position of power there is fragility. If you're leading the country there is vast responsibility and a certain loneliness that I could relate to. I would sit in my office in the afternoon, with my work complete, wanting company. There is a vacuum attached to the job that people don't want to break into. Tony was a young man going into that position.

In his memoirs he wrote that he had asked my opinion on sacking Gordon Brown when he was prime minister and Gordon was next door in No. 11. My recollection is that Tony wasn't specific about Gordon. His question was about superstars and how I dealt with them. My answer was: 'The most important thing in my job is control. The minute they threaten your control, you have to get rid of them.' He did say he was having problems with Gordon but didn't ask me specifically what I thought he should do. I kept my advice general because I didn't want to get into personality issues.

I've always found that you have to take the hard road all the time, whether it's popular or not. If you have a worry about one of your staff, that tells you straight away there is a problem. It never made sense to me to go to bed every night worrying when you could do something to cut the problem away.

Power is useful if you want to use it, but I don't think it resonates with footballers, who are mostly working-class men. But control was my aim. I could use my power if I wished, and I did, but when you reach the station I attained at United, power came with it naturally. The big decisions you make in those jobs are usually seen by outsiders as exercises in power, when control is really what it's about.

Labour politics and the great vineyards aside, America was the source of my main intellectual interests. JFK, the Civil War, Vince Lombardi and the great American ball games: these were among my escapes from the pressures of football. New York was my entry point to American culture. We bought an apartment there, which all the family used, and Manhattan became the ideal venue for short breaks when the international calendar took the players away from Carrington.

The States always intrigued and inspired me. I fed off America's energy and vastness, its variety. My first trip there was in 1983, when Aberdeen won the European Cup Winners' Cup. I took the family to Florida, for a routine kind of holiday. By then, though, America and its history had already entered my blood. The killing of John Kennedy in Dallas in 1963 left its mark on me from the day I heard the news. Over time I developed a forensic interest in how he was killed, by whom, and why.

I remember the day that shook the world. It was a Friday night and I was shaving in the mirror, at the bathroom sink, before going to the dancing with my mates. My dad, who was a bit deaf, called out: 'Is that right that John Kennedy has been shot?'

'Dad, you're deaf. You're imagining it,' I called back, and dried myself off, thinking nothing of it. Half an hour later the news flashed up. He had been taken to Parklands Hospital.

I always remember, at the dancing, at the Flamingo, near Govan, hearing the song that went to No. 1: 'Would You Like to Swing on A Star?' The atmosphere was muted. Instead of dancing we sat upstairs and talked about the murder.

For a young lad like me, Kennedy captured the imagination. He was a good-looking boy and there was a certain spark about him. It resonated that someone as fresh and dynamic as him could become president. Though he stayed in my consciousness, as a defining figure, my interest in the assassination developed along an unexpected route when I was invited to speak at a dinner in Stoke by Brian Cartmel.

Stanley Matthews and Stan Mortensen were both present, along with Jimmy Armfield, and I remember thinking: 'What am I doing here, with all these great players? Surely they'd prefer to listen to Stanley Matthews rather than me?'

But during the dinner, Brian asked me, 'What are your hobbies?'

'I don't have time for hobbies,' I said. I was obsessed with

United. 'I have a snooker table in the house, I like a round of golf and I like watching movies at home.'

He pulled out a card. 'My son has a firm in London, he gets all the early releases. Any time you want a film, give him a call.'

The previous night I had been to the pictures in Wilmslow to see *JFK*. 'Are you interested in that?' asked Brian. By then I had assembled several books on the shooting. 'I was in the fifteenth car in the motorcade,' Brian said. There we were in The Potteries and this guy was telling me he had been in the JFK motorcade.

'How?'

'I was a *Daily Express* journalist. I emigrated to San Francisco and worked for *Time* magazine,' he said. 'I applied to the Kennedy administration in 1958 to work on the election.' Brian had been on the plane when Johnson was sworn in as president.

That personal connection drew me deeper in. I started going to auctions. A lad from America who had read about my interest in the subject sent me the autopsy report. I kept a couple of photographs at the training ground – one I bought in an auction, and another that was given to me. I also bought the Warren Commission report signed by Gerald Ford at auction. That cost me $3,000.

When Cathy and I went back to the States in 1991 for our wedding anniversary we travelled to Chicago, San Francisco, Hawaii, Las Vegas and on to friends in Texas, with New York at the finish. We went most years after that. My book collecting gathered pace. The definitive biography of John Kennedy is probably Robert Dallek's *An Unfinished*

Life, John F. Kennedy 1917–1963. That's an exceptional book. Dallek had access to Kennedy's medical files and showed that he was a walking miracle, with Addison's disease and liver problems.

In the three years of his presidency, plenty of battles came his way, with the failed Bay of Pigs invasion, for which he took the blame, as well as segregation, the Cold War, Vietnam and the Cuban missile crisis. Medicare was another rumbling issue, as it is today. It was some workload. Here's an aside that casts light on the importance of the world's favourite game. Later, in 1969, do you know how the CIA realised the Soviets were at work in Cuba? Football pitches. Aerial shots of football pitches laid out by Soviet workers. The Cubans didn't play football. Henry Kissinger was European in temperament and understood that.

My reading on the Kennedys brought me into contact with some wonderful literature: David Halberstam's *The Best and the Brightest* stands out. It concentrates on the reasons for going into Vietnam, and the lies the Kennedy brothers were told. Even Robert McNamara, US Secretary of Defense and a friend of the family, was misleading them. He apologised, in retirement, to the Kennedy family

On our summer tour of America in 2010, I visited Gettysburg and went to lunch at Princeton University with James M. McPherson, the great Civil War historian who wrote *Battle Cry of Freedom.* I was also shown round the White House. My fascination with the Civil War started when somebody gave me a book about the generals in that conflict. Both sides had dozens. Teachers were made generals. Gordon Brown asked me one day what I was reading about. 'The

Civil War,' I said. Gordon said he would send me some tapes. Soon I was taking delivery of 35 recordings of lectures by Gary Gallagher, who went on to work with James McPherson on the role of the navy in the war, a largely untold story.

Then along came horse racing, another great passion, another outlet. Martin Edwards, the former chairman, had called me one day to say, 'You should take a day off.'

'I'm all right,' I replied.

But I was at the stage where Cathy was saying, 'You're going to kill yourself.' At home, after work, I would be on the phone until 9 o'clock at night and thinking about football every minute.

I bought my first horse in 1996. On our 30th anniversary we went to Cheltenham, where I first met that fantastic man, John Mulhern, the Irish trainer, for lunch. That night I joined them in London for dinner. Inevitably I found myself saying to Cathy in the aftermath, 'Do you fancy buying a horse? I think it'll be a release for me.'

'Where did you get that one from?' she said. 'Alex – the problem with you is that you'll want to buy every bloody horse.'

But it did open this release valve for me. Instead of stagnating in my office or burning time in endless telephone conversations, I could switch my thoughts to the Turf. It was a welcome distraction from the gruelling business of football – and that's why I threw myself into it, to enable me to escape the obsession with my job. Winning two Grade 1 races with What A Friend has been a highlight. The Lexus Chase and the Aintree Bowl. The day before the Aintree race, we had been beaten by Bayern Munich in the

Champions League. One minute my head was on the floor. The next day I was winning a Grade 1 race at Liverpool.

My first horse, Queensland Star, was named after a ship my dad worked on and helped to build. Trainers have told me of owners who've never had a winner. I've had 60 or 70 and I now have shares in around 30 horses. I'm very keen on the Highclere Syndicate: Harry Herbert, who runs it, is a great personality and a fine salesman. You know exactly what's happening with the horses, with information every day.

Rock of Gibraltar was a wonderful horse; he became the first in the northern hemisphere to win seven consecutive Group 1 races, beating Mill Reef's record. He ran in my colours under an agreement I had with the Coolmore racing operation in Ireland. My understanding was that I had a half share in the ownership of the horse; theirs was that I would be entitled to half the prize money. But it was resolved. The matter was closed when we reached a settlement agreeing that there had been a misunderstanding on both sides.

Obviously there was a potential clash between my racing interests and the ownership of the club, and when a man stood up at the AGM and insisted I resign there was awkwardness for me. I have to say that at no point was I sidetracked from my duties as manager of Manchester United. I have an excellent family lawyer in Les Dalgarno and he managed the process on my behalf. It didn't affect my love of racing and I am on good terms now with John Magnier, the leading figure at Coolmore.

Racing taught me to switch off, along with reading books and buying wine. That side of my life developed really from

1997, when I hit that wall and realised I needed to do something else to divert my thoughts from football. Learning about wine also helped in that respect. I started buying with Frank Cohen, a big collector of contemporary art and a neighbour of mine. When Frank went abroad for a while, I started buying on my own.

I could never call myself an expert but I'm not bad. I know the good years and the good wines. I can taste a wine and recognise some of its properties.

My studies took me to Bordeaux and the champagne region, but generally it was through reading that I extended my knowledge, and through conversations with dealers and experts over lunch or dinner. It was exciting. I had dinner with wine writer and TV presenter Oz Clarke and the wine merchant John Armit. Corney & Barrow wine bars put on great lunches. These men would hold conversations about grapes and years that I couldn't hope to follow, but I was always enthralled. I perhaps ought to have learned more about the grapes. That was the essence of it all. But soon I was developing a working knowledge.

In the autumn of 2010 I was asked about retirement, and found myself saying, instinctively: 'Retirement's for young people, because they have other things they can do.' At 70 years of age, with idleness, the system breaks down quickly. You have to have something in place when you retire. Right away, the next day, not after a three-month holiday.

When you're young, the 14-hour days are necessary, because you have to establish yourself, and the only way to do that is by working your balls off. By those means, you establish a work ethic for yourself. If you have family, it's

istiano Ronaldo worked on every aspect of game, even heading. Look at him leap in 2004 FA Cup final win.

Reaching out to our fans. We've just beaten Millwall 3–0 in the 2004 FA Cup final and Mikaël Silvestre is with me.

ork hard, play hard. The dressing room after our victory over Millwall. Ronaldo looks so young.

Rivals to the end. Arsène Wenger and I had our fall-outs but there was more to unite than divide us.

Arsène was livid after we stopped Arsenal's unbeaten 49-match run in October 2004.

Ruud van Nistelrooy opened the scoring as we prevented Arsenal from going 50 games unbeaten. A volcanic day.

afa Benítez turned our rivalry personal. I could ndle that.

When José Mourinho joined Chelsea I thought: 'New kid on the block. Confident.' A new challenge had arrived.

ly hero Denis Law and close friend Bobby Robson at a lunch to celebrate my 20th anniversary United manager. As a player I wanted to be Denis.

Ronaldo was a model student. Carlos Queiroz played an important role in his development.

Ole Gunnar Solskjaer was a natural finisher. I always saw myself in our strikers.

Fergie Time. I pointed to my watch to strike fear into opponents, who knew we often scored in the last minute.

chael Carrick strikes in our thrilling 7–1 win over Roma at Old Trafford in 2007. A near perfect play.

he wonder boys, Ronaldo and Rooney, in that 7–1 victory over Roma. Ronaldo scored twice and ooney once.

Moscow, Roman Abramovich's home town, was the stage for our 2008 Champions League win over Chelsea. Here, Ryan Giggs tucks away his penalty in sudden-death.

My record in penalty shoot-outs wasn't good. At first I couldn't believe we had won when Edwin van der Sar saved from Nicolas Anelka.

e retreat from Moscow. A happy one. Giggs and Ferdinand hold the 2008 Premier League and
ampions League trophies on the tarmac in Manchester.

Labour can always count on my support and Tony Blair and Gordon Brown became friends.

The Glazers were supportive from day one. They let me get on with the job. Avram (*left*), Joel an Bryan joined us at Vale do Lobo in Portugal.

passed on to them. My mother and father conveyed the fruits of their labour to me and I have done so with my own children and beyond. With youth you have the capacity to establish all the stability of later life. With age you have to manage your energy. Keep fit. People should keep fit. Eat the right foods. I was never a great sleeper, but I could get my five to six hours, which was adequate for me. Some people wake up and lie in bed. I could never do that. I wake and jump up. I'm ready to go somewhere. I don't lie there whiling my time away.

You've had your sleep – that's why you woke up. I would be up at six, maybe quarter past six, and be in the training ground for seven. I was only a quarter of an hour away. That was my habit. The routine never changed.

I came out of a wartime generation that said: you're born, that's you. You were safe. You had the library and the swimming baths and football. Your parents worked all the time, so either your granny looked in to make sure you were all right, or you reached an age where you looked after yourself. Your basic pattern was laid down that way. My mother used to say, 'That's the mince, that's the tatties, all you need to do is put it on at half past four.' It would all be ready to cook. You would light the fire for them coming in from work. My dad would get in about quarter to six with the table all set – that was your duty – and you would take the ashes down to the midden. Those were the chores when you came in from school, and we did our homework later, my brother and I, at seven o'clock at night.

It was a simple regime, born of a lack of modern amenities. Now we have more fragile human beings. They've never been in the shipyards, never been in a pit; few have seen manual labour. We have a generation of fathers, my own sons included, who do better for their children than I did for them.

They attend more family events than I did. Picnics, with the kids. I never organised a picnic in my life. I would say, 'Go and play, boys.' There was a school ground beside our house in Aberdeen and the lads would be out there with their pals every day. We didn't have a video recorder until 1980. It was grainy, terrible. Progress brings CDs and DVDs and grandsons who can pull up their fantasy football team on your home computer.

I didn't do enough with my boys. Cathy did it, my wife did it, because she was a great mother. She would say, 'When they get to sixteen, they'll be daddy's boys,' which was true. As they grew older they were very close, and the three brothers were very close, which pleased me greatly, and Cathy would say: 'I told you.'

'But you produced them,' I would tell her. 'If I ever said a bad word about you to those three boys, they would kill me. You're still the boss.'

There's no secret to success in this world. The key is graft. Malcolm Gladwell's book, *Outliers: The Story of Success*, could just have been called Graft. Hard Graft. The examples there run all the way back to Carnegie and Rockefeller. There is a story about Rockefeller I love. The family were big church-goers. One day his son said to him, as the contributions tray was coming round, and each worshipper was donating a dollar: 'Dad, wouldn't it be better if we gave them fifty dollars for the whole year?'

'Yes,' says the father, 'but we'd lose three dollars, son. Interest.'

He also taught his butler how to make a fire that would last an hour longer, how to construct it that way. And he was a billionaire.

Rockefeller's hard work instilled a frugal nature in him. He didn't waste. There is a touch of that in me. Even today, if my grandchildren leave something on the plate, I take it. I was the same with my three sons. 'Don't leave anything on your plate,' was a mantra. Now, if I went near Mark, Jason or Darren's food, they would cut my hand off!

You cannot beat hard work.

Of course, graft and stress place an invisible strain on the body. So does age. From somewhere in that mix I developed heart trouble. In the gymnasium one morning, with the belt on, I saw my heart rate soar from 90 to 160. Summoning the weight trainer, Mike Clegg, I complained: 'There must be something wrong with the belt.'

We tried another. Same numbers. 'You need to see the doc,' Mike said. 'That's not right.'

The doctor referred me to Derek Rowlands, who had looked after Graeme Souness. It was fibrillation. His advice was to try electric shock treatment to control the heart rate. Seven days later it was back to normal. In our next game, however, we lost, and my heart rate shot back up. I blame our players. A victory might have kept me inside normal parameters. The treatment had come with a 50–60 per cent success rate, but now I knew more action was required. The advice was to have a pacemaker fitted and take an aspirin every day.

The insertion in April 2002 took half an hour. I watched it on a screen. I'll always remember the blood spurting up. The device was changed in the autumn of 2010. They last eight years. That time I slept right through the changeover. Throughout these consultations, I was told I could still do what I liked in life: exercise, work, drink my wine.

The initial episode did unsettle me, I admit. The previous year I had taken a health check and returned a heart rate of 48. Albert Morgan, our kit man, had said, 'I always thought you hadn't got a heart.' My fitness was excellent. Yet 12 months later, there I was in need of a pacemaker. What it told me was that getting older comes with penalties. We are all susceptible. You think you are indestructible. I did. You know life's door will slam in your face one day, but consider yourself unbreakable up to that day. All of a sudden, God's drawing the reins in on you.

In my younger days I would be up and down that touch-line, kicking every ball, immersing myself in every nuance of the game. I mellowed with age. By the end I was tending to observe events more than getting caught up in the drama, though some games still had the power to suck me in. From time to time I would offer a reminder that I was still alive. That message would go to referees, my players, opponents.

On health generally I would say: if you get the warning, heed it. Listen to your doctors. Get the check-ups. Pay attention to your weight and what you're eating.

I'm glad to say that the simple act of reading is a marvellous release from the hassles of work and life. If I were to take a guest into my library, they would see books on presidents, prime ministers, Nelson Mandela, Rockefeller, the art of oratory, Nixon and Kissinger, Brown, Blair, Mountbatten, Churchill, Clinton, South Africa and Scottish history. Gordon Brown's book on the Scottish socialist politician James Maxton is in there. Then there would be all the volumes on Kennedy.

Then I have my despots section. What interested me here were the extremes to which humanity will go. *Young Stalin*, Simon Sebag Montefiore; the dictators – Stalin and Hitler, and Lenin; *World War II: Behind Closed Doors* by Laurence Rees; *Stalingrad* and *Berlin: The Downfall 1945* by Antony Beevor.

On a lighter note I can pull out Edmund Hillary and David Niven. Then it's back to the dark side with crime: the Krays and the American Mafia.

I was so immersed in sport in my working life that I tended not to read many books about sport. But there are a few touchstones on the shelves. Reading *When Pride Still Mattered*, the David Maraniss biography of Vince Lombardi, the great Green Bay Packers coach, I was thinking: 'That's me he's writing about, I'm just like Lombardi.' The obsession. I could identify closely with one of Lombardi's greatest sayings: 'We didn't lose the game, we just ran out of time.'

eleven

VAN NISTELROOY

I was at home on a snowy January night in 2010 when my phone beeped with a text message. 'I don't know whether you remember me,' it started, 'but I need to call you.' Ruud van Nistelrooy. Christ, what was this? I said to Cathy, 'He left four years ago.' Cathy's reply: 'What's he wanting? Maybe he'd like to come back to United.'

'No, don't be silly,' I told her.

I had no idea what it might be. But I texted him back: OK. So he rang. First, the small talk. Had some injuries, fit now, not getting a game, blah blah. Then he came out with it. 'I want to apologise for my behaviour in my last year at United.'

I like people who can apologise. I've always admired that. In the modern culture of self-absorption, people forget there is such a word as sorry. Footballers are cocooned by the manager and the club, the media, agents, or pals who just tell then how flipping good they are. It's refreshing to find one who can pick up a phone much later and say, 'I was wrong, and I'm sorry.'

Ruud offered no explanation. Perhaps I should have taken that chance to say, 'Why did it go that way?'

Mulling over Ruud's call to me, that winter night, I knew that two or three Premier League clubs were looking at him, but couldn't see that being a reason for him wanting to speak to me. There would have been no need for him to repair his relationship with Manchester United in order for him to play for another club in England. Perhaps it was a guilt complex. It might have been playing on his mind for ages. Ruud was doubtless a more mature person by that stage.

The first sign of trouble in our relationship had been that Ruud had started to mouth off all the time to Carlos Queiroz about Ronaldo. There were a few stand-up confrontations, but nothing unmanageable. Then Ruud switched his fire to Gary Neville. Gary was ready for that and won the battle. David Bellion was another who seemed to arouse anger in Ruud. There were quite a few altercations all the way through his final season with us, but it was mainly Van Nistelrooy on Ronaldo.

At the end of the previous season, 2004–05, we had reached the final of the FA Cup, against Arsenal. Van Nistelrooy had a horrible game. The previous Wednesday his agent, Rodger Linse, had sought out David Gill and asked for a move. 'Ruud wants to leave.'

David pointed out that we had a Cup final on the Saturday, and that perhaps this wasn't the best moment for our main centre-forward to ask to leave. David asked why he wanted to go. Rodger Linse's reply was that Van Nistelrooy thought the team had stagnated and didn't believe we could win the Champions League. His view was that we couldn't win the European Cup with young players – the likes of Rooney and Ronaldo.

After the Cup final, David called Rodger and asked him to get Ruud in for a meeting with me. Our position was strong because Real Madrid were not going to pay £35 million for him. That was obvious. And it was the reason, I believe, why Ruud was asking to leave. Had Real Madrid been willing to come up with £35 million, there would have been no need for him to push for a move. He was hoping to bargain with the club to find a fee United would find acceptable. Silly idea.

So we had our meeting. His stance was that he wasn't prepared to wait for Ronaldo and Rooney to mature. 'But they're great players,' I told him. 'You should be leading these young players. Helping them.' Ruud still said he didn't want to wait.

'Look, we're going to sign players in the summer to bring us back to our usual level,' I said. 'We don't like losing finals, we don't like losing the League. When you build teams you have to be patient. Not just me, but the players, too. This is going to be a good team.' He accepted my argument and we shook hands.

In that season we had signed Vidić and Evra in the January transfer window. Indirectly, those two acquisitions were to ignite the biggest flashpoint in all the time Ruud was with us. In the Carling Cup I had been playing Louis Saha all the way through. When we reached the final I said to Ruud,

'Look, it's not fair if I don't play Saha. I know you like to play in finals. Hopefully I can get you a bit of the game.' I did say that, no doubt about it.

We were on cruise control against Wigan and I saw an ideal opportunity to give Evra and Vidić a taste of the game. They were my final substitutions. I turned to Ruud and said: 'I'm going to give these two lads a part of the game.' They were going to get a touch, a smell of winning something with Manchester United. 'You —,' said Van Nistelrooy. I'll always remember that. Could not believe it. Carlos Queiroz turned on him. It became fractious in the dug-out. The other players were telling him: 'Behave yourself.'

But that was the end of him. I knew we would never get him back. He'd burned his boats. After that incident, his behaviour became worse and worse.

In the final week of that campaign we needed to win the last game of the season, against Charlton. With Saha's injuries we were walking on eggshells with him. However, I didn't feel I could select Ruud.

Carlos went to Ruud's room and said, 'We're not taking you, go home. The way you've behaved all week – we're not having it.'

Ronaldo had recently lost his father. During that week, Ruud had taken a kick at Ronaldo on the training ground and said: 'What are you going to do? Complain to your daddy?' He meant Carlos, not Cristiano's dad. He probably wasn't thinking. So then Ronaldo was upset, and wanting to have a go at Van Nistelrooy, and Carlos was upset by the insult. Carlos had looked after Ronaldo, as you would expect. He's a coach with Portuguese origins, from the same country.

Here was a young man with a dying father. If he couldn't ask for help from Carlos, who could he seek it from?

The whole episode was very sad. Why Ruud changed, I don't know. I can't say for sure whether it was his way of getting himself out of Old Trafford. It didn't do him any favours or bring him any credit in the sense of respect from the other players.

It was a pity because his numbers were sensational. He was one of our club's greatest goal-scorers. Problems first surfaced after his second season, when he was up for a new contract, in accordance with his original deal. He asked for a clause that would allow him to leave for Real Madrid, specifically, in the event of Real offering a specified sum. A buy-out clause. I pondered this one for a long time. My feeling was that, without that concession, Van Nistelrooy would not have signed his name. Conversely, to concede that ground would give him a controlling hand. We ran the risk of losing him the following season.

So the figure we inserted was £35 million, which, we thought, would deter all-comers, even Real Madrid. They agreed it. To David, I said, 'If they come back next year and pay thirty-five million, at least we'll know we have doubled our money on him. If they don't come, we'll get the two years in his contract out of him, and he will be twenty-nine by that point. We've had him four years. We'll be able to move him on.' Fine, but the moment Ruud signed that contract he changed. In his last season he became a really difficult boy. I don't think he was popular by the end. The alteration in him was dramatic.

My brother Martin had seen him play for Heerenveen

and said: 'I really like this lad, he does look the part.' With that glowing review I needed to get cracking. We went back to see him again but received word he had already signed for PSV a month previously. That confused me. But it seemed a done deal. We kept an eye on him regardless and made our move in 2000.

On a short holiday in Spain, during an international break, I received bad news: a message from our doctor to say Ruud had failed the medical. We were sure we had spotted cruciate ligament damage. PSV disagreed, insisting that all their tests had shown only minor ligament disruption of the kind that would not prevent him passing the examination. Mike Stone, however, would not sign it off. So we sent him back to PSV, who sent him back into training and filmed it, for our benefit. In the practice session Ruud's knee completely went. The footage found its way onto TV, where you could see him screaming. What should we do?

'These days, if you have the right people looking after you, you can be back from this kind of injury in a few months,' I told Martin Edwards.

Van Nistelrooy followed the trusted route to Dr Richard Steadman in Colorado and was out for almost a year. He returned towards the tail end of that season and we signed him in 2001, after I had been to watch him against Ajax. His mobility was not impaired and his pace had not diminished. He wasn't the quickest striker; he was a galloper who had a quick brain in the penalty box.

I'd also been to see him at his home while he was convalescing and had told him we would still be taking him to Old Trafford, irrespective of his injury. That was an important message for him, because I don't think he was the most confident lad at that point in his career. He was a country boy.

He was a typical old-fashioned Italian-type centre-forward. Forget all that running out to the wings and tackling. Back in the early 1960s, Juventus had a centre-forward called Pietro Anastasi, who would contribute little in games before winning them with sudden goal-scoring bursts.

That was the kind of centre-forward who dominated the game in that era. You left them to do their work in the penalty box. Van Nistelrooy was from that template. Opportunities had to be created for him. But he was a flawless finisher who scored some true poacher's goals.

In fact, he was one of the most selfish finishers I ever saw. His personal goal tally was his guiding obsession. That single-mindedness gave him the edge of a great assassin. He had no interest in build-up play or how many yards he had run in a game, how many sprints he had made. The only aspect he was ever interested in was: how many goals did Ruud van Nistelrooy score. He was superb at the 'early hit'. He would dart to the side of the defender and deliver that quick, lethal strike.

If you put my great goal-scorers together (Andy Cole, Eric Cantona, Van Nistelrooy, Rooney), Ruud was the most prolific. But the best natural finisher was Solskjaer. Van Nistelrooy scored some magnificent goals, but many were scabby, six-yard box goals. Andy Cole scored some fine goals, too, but plenty were close in, scrambled, off the leg, just-get-it-in goals. Solskjaer's finishing, though, could be majestic. His thought processes underpinned his skills. He had that analytical mind. As soon as he arrived in a shooting position, he had it all sized up. He had mental pictures everywhere. Yet he didn't play all the time because he wasn't the most aggressive of strikers. He developed more of that later, but was a slender young man without the physique, in his early days, to clear a path.

In games, sitting on the bench, and in training sessions, he would make notes, always. So by the time he came on he had analysed who the opponents were, what positions they were assuming. He had those images all worked out. The game was laid out for him like a diagram and he knew where to go and when.

Ole was a sweet-natured boy who was never looking to be confrontational with me. There was no risk to my office door from Ole wanting to smash it down to demand a place in the first XI. We knew he was content with his role, and that helped us, because if we had a difficult decision to make about the other three strikers, which one to leave out, the fourth was content to play a supporting part. So we just had the three grumpy forwards to deal with. Yorke, Cole and Sheringham.

At first I believed Ruud's range of attributes was wider than it turned out to be. I expected to see from him more of the donkey-work that Manchester United players have to do. There were times when he did his share, and would apply himself to it, but he was not inclined to be that kind of industrious player. He wasn't endowed with great stamina. His test results were never startling. Yet you knew he could always put the ball in the net if you fed it into his path.

In the preceding years we had lost Cantona, Teddy

Sheringham had gone, Ole was having his knee problems, Yorkie had lost a bit of focus and Andy was still fit, fresh. You could always rely on Andy, but I knew when I took Van Nistelrooy on, I was bound to have problems with Cole, because he thought he was the best centre-forward in the world. I say this affectionately, because it was a useful self-image to have, but he was miffed when I started pairing him with Ruud.

Displeasure had been apparent too in Andy's relationship with Cantona. The only colleague he really related to was Yorkie. Their season in 1998–99 was made in heaven. Their partnership, their friendship, was phenomenal. They hadn't known one another when Yorkie came to the club, but they just gelled. In training they would work on runs together, little dummies, one-twos. They synchronised beautifully. I think they scored 53 goals between them.

Pairing up with Van Nistelrooy wasn't going to work for Andy, so I sold him to Blackburn Rovers. He was in his early thirties by that point and we felt we'd had some fine years out of him. We signed him in 1995, got seven years out of him and received £6.5 million from Blackburn. His cost from Newcastle had been £7 million, plus Keith Gillespie, who was worth no more than £1 million. So we almost recovered our money after seven years of productivity. Not bad.

Another striker who ran up against the problem of Ruud's singularity was Forlán, a grand player. Ruud wanted to be the No. 1 finisher. That was his nature. Diego Forlán didn't register on his radar at all, so when you put the two of them out there together there was zero chemistry. Diego was better with a partner. But he scored some priceless goals. Two at

Anfield, a goal with the last kick of the game against Chelsea. He was a good player and a terrific pro.

The other complication I had with him was that his sister was an invalid, in Majorca, and it fell to him to look after her. But he was great about the place, always smiling. Spoke five languages. A breath of fresh air, as a person. We let him go for £2 million, which I thought was too cheap. With his wages, no club was willing to bid any higher. The next thing we knew he was moving on for £15 million. He floated over the ground. He was small but had a good upper body. Tough. He was such a good tennis player that he might have become a pro and had to choose between that and football. I knew that, when he joined. During our pre-season tennis tournament, I tried to get a bet on him. I said to Gary Neville, who ran the book: 'What price is Diego?'

'Why? Why?' said Gary, alarmed. 'Does he play?'

'How would I know?' I said. 'Why don't you ask him?'

But Gary was already on to me. There would be no betting on Diego. He slaughtered them all. Cut them to ribbons.

'You think we're stupid, don't you?' Neville said.

I said, 'Well, it was worth a try. I was hoping you'd say ten-to-one!'

twelve

MOURINHO – THE 'SPECIAL' RIVAL

THE first time I recognised José Mourinho as a potential threat was at his opening press conference as Chelsea manager in the summer of 2004. 'I'm the special one,' José announced. 'What a cheeky young sod,' I thought, as I watched him entertain the press with richly quotable material.

An internal voice told me: New kid on the block. Young. No point in discussing him. No point in taking him on. But he's got the intelligence, the confidence, to deal with the Chelsea job.

I had spoken to Carlos a lot about José and he had told me, 'He is a very clever boy.' His knowledge of Mourinho stretched back to a time they had shared in academia. José was one of Carlos's students in Portugal. 'My best student by far. By far,' Carlos told me. Forearmed with that knowledge, I watched him ride the wave of expectation he had created for himself; the wave that carried him from Porto to London to work for Roman Abramovich. José was one of those guys on a surfboard who can stay longer on the wave than everyone else. I knew straight away it would be unwise to engage him in psychological conflict. I would find another way to tackle him.

In the period from August 2004 to May 2006, we won one trophy: the 2006 League Cup. Chelsea and José won the Premier League in both those campaigns. As Arsenal dropped away, Abramovich's wealth and José's managerial ability became the biggest obstacle to our rebuilding.

Traditionally, our preparation for a new season had emphasised the second half of the 38-game programme. We always finished strongly. There was science as well as spirit behind our talent for winning games in the months that really mattered.

José was fresh in town, working for an employer with stacks of money, and with hype clearing his path. In the autumn of 2004 he needed to make a strong start in his first weeks at Stamford Bridge. Chelsea skated to a six-point lead and we could never make it up. Once they hit the front in the title race, José made sure they won plenty of games narrowly. It was all one- and two-nil victories. They would take the lead in games and then consolidate. Chelsea were becoming an incredibly hard team to break down. They were much better organised than before. I didn't win a game at Stamford Bridge after Mourinho arrived.

José put in lots of pre-season work on the defensive shape and played initially with a back three, two wide men and a midfield diamond. Very hard to play against, that formation.

Our first encounter had been the 2003–04 Champions League campaign, when José's Porto knocked us out. I had a spat with him at the end of the first leg. But I often had disagreements with fellow managers when first running into them. Even George Graham and I clashed after our first meeting when George was at Arsenal. Later, we became good friends. The same is true of Mourinho. I always found him very helpful and very communicative. I think he realised he was dealing with someone who had experienced all the emotional extremes in the game and enjoyed our conversations.

My indignation in that first leg stemmed from all the diving his Porto players were doing. I think he was a bit taken aback by my anger. I went too far. There was no need for me to vent my feelings on José. I was more angry with Keane for being sent off. Playing on my mind was the knowledge that Martin O'Neill had complained about the conduct of José's players in the UEFA Cup final between Porto and Celtic, which Porto won. There was a seed in me. I had watched that final but didn't think they were atypical of a Portuguese team. But when Martin O'Neill kept on and on about it, I started to persuade myself that José's team were cynical.

My first impression in the away leg was that Roy had been the victim of a refereeing misjudgment. On review, it was clear he'd tried to leave his mark on their goalkeeper. That reduced us to ten men and meant Keane was suspended for the return leg.

In the Old Trafford leg, the referee behaved bizarrely. We attacked three or four minutes before the end of the game. Ronaldo beat the full-back and he chopped him down. The linesman flagged but the Russian referee played on. Porto went to the other end and scored.

I congratulated José at the end of that match. When a team knock you out, it's imperative to find a way to say 'all the best'. We had a glass of wine and I told him: 'You were lucky, but good luck in the next leg.'

The next time he appeared at Old Trafford, he brought a bottle of his own wine, a Barca-Velha, and that started a tradition. The wine at Chelsea was awful, which I could never understand. I said to Abramovich once, 'That's paint-stripper.' The next week he sent me a case of Tignanello. A great drop, one of the best.

As for José's gallop along the touchline at Old Trafford, I've done it myself. I think back to when we scored against Sheffield Wednesday and Brian Kidd was on the pitch, on his knees, with me rejoicing on the touchline. I admire people who show you their emotions. It shows you they care.

That Champions League victory over United launched José. Beating Celtic in a UEFA Cup final was an achievement, but defeating Manchester United at Old Trafford and then going on to win the European Cup was a fuller demonstration of his talent. I remember saying to him around 2008, 'I don't know when I'm going to retire. It's difficult when you get older because you're scared to retire.' José said: 'Don't you retire, you're keeping me going.' He said he had other challenges, but definitely wanted to come back to England. He won the Champions League with Inter Milan and La Liga in Spain with Real Madrid before returning to Chelsea in June 2013.

Everyone I speak to tells me that José is exceptionally good with players. He's meticulous in his planning, the detail. He's a likeable person when you get to know him, and he can laugh at himself, turn a joke back on himself. I don't know whether Wenger or Benítez had that capacity.

Watching José tackle the Real Madrid job after his appointment in 2010 was fascinating. It was the most interesting appointment I could remember in the game; the most intriguing match of styles, managerial and playing. Every coach who has worked there has had to adhere to their philosophy. The galáctico philosophy. When they appointed Mourinho, I'm sure they must have accepted that they would need to bend to his thinking if they were to win the European Cup.

It's like any profession. You bring someone in and suddenly everything is altered, and the authors of that appointment say, 'Just a minute, we didn't know we were going to get this.' There would have been a few fans sitting in the Bernabéu thinking: 'I'm not happy with this. I didn't pay for this. I'd rather lose 5–4 than 1–0.'

So the spectacle of José's time in Madrid held me in its grip. It was the greatest challenge of his working life. He had proved the merits of his ways, at Porto, Chelsea and Inter Milan. He had won two European Cups with different clubs. Could he reshape Real Madrid in his own image, to his own thinking? From the beginning, there seemed little prospect of him abandoning his most sacred ideas in favour of all-out attack and celebrity exuberance. He knew that wasn't the way to succeed in modern football. Barcelona would attack beautifully, but they would also hound the ball when possession was lost. They were a hard-working unit, a collective. In that spell when Real reached three Champions League finals in five years, they had the best players: Zidane, Figo, Roberto Carlos. Fernando Hierro, Iker Casillas in goal, Claude Makélélé sitting in the middle of the park to break everything up.

They stayed with the galáctico system after that, importing Dutch players en masse, and David Beckham, Van Nistelrooy, Robinho, but the European Cup eluded them after the Glasgow final of 2002. Mourinho proved he could make big teams win, but the question I wanted answering was whether he would be allowed to do it his way in Madrid.

José was a pragmatist, no question. The starting point in his philosophy is to make sure his team don't lose. Against Barcelona in the previous season's Champions League semi-final, he knew his Inter side were going to cede 65 per cent of possession. All teams knew that. Barcelona's policy was to ensure they were always over-loaded in the midfield area. If you played four there, they would field five, if you played six, they would up the ante to seven. By doing so they could rotate the ball, in and out to the back four. You would end up on their carousel, going round and round, and wind up dizzy. Occasionally you might fall on the ball. Watch a carousel and you will see what I mean. The eyes go woozy.

So José knew Inter would not see much of the ball against Barcelona, but he had weapons of his own, mainly concentration and positioning. Esteban Cambiasso, his central midfielder, was a vital component in that Inter team. If Messi appeared over here, so would Cambiasso. Should Messi pop up in another area, Cambiasso would be there as well. It sounds easy, but as part of a general team plan in which all the defensive duties would connect, it was marvellously effective. Later, I watched a Real Madrid game in which José made three substitutions in the last 15 minutes. They were all defensive in nature, to make sure he won the game.

But all this came much later than our battles in the middle of the decade, when Chelsea won their first League title for 50 years and retained it 12 months later, in the summer of 2006. If 2004–05 was a horrible season, with no trophies, the following year brought only the League Cup. A new team was growing, but I was not to know we could win three Premier League trophies in a row.

Our strategy was to rebuild for the eventual departures of Keane, Giggs, Scholes and Neville. Three of them stayed beyond that plan, while Keane had to go. The intention was to assemble a group of young players who could develop over a number of years, with the experience of Giggs and Scholes and Neville to assist that process. Now I can look back on that policy as an unqualified success.

Yes, we had a barren season in 2004–05, losing the FA Cup final to Arsenal in a penalty shoot-out, but I could see the promise, in that showpiece game, of Rooney and Ronaldo. They toasted Arsenal that day. We had 21 shots at goal. In the Champions League round of 16, we lost 1–0 home and away to Milan, with Hernán Crespo scoring both goals. Rebuilding held no terrors for me. It was second nature. A football club is like family. Sometimes people leave. In football, sometimes they have to, sometimes you want them to, sometimes there is no choice for either side, when age or injury intervene.

I did feel sentimental about great players leaving us. At the same time, my eye would always be on a player who was coming to an end. An internal voice would always ask, 'When's he going to leave, how long will he last?' Experience taught me to stockpile young players in important positions.

So when, on 10 May 2005, we assembled a guard of honour for Chelsea, the new champions, at our ground, I had no intention of surrendering to Abramovich's wealth in the months to come.

Psychologically that was a big moment for Chelsea. They had won the League for the first time in half a century and could see themselves from then on in another light. A lesson we took on board was that slow starts could no longer be tolerated if we were to face down Chelsea, our big new challengers. The following season we made a flying start, though the campaign fizzled out, the lowest point being the game against Lille in Paris, where a proportion of our supporters booed the young players in the warm-up in the wake of Keane's outburst on MUTV about some of our squad not pulling their weight.

That was a killer. Roy had exacerbated the problem of our poor form by making targets of his team-mates. On the pitch we were in shocking form and the 1–0 defeat that night was my lowest point for many years.

In the same month that Roy Keane left the club, in

November 2005, we lost George Best. He was a very nice bloke, George, a very gentle lad, a bit nervous, somehow. Nervous to talk to you. He had an insecurity about him that worried you. I remember sitting in a bar in Japan with him once – he was with a girlfriend – and he could hardly talk. He seemed gripped by shyness. George could have had a good life after football. He could have coached young players, but perhaps lacked the personality to be a tutor. A fact about George that few recognised is how intelligent he was. The funeral was huge and sad and wonderfully orchestrated by the city of Belfast. It had the feel and the grandeur of a state funeral. I remember looking at George's father, a wee, humble man, and thinking: 'He produced one of the greatest players of all time.' A small man from Belfast, a quiet man. You could see where George got his reticence.

The football public in his country is basically working class, and for some reason they like people who are flawed. Best, Gascoigne, Jimmy Johnstone. They see reflections of themselves in these imperfect heroes. They understand the frailty. Jimmy was such a likeable lad you could never fail to be amused by his mischief.

Jock Stein would stare at his telephone every Friday night and his wife Jean would say, 'What are you looking at the telephone for?'

'It's going to ring,' Jock would say. 'The phone's going to ring.'

A typical call would start: 'Lanarkshire police here, Mr Stein. We've got young Jimmy here.'

George Best, of course, was one of United's great European Cup winners. But we were a long way off that pinnacle in this campaign. Wayne Rooney was sent off in a 0–0 draw at Villarreal in September 2005 for sarcastically clapping Kim Milton Nielsen, who had also dismissed David Beckham in the 1998 World Cup. Not my favourite referee. Nielsen was one of the most infuriating match officials. You were petrified when you saw his name on the list. On another occasion, Rooney swore at Graham Poll ten times. Poll, who could have sent him off, probably enjoyed having the TV cameras on him. But at least he had the common sense to handle Wayne as a human being and not be bothered by his effing and jeffing. In that respect, Rooney would have more respect for Poll than he would for Nielsen. That was the game in which Heinze ruptured his knee ligament after his agent had asked us for a transfer.

Meanwhile, after we had been knocked out of the Champions League with a 2–1 defeat at Benfica in December, the press were rolling out the sell-by-date theory. To be criticised for continual negligence in the job would have made sense to me, but the suggestion was that I had lost it because of my age, which was disgusting. As people grow older, they gain experience. There was a phase in football when top players were being hired as Premier League managers straight away with no apprenticeship. Managers with experience were tossed aside. Look at Bobby Robson, who was pushed out by Newcastle. Sam Allardyce, a proven manager, was given six months at the same club. Ridiculous. Having to face the press on a Friday was galling. None would ask me to my face: 'Aren't you past your sell-by date?' But they would write it. They would use the power of the pen to destroy a manager.

Momentum had its own logic. Supporters would say: 'What they're reporting is right, you know, I've been saying that for years.' I knew where we were going. I knew we needed a bit of time. Not too much, because at that time in my career I wouldn't have been granted unlimited leeway. Had I not felt I was on the verge of building another good team, I would have walked of my own volition. I was confident in Rooney and Ronaldo. I was sure the scouting structure was strong. Players would be found to take us back to our natural level. Though we only won the League Cup, there were some good performances in 2006.

Our form recovered after the Benfica defeat, with wins against Wigan, Aston Villa, West Brom and Bolton, which left us nine points behind Chelsea in the League. Then Evra and Vidić joined. At the back, we practised defensive drills almost every week, especially with crosses: position, attacking the ball, movement of strikers against them, with the full-backs coming into it. We would start off at the centre circle, with two strikers and two sets of wide players, right and left. We'd start off by knocking the ball up to one of the strikers, who would have a shot. As soon as that happened, a second ball would be played out to the side position, from where they would cross, and then a third ball would come from the edge of the box back in again; so they had to react to the shot, the first cross and the ball coming into the box. Three tests in one.

The culture of our game has changed. How many centre-halves can you name who actually like defending? Vidić liked it. He loved the challenge of sticking his head in there. You could tell that the thrill of contesting those 50–50 balls animated him. Smalling is a bit like that: he enjoys defending. Vidić was a dour, uncompromising sod. He was a proud Serb. In 2009 he came to see me to say he might be getting called up.

'What do you mean, called up?' I said, alarmed.

'Kosovo. I am going,' he said. 'It's my duty.'

He had the eyes for it.

The search for new talent crossed continents and frontiers. Gérard Piqué was one we picked out at a youth tournament. The door to good young Barcelona players had been opened by Arsenal's acquisition of Cesc Fàbregas, so we were sure of our ground in dealing with the Piqué family. Our problem was that the player's grandfather had been a member of the Nou Camp ruling hierarchy. Gérard's family were embedded in Barcelona's history.

Equally they had changed the first-team coach several times, so there was flux. Piqué was a terrific player and I was deeply disappointed when he told us he wanted to move back to Spain. He was an exceptional passer of the ball and a great personality with a winning mentality. His family are all winners: they are successful people. That shone from his mother and father. Unfortunately, he didn't want to wait for Ferdinand and Vidić to fall apart. That was my problem. Piqué and Evans would have made a fine partnership for the next ten years.

When we played Barcelona in the Champions League semi-final and drew 0–0, Gérard's father came to see me in the team hotel – they were really lovely people – and explained that Barcelona would like to take his son back. His parents were also keen to see him come home. They missed him. And Gérard was missing first-team football and believed he could earn a starting place at Barcelona. It was all straightforward. The eventual fee was 8 million euros. He had cost us £180,000 on account of the FIFA regulations in place at the time.

The big clubs in Europe subsequently raised their barriers to stop English raids. They were never likely to allow the likes of Piqué and Fàbregas to leave the country year after year. At our end, spotting young talent in England, we would have paid £5 million for a first-team player. But why were we asked to pay £500,000 for one who subsequently failed to make the grade? Richard Eckersley was an interesting case: Burnley offered us £500,000 for him. We wanted £1 million. We'd spent 12 years developing the boy. The compensation should really kick in when the player makes the first team. I don't think the selling club would complain, especially with a sell-on clause.

We are all subject to errors of judgment, and I made a few in those years, with Kléberson, Djemba-Djemba, and so on. I was castigated right to the end over Ralph Milne – and he cost me £170,000. I get pelters for that. The coaching staff would tease me: 'We need another Ralphy Milne, boss.' All my staff had been with me for 20 years plus. They don't forget. William Prunier was another one I was mocked for. Even Patrice Evra, in that high-pitched way, said to me one day: 'Boss, did you have William Prunier?'

Ryan Giggs' face dropped as he waited for the response.

'Aye, we had him on trial once,' I snapped.

'On trial?' Evra squeaked back. He was not going to let it drop. 'How long?'

'Two games.'

'A two-game trial?'

'Yes, and it was a disaster!'

Patrice had found the target.

The first thing you do with a new player is help him settle: banking, housing, language, transport, and so on. There is a process. Language is always the biggest barrier. Valencia's grasp of English, for example, was a problem. With Antonio it was purely a confidence issue. I can write and read in French, but I lack confidence speaking it. Antonio knew this. 'How's your French?' he said one day. Point taken. But I did point out to him that had I been working in France, I would have made an effort to speak the language. Valencia was working in England, so the same applied to him.

As a player, though, he was as brave as hell. You couldn't intimidate Valencia. He's a boy from the favela. He's obviously scrapped in his life. Tough as anything. In a 50–50, he would be right in there, arms across the opponent.

Another marquee signing in the summer of 2006 was Michael Carrick. We had admired Carrick for a while and David Gill was receiving feedback from Spurs that they might be willing to sell. 'What value would you put on him?' asked David.

'If you got him for eight million you would be doing well,' I said.

I'll always remember the words David came back with: 'Daniel Levy says you'll have to go a bit north before they can accept it.'

We haggled for weeks. We had watched Michael playing against Arsenal at the end of the season and Martin told me, 'He's definitely a Manchester United player.' He was the star man. I think the initial fee was £14 million, with clauses running to £18 million.

Michael was a natural passer of the ball at a time when Scholes was inching towards his mid-thirties. What impressed me about Carrick was that he was always looking to play that forward pass. His range was expansive and he could switch the play. The long passes were the ones I felt we could utilise with the players we had. After a couple of months we told him we couldn't understand why he had not yet scored for us. In training he struck the ball well, but in games he was not a threat from shooting positions. We improved him in that department. We offered him more freedom and tried to release strengths he was perhaps unaware he had. Maybe he had been in a routine at Spurs, where he was the deeper midfield player and seldom found his way into the box. With us, he found new qualities in his game.

He's a fine player, Michael. He was a shy boy who needed to be shaken at times. He doesn't start seasons particularly well, for reasons we struggled to understand and which we talked to him about, but generally came right about the end of October. There is a casualness about him that causes people to misunderstand his value and his constitution.

As I left, Mourinho returned to Chelsea, who, in an earlier phase, were home to my favourite foreign player in the Premier League – outside United, of course. Gianfranco Zola was a marvel. I will always remember a goal he scored against us at Stamford Bridge when he drew his foot back to shoot and then paused before the execution. While Zola was devising his artistic finish, Big Pally came sliding in and carried on going while Zola dragged it back. Oh, the stick Pally got that day. Bryan Robson said: 'Any chance of you staying on your feet?' But I loved Zola, because he played with a smile.

thirteen

COMPETING WITH WENGER

You're not the same on the battlefield as you are in church. Away from the game, Arsène Wenger is a cool customer. He's good company and has a broad spread of conversational topics. We can talk about wine and other things in life. In UEFA gatherings he made it his business to help other managers. He is a conscientious member of our trade. But when it comes to his team – to match-day – he is a completely different animal.

I've always felt I could understand Arsène. I could identify with the sharp change in him when that whistle blew. There was a bit of that in me too. If we shared one characteristic it was an absolute hatred of losing. When I lost to Raith Rovers early in my career at St Mirren (they were booting lumps out of us), I refused to shake hands with Bertie Paton, the Raith Rovers manager, who was my great mate and accomplice on the pitch at Dunfermline. Well, Bertie ran after me to remonstrate. Oh, aye. Sometimes you need a wee lesson that you're wrong, and I was wrong that day. It was a small reminder that life is bigger than the game. When you behave that way, it's petty and lacks dignity.

By the end, Arsène and I were on very friendly terms. We had survived together and respected each other's efforts to play good football. But we had conflicts down the years. The opening shot was him complaining about me complaining about the fixture list. A complaint about a complaint. So I fired back with a crafted put-down: 'He's just arrived from Japan, what does he know about it?' Which was true.

For the next two years, it was Arsène complaining about congestion in our fixture list. A foreign coach who comes in and thinks he can play 55 games a season in our League without adjusting is kidding himself. It's a gruelling, energy-sapping League. That's why, in the modern game, you have to change the team to spread the load. Arsène learned to adapt to that culture. He overcame the early shock of playing Saturday, Wednesday, Saturday.

The first time his Arsenal side played us at Old Trafford, he came into my office. Our relationship was fine at first. The problems started when he lost a game with one of his good Arsenal sides. He found it hard to accept fault in his team and looked to blame the opponent. He would often do it by concentrating on physical challenges. It was hard for him to accept that opponents might adopt a robust approach against his men. His interpretation of physical challenges extended sometimes to the very act of tackling. He would fix in his mind the idea that no one should actually be tackling his boys.

I watched his best Arsenal teams, though, and was thrilled. I always liked watching Arsène's sides. Playing against them presented special challenges that I burned many hours thinking about. I always felt I had to examine everything Arsenal did because they presented so many threats across the park. Chelsea presented a different set of problems. There we would be facing experienced players, who knew every trick in the book. Arsenal, on the other hand, played the right way.

They had one of the worst disciplinary records in football in Arsène's early years, but you could never say they were dirty players or a dirty team. Steve Bould and Tony Adams would kick the life out of you – everyone knew that. They would come through the back of you all the time. But in essence, his teams were never filthy. Volatile and macho would be a more accurate term. They were a combative bunch. Bould and Adams, I've mentioned. Then they bought Patrick Vieira, a big competitor who could mix it, get about people. And Nigel Winterburn was a bit of a nark; always chipping away. Ian Wright, their leading striker in those early days, also had a nasty streak.

In 2010, Arsène delivered a surprising criticism of Paul Scholes, telling reporters he had a 'dark side'. There was no reason for him to pronounce on one of my players. We were not due to play Arsenal that week, and there had been no friction between us. At that time Paul Scholes had won ten Premier League titles and a European Cup, and there was Arsène discussing his 'dark side'. Baffling.

Players surprise you. They can surprise you in the level of performance they rise to and the levels to which they sink. Arsène struggled to accept that as a contributing factor in a defeat. Football brings out the best and the worst in people because the emotional stakes are so high. In a high-stakes game, a player can lose his nerve for a minute and he can lose his temper too. And you're left regretting it. Arsenal had a lot of those moments, but Arsène struggled to believe that internal failings and weaknesses can some-times cause you to lose. The explanation is sometimes within.

I'm not saying managers see everything, but we see most things, so Arsène's stock defence after a game of, 'I didn't see it' was not one I used. My preferred line was: 'I'll need to look at it again.' It was the same basic message, but this one bought you time. By the next day, or soon after, it's likely to be old news. Something else will have happened in the great churn of events to move the attention away from you.

I was sent off eight times in my career – and the last one was the most stupid, because I was the manager. An opponent had been kicking lumps out of one of our players and I said to my right-hand man Davie Provan, 'I'm going to go on and do that guy.' Davie said, 'Don't be so stupid, sit still.'

'If he takes our boy Torrance on again, I'm on.' And, of course, he did. 'That's it,' I said, 'I'm on.'

Two minutes later I was back off again.

In the dressing room I said: 'If. I. Ever. Hear. A. Word. Of this getting out, you're all dead.' I thought the referee's back was turned when I whacked him. He was 6 feet 3 inches, an army player.

My first clash with an Arsenal manager was with George

Graham. I watched the denouement to the 1989 title race upstairs in my bedroom and told Cathy, 'No calls, don't put anyone through.' When Michael Thomas scored the goal against Liverpool that won Arsenal the title, I went berserk. Two years later, Arsenal won it again, beating us 3–1 in the year we won the European Cup Winners' Cup. I stayed with George after our Highbury game one year. He has this fantastic collection of malt whiskies. 'Do you want one? he asked. 'I don't drink whisky,' I said. So George opened a bottle of wine.

'Which of those malts do you open for guests?' I wondered.

'None of them. Nobody gets a malt,' he said. 'I've got blended Bell's here.'

'Typical Scot,' I said.

George laughed. 'This is my pension.'

Our first meeting at Old Trafford was a war. Afterwards, George was persuaded by a mutual friend to come up to my office. My word, it was hard playing against his Arsenal teams at that time. When Arsène took over after Bruce Rioch's brief spell, I didn't know much about him.

One day I asked Eric Cantona: 'What is Wenger like?' Eric said: 'I think he's overdefensive.' 'Oh, that's all right,' I thought. And the way he started at Arsenal was with five at the back. But when you see his teams now, you can't argue for a second that his teams are defensive. Eric's critique still makes me smile.

At the end of the 1990s, and for the first part of the new millennium, Arsenal were our challengers. There was no one else on the horizon. Liverpool and Newcastle had brief spells of prominence. Blackburn had their title-winning year. But if you look at our history prior to José Mourinho's arrival at Chelsea, there was no consistent threat to our dominance outside of Arsenal. Chelsea were a good Cup team, but they could never quite scale the peak of the Premier League.

When Blackburn came with an assault we knew it was unlikely to last because there was no history to sustain an achievement of that magnitude. Their League title win was great for football and for Jack Walker, the benefactor who brought such fine players to the club, Alan Shearer especially. That was a tremendous time for Blackburn. Experience tells you, though, only to worry about the challengers who have a tradition of bidding for the big prizes. When Arsenal and United were locked together for so long, you knew the Gunners were sustained by history and a strong identity.

At their ground, in my penultimate year as United manager, I had lunch in the boardroom and said to myself: 'This is class. Real class.' At Highbury I would study the bust of Herbert Chapman and feel that any suspicion of nostalgia was outweighed by the sense of solidity and purpose those marble halls conveyed. Achievement was always there, from Herbert Chapman and the 1930s, all the way through.

Their dressing rooms are marvellous. The advantages of building a new stadium from scratch are enormous. You have a blank sheet. Every detail you see in the Arsenal home dressing room reflects Arsène's specifications. He has covered every requirement for a football team. In the centre of the room is a marble-topped table where they put all the food. After a game, everyone tucks in. Another expression of class. The staff have their own quarters.

So I never ceased to be concerned at the high quality Arsenal could bring to our tussles. History helped us, but it helped them too, and they had the right manager. Arsène was the right one because you always felt that, having been given the chance to manage in England, he put his tent down and was never going to move it. All the while, there was speculation that he might leave one day to join Real Madrid. I never thought Arsène would leave Arsenal. Ever. I'd say to myself: 'We're going to have to put up with it. He's going to be here forever. I'd better get used to it.'

At times it was very edgy. Although Arsène would never come in for a drink after games, Pat Rice, his assistant, would always cross the threshold for a glass, until the pizza fight at Old Trafford.

My recollection of that fabled incident is that when Ruud van Nistelrooy came into the dressing room, he complained that Wenger had been giving him stick as he left the pitch. Right away I rushed out to say to Arsène: 'You leave my players alone.' He was incensed at losing the game. That was the reason for his combative behaviour.

'You should attend to your own players,' I told him. He was livid. His fists were clenched. I was in control, I knew it. Arsène had a thing about Van Nistelrooy. I remember him saying he'd had a chance to sign Ruud but had decided he was not good enough to play for Arsenal. I agreed with him in the sense that Van Nistelrooy may not have been a great footballer. But he was a great goal-scorer.

Anyway, the next thing I knew I had pizza all over me.

We put food into the away dressing room after every game. Pizza, chicken. Most clubs do it. Arsenal's food was the best.

They say it was Cesc Fàbregas who threw the pizza at me but, to this day, I have no idea who the culprit was.

The corridor outside the dressing room turned into a rabble. Arsenal had been defending a 49-game unbeaten record and had been hoping to make it 50 on our turf. It seemed to me that losing the game scrambled Arsène's brain.

That day created a division between us, without doubt, and that rift extended to Pat Rice, who stopped coming in for a drink after games. The wound was not fully healed until the Champions League semi-final in 2009, when Arsène invited us into his room after the game and congratulated us. When we played them at Old Trafford a few weeks later, Arsène came in with Pat, just for a few minutes.

In football you do see incidents that reflect normal conflicts in life. In our home lives, sometimes. You know when your wife turns that machine off and won't talk to you. 'Christ, what have I done?' you think.

'Have you had a good day?' you ask. 'Yeah,' she mumbles. Then the anger passes and normality returns. Football is like that. I would have hated the silence between Arsène and me to go on so long that it became poisonous.

At my end of it, I had a formula for defeat. After saying my bit in the dressing room, always, before going through that door to face the press, to face the television, to speak to the other manager, I said to myself, 'Forget it. The game's gone.' I always did that.

Whenever people came to my room at the ground after a game, I always made sure there was a good atmosphere. There was no gloom, no frostiness. No blaming the referee.

When Aston Villa beat us at Old Trafford in the 2009–10 season, it was the first time they had beaten us on our turf in decades. Martin O'Neill, whose conversation I always enjoy, practically moved into my office with his wife and daughter. It felt like an hour and a half. It was a really good night. John Robertson, Martin's assistant, and a few of my friends joined us and it turned into a real get-together. I ended up needing a driver to take me home.

When we lost in the FA Cup third round to Leeds United, the Leeds physio, Alan Sutton, couldn't stop laughing and smiling in my office. As he left I said, 'You're still bloody laughing!'

'I can't help it,' he said. It was the first time in my Old Trafford career that Leeds had beaten us on our soil and he was just incapable of not grinning. His pleasure was infectious. You have to say to yourself, I'm a human being, I must keep my dignity.

I was hospitable in that way to all the managers who joined me after the game.

I saw a change in Arsène in the last few years. When the Invincibles were forming, we were in transition. Around 2002, we were rebuilding the side. The Arsenal side of 2001–02 won the title at our ground, of course, and were accorded a standing ovation by our supporters. An attribute of Manchester United fans is that they will always acknowledge class. There were times when I would think, bitterly, 'Go on, go and applaud them, why don't you? Meanwhile, I'll go into the dressing room and pick our players up.' But that is how they are. I remember their standing ovation for the Brazilian Ronaldo after his Champions League hat-trick against us. As he left the pitch, Ronaldo seemed bemused, like his manager. 'Strange club, this,' they must have thought. Gary Lineker's last game in

England for Spurs was also warmly received. But there is a lot to be said for it. It brings football to its zenith. If you see class, excitement, entertainment, there is an obligation to acknowledge it.

Those people have seen all the best United teams, so they know what a good side is. They have the necessary reference points. They know what a top player is as well. On top of that, you have to acknowledge when you are beaten. There is nothing to be done. Sulking is futile. The Old Trafford game in 2002 was a non-event for me, in one sense, even if we were chasing second place. It was already obvious that Arsène's team were going to win the League. There was a sense of destiny.

In those moments of defeat and acceptance, there would be a dawning, for me, of where we needed to go. My feeling was always: 'I don't like this, but we'll have to meet the challenge. We'll have to step up a mark.' It wouldn't have been me, or the club, to submit to apocalyptic thoughts about that being the end, the finish of all our work. We could never allow that.

Every time those moments poked us in the eye, we accepted the invitation to regroup and advance again. Those were motivating passages. They forced me on. I'll go further: I can't be sure that without those provocations I would have enjoyed the job so much.

In later years we learned more about Arsenal's thinking. Arsène had a template of how he sees his players and the way they play. We didn't need to win the ball against Arsenal, we needed to intercept it. You need good players who can intercept. We worked out that when the ball was played into

Fàbregas with his back to goal, he would turn it round the corner and meet the return pass. He would twist the pass round the corner then run to get it back on the other side of the defender. So we would say to our players: 'Stay with the runner, then intercept the pass.' Then we counter-attacked quickly.

They were more dangerous at Old Trafford than their own ground. Away from home, they didn't feel obliged to throw everything at us. They were more conservative.

Barcelona were far more organised than Arsenal. When they lost the ball they would hound it. Every one of their players would be after it to win it back. Arsenal didn't have quite that dedication to the task of regaining possession. Then again, sometimes Barcelona would imitate Arsenal in over-elaborating, because they enjoyed it so much. Against Real Madrid at the Bernabéu in 2009, Messi was playing one-twos in the Real Madrid penalty box: not just one but two or three, while the Madrid defenders were all over the place. They won 6–2, but for a time I thought they would throw the game away.

We all have to put our hands up to having players who were over-physical at times, but Arsène could never do that, which was a weakness. It's not a crime to admit guilt when a player is sent off. You should feel bad, because he's let his team down. I had some issues with Paul Scholes. I even fined him for the silly things. I don't get upset when a player is booked when he was on for the tackle, but if he is sent off for a stupid challenge – and Scholesy was guilty of that – he would be fined. But if you expect a player to go through a season without infringing the laws of the game, you're asking for miracles.

Arsène's softer centre in my later years reflected the players he brought to the club. Samir Nasri becomes available, so Arsène takes him. Rosický becomes available, so he takes him, because he's his type of player. Arshavin becomes available, so in he comes. When you acquire a lot of those players, they are almost clones. The team Arsène inherited gave him a start in English football.

We stayed on these parallel tracks right to the end. And of course we were united by a desire to find and develop young players in our own image.

Then again, Aaron Ramsey said before we played Arsenal one time that he had chosen Arsène's team over mine because Arsenal produce more players than Man Utd.

I thought: 'What world is he in?' I think a young boy can get manipulated into saying things. It was his own decision to reject United, and I have no problem with that. I thought he made the wrong choice, I must say, though he would have faced more competition at our place to make the first team. Arsenal had not produced many of their own players. They had developed players, which is not the same thing. They bought them from clubs in France and all over the place. The only truly homegrown player I could think of was Jack Wilshere.

Giggs, Neville, Scholes, Fletcher, O'Shea, Brown, Welbeck: all produced at Man Utd.

There I go again. I could never be anything other than competitive with Arsène, my rival for 17 years.

fourteen

THE CLASS OF '92

Each time a member of our great homegrown generation left the club, I would count those left. Two managed to stay to the end of my time: Paul Scholes and Ryan Giggs. Gary Neville almost made it through with me. Even now I can visualise the six of them taking the mickey out of each other as boys after training. Scholesy would try to hit the back of Nicky Butt's head with the ball – or Gary's head more often. He was a devil for that. Those half-dozen young men were inseparable.

These were solid human beings: the sort you hated losing. They understood the club and its purpose. They would march with you, defend the principles on which we operated. Any parent would recognise that moment when a 21-year-old walks in and says they are going to buy their own place, or move in with their girlfriend or take a job in some other town. They leave you. Football was the same for me.

I became greatly attached to the men who were with me from their teenage years, the so-called Class of '92. I saw them grow from 13 years of age.

Nicky Butt was a prime example. He always reminded us of the cartoon character with the freckles, big ears and buck teeth on the front page of the comic, *Mad*. That mischief, that devilment. They were so long under my care that they felt like family to me. I would chastise them more than other players because they felt like relatives more than employees. Nicky was always up to something, a jack the lad. He was also brave as a lion, incapable of shirking any challenge.

He was one of the most popular players to have played at our club. He was a real Manchester lad. Down to earth and mentally tough. Like Phil Neville, Nicky reached the point where he wasn't playing often enough to satisfy his competitive urges. That prompted him to look elsewhere for openings. Once again we let him go very cheaply, for £2 million. Those men didn't owe us a penny. We had acquired them for nothing through our academy. The money for Nicky was a token sum to ensure he left for the best deal. Right to the end of his playing days, he would refer to us as his club.

Behind my back, I'm sure those lads resented bearing the brunt of my annoyance. 'Oh, me again,' they probably thought. 'Why don't you give him over there some?'

The first person I would give stick to was Giggsy, bless him. As youngsters they would never answer back. With time, Ryan learned to defend himself. Nicky might also retaliate now and then. Gary would have a go. But then Gary would answer his shadow back. He has to have an argument every day. He would be up at six o'clock with the papers, texting Di Law or later Karen Shotbolt, our press officers: 'Have you read this in the *Telegraph* or *The Times?*'

We always said of Gary that he woke up angry. His was an argumentative nature. He is a forthright guy. Where he sees error, sees flaws, he attacks them. His instinct was not to negotiate his way through an impasse, but strike hard with his opinions. There was no consensus with Gary. He was explosive. I would see a small issue escalate in his mind. But with me he knew where the limits of my patience were. I would say: 'Gary, go and annoy someone else.' Then he would laugh and the drama would be defused.

If I try to imagine those 20 years without the homegrown lads, I find it hard to visualise the base of the team. They provided our stability. Manchester United are recognised for the great players we found in the 26 years I was there, from Bryan Robson and Norman Whiteside and Paul McGrath onwards, through to Cantona and Ronaldo. But those homegrown boys carried the spirit of Manchester United inside them. That's what they gave the club: spirit. They were a great example to our coaching staff of what could be achieved through youth development, and a beacon to the young players coming through. Their presence told the next 19-year-old coming up the line: 'This can be done. The next Cantona can be created here at our academy, on our training ground.'

I will always remember Paul Scholes' first day at our club. He came in with a little guy called Paul O'Keefe. His father, Eamonn, had played at Everton. They were standing behind Brian Kidd, who had told me he was bringing in two lads he liked the look of. They were 13. 'Where are these two young kids?' I asked Brian. They were so small they were invisible behind Brian's frame.

They were about 4 feet 8 inches tall. I looked at this tiny pair and thought: 'How are these two going to become footballers?' It became a standing joke at the club. When Scholesy came into the youth team, I said, in the coaches' room: 'That Scholes has got no chance. Too small.' When he joined us properly at 16 he was still minuscule. But he really did shoot up. By 18, he had risen three or four inches.

Paul never said a word. He was exceptionally shy. His father had been a good player and they had shared a nickname, Archie. When I harboured those initial doubts about his size, I had never seen him play in a game, though I had looked at him in training at the school of excellence. At the indoor centre we mainly taught technical skills. When he progressed to play for the A youth team, he was a centre-forward. 'He's not got the pace to play centre-forward,' I said. They played him just behind a striker. In one of the early games at The Cliff, he hit one on the drop just outside the box and it stopped my breath with its power.

'He's good, but I don't think he has any chance of making it. Too small,' said Jim Ryan, who was watching with me. It became a stock phrase at the club. Scholesy: too small.

As his time with us rolled on, Paul Scholes encountered problems with his asthma. He didn't play in the youth team the year they won the FA Youth Cup. Beckham joined the team only in the later rounds because he had grown gangly and weak. Simon Davies, who played for Wales, was the captain. Robbie Savage was also in the side. The majority of them went on to be internationals. Another, Ben Thornley, would have earned a cap, but for major knee trouble.

As a young forward, in the hole, Scholes would be guaranteed 15 goals a season. When he developed into a central midfield player, he had the brain for the passing game and a talent for orchestration. He must have been a natural. I loved watching teams trying to mark him out of the game. He would take them into positions they didn't want to go to, and with a single touch would turn the ball round the corner, or feint away and hit the reverse pass. Opponents would spend a minute tracking him and then be made to appear inconsequential and sometimes even foolish. They would end up galloping back to their own box. He would destroy a marker that way.

Paul endured several disappointments with long-term injuries but would always come back better. He was a superior player after his eye problem and after his knee injury. He would return re-energised.

In his early thirties, he was prone to occasional bouts of frustration as the competition for midfield places intensified. I had Darren Fletcher and Michael Carrick to consider in the two central positions. I confess, I made an error here. Taking people for granted is not a mistake you are necessarily aware of at the time, and it is hard to correct until you are confronted by the effect on the victim. My attitude was that in times of need I could always go back to Scholesy. He was a loyal servant, always ready and willing to step in. Carrick and Fletcher would be my new first-choice pairing and Scholes would be the ageing support. It was in my mind for too long that Paul was coming to the end of his career.

In the 2009 Champions League final in Rome, which we lost to Barcelona, I sent Paul on in the second half. Anderson had made only three passes in the first half. Scholes made 25 in the last 20 minutes of the game. You think you know everything in this game. You don't. Taking people for granted and thinking you can always go back to them as they approach the end is wrong. You forget how good they are.

At the end, consequently, I used him a lot more and rested him at the right times. People would ask me to pick my best Man United team. I would find it incredibly difficult. You couldn't leave out Scholes and you couldn't leave out Bryan Robson. They would both give you at least ten goals a season. But then that raises the question: how can you leave out Keane? You would have to play the three of them. But if you do that, who do you play with Cantona, who was always better playing with another forward? Try picking one striker from McClair, Hughes, Solskjaer, Van Nistelrooy, Sheringham, Yorke, Cole, Rooney and Van Persie. You couldn't disregard Giggs. So it always felt like an impossible task to select a best XI, yet you would have to say Cantona, Giggs, Scholes, Robson and Cristiano Ronaldo could never be left out of a Man United side.

Scholes was probably the best English midfielder since Bobby Charlton. Since I have been in England, Paul Gascoigne was the best of those who could lift you from your seat. In his last few years, Paul Scholes elevated himself above Gascoigne. One, for longevity, and two, for improving himself in his thirties.

He was such a brilliant long passer that he could choose

a hair on the head of any team-mate answering the call of nature at our training ground. Gary Neville once thought he had found refuge in a bush, but Scholesy found him from 40 yards. He inflicted a similar long-range missile strike, once, on Peter Schmeichel, and was chased round the training ground for his impertinence. Scholesy would have made a first-class sniper.

As a player myself, I never possessed the innate ability of a Cantona or a Paul Scholes: eyes in the back of the head. But I could see it in others because I watched so many games. I knew how important those players were to a team.

Scholes, Cantona, Verón. Beckham had good vision too. He was not the sort who could thread great passes through, but he could see the other side of the pitch all right. Laurent Blanc had good vision. Teddy Sheringham and Dwight Yorke could see what was happening all around them. But of the players in the top echelon, Scholes was the best of that type. When we were winning easily, Scholes would sometimes try something daft, and I would say, 'Look, he's getting bored now.'

Ryan Giggs was the biggest noise from that generation. He was the one most likely to be identified as a wonder boy. Awarding him a first-team debut at 16 landed us with a problem we had not expected: the Giggs phenomenon.

An Italian agent phoned me when Ryan was a kid and asked, 'What do your sons do?' I said: 'Mark's doing a degree, Jason's going into television, Darren is an apprentice here.' He said: 'Sell me Giggs and I can make them rich.' Naturally I declined the offer.

The George Best comparison stuck to him immediately

and was impossible to dislodge. Everyone wanted a piece of him. But Giggs was smart. 'See the manager,' he would say to anyone seeking an interview or a tie-up. He didn't want to grant interviews and found a way to transfer the blame for the refusal on to me. He was clever.

Bryan Robson approached Ryan one day to recommend Harry Swales as an agent. He had checked it with me first. Bryan was coming to the end and was sure Harry was the right man for Giggs. He was right. Harry is fantastic. Got engaged at 81 to a Swiss lady he met on the platform of a railway station. She was lost. He is a former sergeant-major with a handlebar moustache. He looked after Ryan really well. Ryan has a strong mother, too, and his grandparents were very, very good people.

To stretch his first-team career to two decades, Ryan had to develop a meticulous fitness programme. Yoga, and his preparation routines, were at the root of his longevity. Ryan was religious about yoga. Twice a week after training, an expert would come in to guide him through the exercises. That became vital to him. In the days when he was susceptible to hamstring injuries, we were never sure how much we could play him. His hamstrings were a constant concern. We would leave him out of games to have him ready for others. By the end, only his age would prompt us to give him a rest. He would play 35 games a season because his fitness was fantastic.

Ryan's intelligence helped him make the sacrifices in his social life. He is a reserved kind of guy but, of all that bunch, he was the one they looked up to. He was the king, the man. There was a brief period when he and Paul Ince would wear daft suits but it soon passed. Ryan still has the suit that caused me to blurt, 'What the hell is that?'

Incey was a fan of flash dressing and he and Giggs were good pals. They were a duo. But Ryan has led a highly professional life. He is revered around the club, where everyone defers and looks up to him.

When his pace deteriorated we played him more in the centre of the park. We no longer expected him to flash round the outside of defenders the way he did as a boy. Not many people noticed that even in his later incarnation he retained his change of pace, which is sometimes more important than raw speed. His balance, too, was unaffected.

In the autumn of 2010 he was brought down by West Ham's Jonathan Spector in the penalty box, and I seized my chance to set a quiz question. How many penalties had Ryan Giggs won in his Manchester United career? Answer: five. Because he always stays on his feet. He stumbles but never goes down. I would ask him, after a heavy foul in the box, why he had declined to go down, which he would have been entitled to do, and he would look at me as if I had horns. He would wear that vacant look. 'I don't go down,' he would say.

Ryan is a calm boy, very even-tempered in adversity. Strange to say, he was never a great substitute until his later years. He was always better starting a game. But he played a great role as a sub in the 2008 Champions League final in Moscow, and against Wigan when we won the League, coming on to score our second goal. He removed the doubt we had about him being a good impact player and was an amazing asset to have off the bench.

Giggs turned his back on the fame and the branding; he lacked the temperament for that level of exposure. His personality was more introverted. To lead that life, you need great energy to be trotting all over the world and putting your face in front of a camera. It also requires a certain vanity: the belief that this is what you were made for. You read about actors always knowing they wanted to be on the stage or in films. I never had that magnetic attraction to fame.

My hope was that players who had grown up with us would carry things on at Carrington and maintain the continuity, much as Uli Hoeness and Karl-Heinz Rummenigge, say, had at Bayern Munich. They understand how the club functions and the standard of player needed to keep the show rolling along. Whether that leads in the end to management cannot be known, because it depends how the coaching side develops. But Giggs and Scholes are both intelligent men who understand United's soul and were great players them-selves, so all the right stuff was there.

Ryan could definitely be a manager because he's so wise and players invariably respect him. His relative quietness would not be a barrier. There are plenty of non-vocal managers. But your character must be strong. To deal with a club like Manchester United, your personality has to be bigger than those of the players. Or, you have to believe it is, to control the whole picture. You have big players, wealthy players, world-famous players, and you have to rule over them, stay on top of them. There is only one boss of Manchester United, and that's the manager. Ryan would need to cultivate that side of himself. But so did I, from 32 years of age.

At school we would be asked: 'What do you want to be when you grow up?' I would say: 'A footballer.' 'Fireman' was a more popular answer. To say 'footballer' implied no urge to be known across the world, merely to earn a living by playing the game. Giggs would have been that type.

You can be destined by your nature to chase a certain ending, and David Beckham always had that air of knowing where he was going. He was comfortable with that lifestyle and keen to attain that status. None of the others would have even dreamed about worldwide recognition. It was not part of them. Imagine Gary Neville with fashion photographers: 'Can you bloody hurry up?'

They were all lucky to have the protection of really good families. The Nevilles are really solid people. The same was true for all of them. It was a blessing, for them and for us. They know the value of a good upbringing: keeping your feet on the ground; manners; respect for older generations. If I had called someone from an older generation by their first name, my dad would have clipped me on the ear. 'Mister, to you,' he would have said.

All that has disappeared now. All my players would call me 'gaffer' or 'boss'. Lee Sharpe came in one day and asked, 'How you doing, Alex?' I said: 'Were you at school with me?'

Even better, a young Irish boy, Paddy Lee, saw me moving up the stairs of The Cliff, as he was coming down, with Bryan Robson behind me, and said, 'All right, Alex?'

I said: 'Were you at school with me?'

'No,' he said, perturbed.

'Well don't call me Alex!'

I get the giggles now recalling these moments. Behind

the fierce response I would be laughing inside. Wee Paddy Lee was terrific at animal impressions. Every Christmas he would do ducks, cows, birds, lions, tigers – everything. Even ostriches. The players would be rolling about. Paddy went to Middlesbrough for a year but didn't quite make it.

Wee George Switzer was another. Typical Salford boy. In the training ground canteen he was brilliant at barking things out and disguising where it had come from, so the victim would scan the room trying to spot the perpetrator.

'Hi boss!' Or 'Archie!' to Archie Knox. For a long time it was impossible to nail the culprit. There were no clues in the sea of faces at mealtimes.

But one day I caught him. 'All right, son?' I said. 'You do that again and you'll run round the pitch till you're dizzy.'

'Sorry, boss,' Switz stuttered.

Despite the image of me as someone who wanted obedience at all times, I loved people with a bit of devil in them. It was refreshing. You need self-confidence, a bit of nerve. If you're surrounded by people who are scared to express themselves in life, they will be equally frightened when it really matters, on the pitch, in games. Those lads from the 1992 class were never scared of anything. They were mighty allies.

fifteen

LIVERPOOL – A GREAT TRADITION

F ROM adversity, the really illustrious clubs return to their cycle of winning. Maybe I was lucky to have joined United in a troubled phase of their history. The League title had not been won for 19 years and I inherited a culture of low expectation. We had become a Cup team, and the fans anticipated a good run in the knock-out competitions more than in League action, where their hopes were kept in check.

My predecessors Dave Sexton, Tommy Docherty and Ron Atkinson were successful men, but in their years there was no consistent or sustained challenge for the championship. The same was true of Liverpool in the years when United were on top from 1993 onwards, but I could always feel their breath on my neck from 25 miles away.

When a club of Liverpool's history and tradition pull off a treble of cup wins, as they did in 2001, with the FA, League and UEFA trophies under Gérard Houllier, you are bound to feel a tremor of dread. My thought that year was: 'Oh, no, not them. Anybody but them.' With their background, their heritage and their fanatical support, as well as their terrific home record, Liverpool were implacable opponents, even in their fallow years.

I liked and respected Gérard Houllier, the Frenchman who took sole charge when the joint-manager experiment with Roy Evans was ended by the Anfield board. Steven Gerrard was starting to emerge as a youthful force in midfield, and they could summon two sensational goal-scorers in Michael Owen and Robbie Fowler.

The big cultural change was investing power in someone from outside the Liverpool religion. The succession of internal appointments from Shanks to Bob Paisley to Joe Fagan to Kenny Dalglish to Graeme Souness to Roy Evans maintained consistency of purpose. Towards the end of Kenny's first spell in charge, you could sense a shift. The team had grown old and Liverpool were starting to make unusual purchases: Jimmy Carter, David Speedie. These were untypical Liverpool signings. Graeme Souness made the right move but too quickly, breaking up an ageing team too fast. One mistake was to discard one of the best young players, Steve Staunton. Graeme would admit that himself. There was no need to let Staunton go. Graeme is a good guy but he's impetuous. He can't get there quickly enough. And his impetuosity cost him in that period.

A virtue of dealing with Liverpool back then was that they

would all come into my office mob-handed after the game. I inherited the tradition of every member of our staff going in to see them at Anfield and each one on their side reciprocating at Old Trafford. The Liverpool boot-room men had far more experience in that regard than me, but I learned quickly. Win, lose or draw, there would be a full turn-out and a rapport between the two managerial clans. Because there was such a divide between the two cities and such competitive tension on the field, it was even more important to retain our dignity, whatever the result. It was vital, too, that we concealed our weak points, and Liverpool were equally guarded in that respect.

Gérard had been a visiting trainee teacher in Liverpool during his course at Lille University, and had examined the club with an academic's eye. He was not entering Anfield blind to its traditions. He understood the ethos, the expectations. He was a clever man; affable, too. After he was rushed to hospital following a serious heart attack, I said to him, 'Why don't you just step upstairs?'

'I can't do that,' Gérard replied. 'I like working.' He was a football man. Heart trouble could not break his addiction.

Expectation always bears down on Liverpool managers and I think that brand of pressure pierced Kenny's defences in the end. At the time he abandoned the role of iconic player and moved into the dug-out, he possessed no managerial background. The same disparity undermined John Greig at Rangers. Possibly the greatest Rangers player of all time, John inherited a disintegrating team that could not be restored to an even keel. The emergence of Aberdeen and Dundee United was no help. Playing in the glamour role up front as one of Liverpool's finest players and then graduating to manager almost the next day was very difficult for Kenny. I remember him coming to see me in the Scotland camp and asking for advice about a job he had been offered in management. It was only later I realised he had been talking about the big one.

'Is it a good club?' I had asked him.

'Aye, it's a good club,' he said.

So I told him: if it was a good club, with good history, some financial leeway, and a chairman who understands the game, he would have a chance. If only two of those variables could be ticked off, he was in for a battle.

Without my intensive education at Aberdeen, I would have been poorly qualified to take over at Manchester United. I started at East Stirling without a penny. I enjoyed that, with 11 or 12 players. Then I went to St Mirren without a dime. I freed 17 players in my first season: they weren't good enough. They had 35 before I started swinging my machete. There, I would order the pies and the cleaning materials and the programmes. It was a full education.

When Gérard started importing large numbers of foreign players, I thought the treble-winning season offered proof that the policy might restore the club to its pomp. The likes of Vladimír Šmicer, Sami Hyypiä and Dietmar Hamann had established a strong platform on which Houllier could build. Any Cup treble has to be taken seriously. You might say fortune smiled on them in the FA Cup final against Arsenal, because Arsène Wenger's team battered them in that match before Michael Owen won it with the second of his two goals. It wasn't the individuals that worried me around that time so much as the name: Liverpool. The history. I knew that if this upsurge continued they would become our biggest rivals again, ahead of Arsenal and Chelsea.

A year after that Cup treble, they finished runners-up, but then fell away to fifth after Gérard brought in El Hadji Diouf, Salif Diao and Bruno Cheyrou, from which many commentators drew a line of cause and effect. Cheyrou was one we looked at when he was at Lille. He had no pace but a nice left foot. A strong lad, but not quick. Diouf had a good World Cup with Senegal and made a name for himself. You could understand Gérard's antennae twitching. I was always wary of buying players on the back of good tournament performances. I did it at the 1996 European Championship, which prompted me to move for Jordi Cruyff and Karel Poborský. Both had excellent runs in that tournament, but I didn't receive the kind of value their countries did that summer. They weren't bad buys, but sometimes players get themselves motivated and prepared for World Cups and European Championships and after that there can be a levelling off.

With Diouf there was a talent but it needed nurturing. He was a persistent thorn in your flesh, and not always in a nice way. He'd be silly on the pitch, but he had a right competitive edge about him, and he had ability. Joining an august club like Liverpool was not compatible with his rebellious side because he found it hard to conform to the discipline you need to be successful. Gérard soon found that out. With the number of high-intensity games you are going to play against Arsenal and Chelsea, you need players of a good temperament. And, in my opinion, Diouf had a dodgy one. Cheyrou just never made it. He didn't have the pace to play in the Premier League.

The Spice Boy culture was another dragon Gérard had to slay. I would hear stories of Liverpool players nipping across to Dublin for recreation. I felt that Stan Collymore's arrival was hardly conducive to stability. I nearly bought Collymore myself because there was an incredible talent. But when I watched him play for Liverpool, there was no great urgency about him, and I began to think what a lucky guy I had been for not buying him. I can only assume he would have been the same at United. Instead I took Andy Cole, who was always brave as a lion and always gave his best.

Before the upswing under Houllier, Liverpool had fallen into the trap that had caught United years before. They would buy players to fit a jigsaw. If you look at Man United from the mid-1970s to the mid-1980s, they were buying players such as Garry Birtles, Arthur Graham from Leeds United, Peter Davenport, Terry Gibson, Alan Brazil: there seemed to be a desperation. If someone scored against United they would be signed: it was that kind of short-term thinking. Liverpool acquired the same habit. Ronny Rosenthal, David Speedie, Jimmy Carter. A succession of players arrived who weren't readily identifiable as Liverpool players. Collymore, Phil Babb, Neil Ruddock, Mark Wright, Julian Dicks.

Gérard bought a wide mix of players to Anfield: Milan Baroš, Luis García, Šmicer and Hamann, who did a fine job for him. I could see a pattern emerging in Gérard's recruiting. Under Benítez I could observe no such strategy. Players came and went. There was a time when I looked at his first XI and felt they were the most unimaginative

Liverpool side I ever went up against. In one game against us, he played Javier Mascherano in central midfield and had his back four, as usual, but played Steven Gerrard wide left, with Alberto Aquilani off the front. He took Dirk Kuyt off and put Ryan Babel on the left, moving Gerrard to the right. The three played in a pack through the middle. Babel was on as an outside-left but not once did he work the touchline. I can't know what his orders were, but on the bench I remember saying it was a good time to bring him on, wide left, against Gary Neville. I told Scholes: warn Gary to concentrate. But Liverpool played with hardly any width at all.

Apparently Benítez came to our training ground as a guest of Steve McClaren, but I don't remember meeting him. We received lots of visits from overseas coaches and it was hard to keep track of them all. We had people from China and Malta and groups of three and four from Scandinavian countries. There was also a steady flow of other sportsmen: the Australia cricket team, NBA players, Michael Johnson, Usain Bolt. Johnson, who runs a spring training programme in Texas, impressed me with his knowledge.

Soon after Benítez arrived, I attended a Liverpool game and he and his wife invited me in for a drink. So far, so good. But our relationship frayed. The mistake he made was to turn our rivalry personal. Once you made it personal, you had no chance, because I could wait. I had success on my side. Benítez was striving for trophies while also taking me on. That was unwise.

On the day he produced his famous list of 'facts' detailing my influence over referees, we received a tip-off that Liverpool would stage-manage a question that would enable Benítez to go on the attack. That's not unusual in football. I had been known to plant a question myself. Put it this way, our press office had warned me, 'We think Benítez is going to have a go at you today.'

'What about?' I asked.

'I don't know, but we've been tipped off,' they said.

So, on television, Benítez puts his glasses on and produces this sheet of paper.

Facts.

The facts were all wrong.

First, he said I intimidate referees. The FA were scared of me, according to Rafa, even though I had just been fined £10,000 by the FA two weeks previously, and I was failing to support the Respect campaign. The Respect initiative had started that season, yet Rafa was going on about my criticism of Martin Atkinson in a Cup tie the previous year, before the new guidelines had come into place. So he was wrong in the first two things he said. The media loved it, even though the facts were inaccurate. They were hoping it would start a war, that I would launch a rocket back.

In fact, all I said in reply was that Rafa was obviously 'bitter' about something and that I was at a loss to explain what that might be. That was me saying to him: look, you're a silly man. You should never make it personal. That was the first time he tried those tactics, and each subsequent attack bore the same personal edge.

My inquiries told me that he had been irritated by me questioning whether Liverpool would be able to handle the title run in, whether they would buckle under the pressure. Had I been the Liverpool manager, I would have taken that as a compliment. Instead Benítez interpreted it as an insult. If I, as Manchester United manager, was talking about Liverpool and dropping in remarks to make them wobble, my Anfield counterpart ought to know they'd got me worried.

When Kenny was in charge at Blackburn, and they were out in front in the title race, I piped up: 'Well, we're hoping for a Devon Loch now.' That stuck. Devon Loch popped up in every newspaper article. And Blackburn started to drop points. We ought to have won the League that year but Rovers held on. There is no doubt we made it harder for them by raising the spectre of the Queen Mother's horse performing the splits on the Aintree run-in.

The advance publicity had been that Benítez was a control freak, which turned out to be correct, to a point that made no sense. He displayed no interest in forming friendships with other managers: a dangerous policy, because there would have been plenty from lesser clubs who would have loved to share a drink and learn from him.

In the 2009–10 season he did come in for a glass at Anfield, but looked uncomfortable, and, after a short while, said he needed to go, and that was that. To Sammy Lee, his assistant, I said: 'At least that's a start.'

On the day Roberto Martínez, manager of Wigan Athletic, was quoted as saying I had 'friends' who did my bidding in relation to Benítez (big Sam Allardyce was one he was referring to), Roberto phoned me and put a call into the LMA to ask whether he should make a statement correcting the story. Roberto told me he had no connection with Benítez, who had not helped him in any way. I think Martínez had spoken to a Spanish paper about the way Benítez saw us, his rivals in England, but was not endorsing that view himself. He was merely the messenger. You would think Benítez and Martínez would have struck up an affinity, being the only Spanish managers in England.

Benítez would complain about having no money to spend, but from the day he landed, he doled out more than me. Far more. It amazed me that he used to walk into press conferences and say he had no money to spend. He was given plenty. It was the quality of his buys that let him down. If you set aside Torres and Reina, few of his acquisitions were of true Liverpool standard. There were serviceable players – Mascherano and Kuyt, hard-working players – but not real Liverpool quality. There was no Souness or Dalglish or Ronnie Whelan or Jimmy Case.

Benítez did score two great successes in the transfer market: Pepe Reina, the goalkeeper, and Fernando Torres, their striker. Torres was a very, very talented individual. We watched him many times and tried to sign him when he was 16. We expressed our interest two years before he joined Liverpool, but we always felt that our contact with him would end only in him receiving an improved contract at Atlético Madrid. We watched him in many youth tournaments and always fancied him. He was ingrained in the fabric at Atlético, so I was surprised Liverpool were able to prise him away. Benítez's Spanish connections must have helped.

Torres was blessed with great cunning: a shrewdness that was borderline Machiavellian. He had a touch of evil, though not in a physical sense, and he had that total change of pace. In a 45-yard sprint he was no faster than several Liverpool players, but he had that change of pace, which can be lethal.

His stride was deceptively long. Without warning he would accelerate and slice across you. Conversely, I'm not sure he was at his best when things were going against him because his reactions could become petty. Perhaps he was spoilt at Atlético Madrid, where he was the golden boy for so long. He was captain there at 21.

He had a fine physique: a striker's height and frame. And he was Liverpool's best centre-forward since Owen or Fowler. Another star, of course, was Steven Gerrard, who didn't always play well against Man United, but was capable of winning matches by himself. We made a show for him in the transfer market, as did Chelsea, because the vibe was that he wanted to move from Anfield, but there seemed to be some restraining influence from people outside the club and it reached a dead end.

His move to Chelsea seemed all set up. A question kept nagging at me: why did Benítez not trust Gerrard as a central midfield player? The one thing we could be sure of in my later years against Liverpool was that if their two central midfielders won it off you they would not do much with it. If Gerrard was in there and he won it against you, you knew he had the legs and the ambition to go right forward and hurt you. I could never understand why Liverpool so often neglected to play him centre-mid. In 2008–09, when they finished second with 86 points, they had Alonso to make the passes and Gerrard further up the pitch behind Torres.

Another of our advantages was that they stopped producing homegrown talents. Michael Owen was probably the last. If Michael had joined us at 12 years old, he would have been one of the great strikers. In the year he played in the

Malaysian youth finals we had Ronnie Wallwork and John Curtis there on England duty. When they returned I gave them a month off – sent them on holiday. Michael Owen was straight into the Liverpool first team, with no rest and no technical development. Michael improved as a footballer in the two years he had with us. He was terrific in the dressing room and was a nice boy.

I think that lack of rest and technical development in his early years counted against him. By the time Houllier inherited him, he was already formed and was the icon of the team. There was no opportunity by then to take him aside and work on him from a technical point of view. I made a mistake with Michael in the sense that I should have signed him earlier. There would have been no chance of him coming straight to Man United from Liverpool, but we should have stepped in when he left Real Madrid for Newcastle. He's a fine young man.

Of the other Liverpool players who gave us trouble, Dirk Kuyt was as honest a player as you could meet. I'm sure he was 6 feet 2 inches when he arrived and ended up 5 feet 8 inches because he ran his legs into stumps. I've never known a forward player work so hard at defending. Benítez picked him every game. But then, if something happens in the opposition penalty box, will he be sharp enough or is he exhausted from all the scuffling?

Despite my reservations about him as a person and a manager, Benítez persuaded his players to work their socks off for him, so there must be some inspirational quality there: fear, or respect, or skill on his part. You never saw his teams throw in the towel, and he deserves credit for that.

Why did he not do as well as he might have at Anfield, from my perspective? Benítez had more regard for defending and destroying a game than winning it. You can't be totally successful these days with that approach.

José Mourinho was far more astute in his handling of players. And he has personality. If you saw José and Rafa standing together on the touchline, you knew you could pick the winner. You always had to respect a Liverpool side. The same goes for some of the work Benítez put in, because they were a very hard side to beat, and because he won a European Cup there. There were plus points. He got lucky, but so did I, sometimes.

His mode on the touchline was to constantly move his players around the pitch, but I doubt whether they were always watching him or acting on those instructions. No one could have understood all those gesticulations. On the other hand, with Mourinho, in a Chelsea–Inter match, I noticed the players sprinted over to him, as if to say, 'What, boss?' They were attentive to his wishes.

You need a strong manager. That's vital. And Benítez is strong. He has great faith in himself and he's sufficiently stubborn to ignore his critics. He does that time and again. But he did win a European Cup, against AC Milan in Istanbul in 2005, which offered him some protection against those who dismissed his methods.

When Milan led 3–0 at half-time in that game, so the story goes, some of the Milan players were already celebrating, pulling on commemorative T-shirts and jigging about. I was told Paolo Maldini and Gennaro 'Rino' Gattuso were going crackers, urging their team-mates not to presume the game was over.

Liverpool won the Cup that night with a marvellous show of defiance.

After a brief spell in charge at Anfield, Roy Hodgson gave way to Kenny again and Liverpool embarked on another phase of major rebuilding. Yet few of the signings made in Kenny's time haunted me at night. We looked at Jordan Henderson a lot and Steve Bruce was unfailingly enthusiastic about him. Against that we noticed that Henderson runs from his knees, with a straight back, while the modern footballer runs from his hips. We thought his gait might cause him problems later in his career.

Stewart Downing cost Liverpool £20 million. He had a talent but he was not the bravest or the quickest. He was a good crosser and striker of the ball. But £20 million? Andy Carroll, who also joined for £35 million, was in our northeast school of excellence, along with Downing and James Morrison, who went on to play for Middlesbrough, West Brom and Scotland. The FA closed it down after complaints from Sunderland and Newcastle. This was at the time academies started. The Carroll signing was a reaction to the Torres windfall of £50 million. Andy's problem was his mobility, his speed across the ground. Unless the ball is going to be in the box the whole time, it's very difficult to play the way Andy Carroll does because defenders push out so well these days. You look for movement in the modern striker. Suárez was not quick on his feet but has a fast brain.

The boys Kenny brought in from the youth set-up did well. Jay Spearing, especially, was terrific. As a boy Spearing was a centre-back, with John Flanagan at full-back, and Spearing was easily the best of them: feisty, quick, a leader.

You could see he had something. He was all right in the centre of midfield, but it was hard to visualise his long-term future. His physique perhaps counted against him.

Kenny won the League Cup, of course, and reached the final of the FA Cup, but when I heard that he and his assistant Steve Clarke had been summoned to Boston to meet the club's owners, I feared the worst for them. I don't think the protest T-shirts and defending Suárez in the Patrice Evra saga helped Kenny. As a manager your head can go in the sand a bit, especially with a great player. If it had been a reserve player rather than Suárez, would Kenny have gone to such lengths to defend him?

The *New York Times* and *Boston Globe* editorials about the subsequent Evra–Suárez non-handshake showed the way the debate was going. Kenny's problem, I feel, was that too many young people in the club idolised him. Peter Robinson, the club's chief executive in the glory years, would have stopped the situation escalating to the degree it did. The club has to take precedence over any individual.

The next man in, Brendan Rodgers, was only 39. I was surprised they gave it to such a young coach. A mistake I felt John Henry made in Brendan's first weeks in charge in June 2012 was to sanction a fly-on-the wall documentary designed to reveal the intimacies of life at Liverpool. To put that spotlight on such a young guy was hard and it came across badly. It made no great impact in America, so I could not work out what the point of it was. My understanding is that the players were told they were obliged to give the interviews we saw on our screens.

Brendan certainly gave youth a chance, which was

admirable. And he achieved a reasonable response from his squad. I think he knew there had been some sub-standard buys. Henderson and Downing were among those who would need to prove their credentials. In general you have to give players you might not rate a chance.

Our rivalry with Liverpool was so intense. Always. Underpinning the animosity, though, was mutual respect. I was proud of my club the day we marked the publication of the Hillsborough report in 2012: a momentous week for Liverpool and those who had fought for justice. Whatever Liverpool asked for in terms of commemoration, we agreed to, and our hosts made plain their appreciation for our efforts.

I told my players that day – no provocative goal celebrations, and if you foul a Liverpool player, pick him up. Mark Halsey, the referee, struck the right note with his marshalling of the game. Before the kick-off, Bobby Charlton emerged with a wreath which he presented to Ian Rush, who laid it at the Hillsborough Memorial by the Shankly Gates. The wreath was composed of 96 roses, one for each Liverpool supporter who died at Hillsborough. Originally, Liverpool wanted me and Ian Rush to perform that ceremony, but I thought Bobby was a more appropriate choice. The day went well, despite some minor slanging at the end by a tiny minority.

For Liverpool to return to the level of us and Manchester City was clearly going to require huge investment. The stadium was another inhibiting factor. The club's American owners elected to refurbish Fenway Park, home of the Boston Red Sox, rather than build a new arena. To construct a major stadium these days is perhaps a £700 million enterprise. Anfield has not moved on. Even the dressing rooms are the same as 20 years ago. At the same time, my reading of their squad was that they needed eight players to come up to title-winning standard. And if you have made mistakes in the transfer market, you often end up giving those players away for very little.

While Brendan Rodgers went about his work, Rafa Benítez and I had not seen the last of one another. He returned to English football as Chelsea's interim manager when Roberto Di Matteo, who had won the Champions League in May, was sacked in the autumn of 2012. In a United press conference soon after Benítez's unveiling, I made the point that he was fortunate to inherit ready-made sides.

I felt his record needed placing in context. He won the Spanish League with 51 goals, in 2001–02, which suggested he was a skilled pragmatist. But I found Liverpool hard to watch when he was manager there. I found them dull. It was a surprise to me that Chelsea called him. When Benítez placed his record alongside Di Matteo's, it would have been two League titles with Valencia, a European Cup and an FA Cup with Liverpool. In six months, Di Matteo had won the FA Cup and the European Cup.

They were comparable records. Yet Rafa had landed on his feet again.

sixteen

A WORLD OF TALENT

FROM the moment Manchester United became a Plc in 1990, I was certain the club would be bought and taken into private ownership. Rupert Murdoch's BSkyB were the largest of the private bidders before Malcolm Glazer first took a stake in 2003. With our history and our aura, we were too big a prize to be ignored by individual investors. The only surprise to me, when the Glazer family moved in to take control, was that there had not been a host of wealthy suitors.

Once the Glazers had seized their opportunity, Andy Walsh of the United supporters' group called me to say: 'You have to resign.' Andy's a nice lad but there was no temptation for me to agree to that request. I was the manager, not a director. Nor was I one of the shareholders who had sold the club. The takeover was not down to me in any way.

'We'll all be behind you,' Andy said. My reply was: 'But what do you think would happen to all my staff?' The moment I left, most of my assistants would have been out as well. Some had been with me for 20 years. The impact made on others when a manager changes his position is sometimes lost on those outside the circle.

It was a worrying time, I admit. One of my concerns was how much money we might have to invest in the team. But I had to be confident both in my own ability to spot good players and the structure of the organisation. The Glazers were buying a good solid club and they understood that from the start.

My first contact was a phone call from the father, Malcolm. Two weeks later his sons Joel and Avi came over to set out their position. They told me there would be no changes to the way the football side was run. In their view, the club was in good hands. I was a successful manager. They had no concerns. They were totally behind me. All the things I wanted to hear from them, I heard that day. I know there is always an element of window dressing. People tell you everything is fine, then make a million alterations. People lose their jobs; there are cutbacks because debts need to be repaid. But United stayed solid under the new ownership, irrespective of the borrowings people talked about and the interest payments incurred.

Over the years, several supporter groups challenged me to define my stance in relation to the club's debts and my answer was always: 'I'm the manager. I'm working for a club owned by people in America.' That was my standpoint. I never thought it sensible to upset the management side of the club by adding to the debate on models of ownership. If the Glazers had taken a more confrontational path, then it might have been different – if, for example, they had instructed me to get rid of one of my coaches. Any changes that might have undermined my ability to run the club would have altered the whole dynamic, but there was never that kind of pressure. So do you throw down your tools because some supporters want you to walk away from a lifetime's work?

When I first joined United, there was a group of supporters known as the Second Board. They would meet in the Grill Room and decide what they thought was wrong with Manchester United. Back then, when my position was more fragile, I was more attuned to the damage that might be done to my position should they turn against me. Other United managers before me had felt the same way. In my playing days at Rangers, a group of powerful fans travelled with the first team and were influential lobbyists. At United there was a larger array of supporters' voices. In disgust at the Glazer takeover, some handed in their season tickets and started FC United of Manchester.

There is a price to pay when you support a football club, and the price is that you can't win every game. You are not going to be a manager for a lifetime. United are lucky to have had two for half a century. With losing and winning games, the emotions rise and fall. Football naturally generates dissent. I remember us losing a game at Rangers and the supporters throwing bricks through the windows.

There was no reason, beyond my age, for the Glazers to consider a change of manager in the summer of 2005. I never considered that possibility, never felt under threat.

The tens of millions of pounds paid out in interest to service the loans did arouse protective feelings towards the club. I understood that, but at no stage did it translate into pressure to sell a player or excessive caution on the purchasing front. One of their strengths was their commercial department in London, which brought in dozens of sponsorships globally. We had Turkish airlines, telephone companies in Saudi Arabia, Hong Kong, Thailand, beer companies in the Far East. That sucked in tens of millions and helped service the debt. On the football side we generated huge earnings. The 76,000 crowds helped a great deal.

So at no stage was I held back by the Glazer ownership. Often we would lose interest in a player because the transfer fee or wage demands had become silly. Those decisions were taken by me and David Gill. There was no edict from above to spend only in line with the club's debts.

Instead our galaxy went on expanding. From 2007 more foreign talent poured into Carrington from South America, Portugal and Bulgaria. No imported player in those years attracted more attention than Carlos Tévez, who was at the heart of a major controversy over the relegation of Sheffield United from the Premier League and was to end up in opposition to us at Manchester City, staring down from that provocative billboard in his sky-blue shirt, underneath the message: 'Welcome to Manchester.'

The tale begins when Tévez was at West Ham and David Gill was receiving calls from his agent, Kia Joorabchian, saying the boy would love to play for Man United. We had heard that kind of story many times. It was almost routine for agents to call saying their client had a special feeling for our crest. My advice was that we should not involve ourselves in any complicated dealings with the Tévez camp. David agreed. It was clear that a consortium of people owned the player. But, to David, I also remarked: 'He does make an impact in games with his energy and he has a decent scoring record. It would depend what the deal was.'

David told me he could acquire Tévez on loan for two years, for a fee. That was the way it turned out and Carlos did well for us in his first season. He scored a lot of important goals, against Lyon, Blackburn, Tottenham and Chelsea. There was a real enthusiasm and energy about him. He wasn't blessed with great pace and wasn't a great trainer. He would always like a wee break, saying his calf was sore. In the context of the way we prepared, that sometimes annoyed us. We wanted to see a genuine desire to train all the time. Top players have that. But Tévez compensated quite well with his enthusiasm in games.

In the 2008 European Cup final in Moscow, he played and scored in the penalty shoot-out against Chelsea. He was our first taker. In the game itself, I took Rooney off and left Tévez on because he was playing better than Wayne. What planted a doubt in my mind was that in his second season I signed Dimitar Berbatov, and the emphasis was on Berbatov and Rooney as our forward partnership.

Watching Dimitar at Tottenham, I felt he would make a difference because he had a certain composure and awareness that we lacked among our group of strikers. He displayed the ability of Cantona or Teddy Sheringham: not lightning quick, but he could lift his head and make a creative pass. I thought he could bring us up a level and extend our range of talents.

So Berbatov's arrival relegated Tévez to more of a backup role. And around December in his second season, we started to feel he wasn't doing especially well. The reason, I think, was that he's the type of animal that needs to play all the time. If you're not training intensively, which he wasn't, you need to play regularly. During that winter, David Gill asked, 'What do you want to do?' I felt we ought to wait until later in the season to make a decision. 'They want one now,' David said.

I replied, 'Just tell them I'm trying to get him more games so we can assess it properly, because Berbatov is in the team a lot.'

Tévez did influence plenty of outcomes in the second half of the 2008–09 campaign, especially against Spurs at home, when we were 2–0 down, and I sent him on to shake things up. He chased absolutely everything. He brought huge enthusiasm to the cause and was the one responsible for us winning that match 5–2. His impact changed the course of events.

The 2009 Champions League semi-final pitted us against Arsenal and I was playing a three of Ronaldo, Rooney and Park. That was my chosen group for the final and apparently Tévez was not impressed. We made a mess of the final in Rome against Barcelona. We chose a bad hotel. It was a shambles. We have to hold our hands up about our poor planning.

Anyway, I brought Tévez on at half-time and just felt he was playing for himself a bit. From what I could gather, he had already made his mind up before joining City. After the game in Rome he said to me: 'You never showed any great desire to sign me permanently.' I explained that I had to see how the season played out and that he hadn't played enough games for me to be sure. David offered the £25 million fee for him, but from what I can gather it was as if he were talking to the wall. That led us to think he had already elected to move across town.

The rumour, not confirmed, was that our Manchester rivals had paid £47 million. Tévez spoke to Chelsea at some point, too, and I think his advisers played one against the other. The word was that Chelsea offered £35 million but that City outbid them. To me these were incredible sums. I wouldn't have paid that kind of money, fine player though he was. To me he was an impact maker. It was a mistake on my part, in the sense that Berbatov was a player I fancied strongly and I wanted to see him succeed. But he is also the sort who wants to be assured he is a great player. The conundrum with him and Tévez was always there.

There was no disciplinary problem with Tévez of the sort Roberto Mancini encountered when the boy declined to warm up for City, apparently, in a Champions League game in Germany, but there was a major hoo-ha over his supposed role in Sheffield United's demotion to the Championship in 2007. Tévez's goals had been saving West Ham from relegation when they came to our ground at the end of that season. They were fined for breaching third-party ownership rules with Tévez, but no points were deducted by the Premier League. Inevitably Tévez scored against us for West Ham, which helped send Sheffield United down, and Neil Warnock, their manager, tried to load the blame on us for playing a supposedly weakened team against the Hammers.

We had a Cup final the week after that West Ham game. Our squad was one of the strongest in the League and I had been changing the team all season according to circumstance. If you watch that match, we had two or three penalties turned down and their goalkeeper had a fantastic game. They broke away and Tévez scored. West Ham were never in the game. We battered them. I brought on Ronaldo, Rooney and Giggs in the second half but still we couldn't knock them over.

Meanwhile Mr Warnock accuses us of throwing the game away. In their last game they faced Wigan at home and all they needed was a draw. In early January, Warnock had let David Unsworth go on a free transfer to Wigan, and Unsworth takes the penalty kick that knocks Sheffield United out of the Premier League. Could anyone with an open mind not say: I made a mess of that, there? Has he ever looked at himself in the mirror and said, 'All we needed was a draw at home and we weren't good enough to take a point off Wigan?' The accusation was ridiculous.

In January 2007 we acquired a real aristocrat – for a two-month spell, at any rate. Louis Saha had returned at the start of the season full of promise but picked up another injury. In October Jim Lawlor, United's chief scout, pointed out to us that it was a waste for Henrik Larsson to be playing in Sweden when he still had so much to offer on a bigger stage. Helsingborgs, where Henrik was playing, would not sell him, but I asked Jim to ask their chairman what they would think about him coming on loan in January. Henrik pushed the boat in that direction with his employers.

On arrival at United, he seemed a bit of a cult figure with our players. They would say his name in awed tones. For a man of 35 years of age, his receptiveness to information on the coaching side was amazing. At every session he was rapt. He wanted to listen to Carlos, the tactics lectures; he was into every nuance of what we did.

In training he was superb: his movement, his positional play. His three goals for us were no measure of his contribution. In his last game in our colours at Middlesbrough, we were winning 2–1 and Henrik went back to play in midfield and ran his balls off. On his return to the dressing room, all the players stood up and applauded him, and the staff joined in. It takes some player to make that kind of impact in two months. Cult status can vanish in two minutes if a player isn't doing his job, yet Henrik retained that aura in his time with us. He looked a natural Man United player, with his movement and courage. He also had a great spring for a little lad.

I could have signed him earlier. I was ready to make the bid when he was at Celtic but Dermot Desmond, Celtic's majority shareholder, rang me and said, 'You've let me down, Alex, you've got tons of players, we need him.'

A month after Henrik went back to Sweden, we registered one of our greatest European victories: the 7–1 win over Roma on 10 April, our highest Champions League score. There were two goals each for Michael Carrick and Ronaldo, one from Rooney, Alan Smith and even Patrice Evra, who scored for the first time in Europe.

Top games of football are generally won by eight players. Three players can be carried if they're having an off night and work their socks off, or are playing a purely tactical role for the team in order to secure the result. But half a dozen times in your career you achieve perfection where all 11 are on song.

Everything we did that night came off. For the second goal we produced a six-man move of one-touch passing. Alan Smith scored from a Ryan Giggs pass between the two centre-backs. First time – bang, in the net. Brilliant goal. So you have these moments when you say: we could not have improved on that.

I remember taking a team to Nottingham Forest in 1999 and winning 8–1. It could have been 20. Roma were a bloody good side too. They had Daniele De Rossi, Cristian Chivu and Francesco Totti, and we absolutely slaughtered them. We had been beaten 2–1 in Rome, where Scholes had been sent off for a suicidal tackle right on the touchline. The boy was practically off the pitch when Paul arrived with his challenge. So we were under some pressure in the return leg. Until the goals started flying in.

Wimbledon away in the FA Cup in February 1994 was another classic. In a 3–0 win we scored one goal with 38 passes. People talk of the best Man United goal being Ryan Giggs' in that FA Cup semi-final against Arsenal, or Rooney's overhead kick against Manchester City, but for me that goal at Wimbledon was sublime. Every player in the team touched the ball. In the first minute of the game, Vinnie Jones tried to do Cantona. Crack. Down went Eric. All our players ran towards Jones, but Cantona said, 'Leave him alone,' because he was a fellow ex-Leeds player, and may have felt a kinship. Then he patted Jones on the back as if to say, 'You can kick me if you like but you won't stop me.' Cantona was marvellous that day and scored our first goal with a beautiful volley that he teed up for himself with his right foot.

People always said Wimbledon couldn't play. That's not true. The quality of the service to their front players was high, especially the crosses. Their set-piece delivery was terrific. They were not devoid of talent. What they did was use those talents as a weapon against weaker people. If you didn't head the ball, you were dead. If you couldn't handle set pieces you were dead. If you wanted to get into a 50–50 with them – no chance. They were hard to play against. So that 3–0 win in their ground was special to us.

Two big wins over Arsenal also stand out. In a 6–2 win at Highbury in the League Cup in 1990, Lee Sharpe scored a hat-trick. On another occasion, in February 2001, we beat them 6–1 at Old Trafford. An Irish family had bought an auction prize to see us play at Liverpool in December 2000, but were fog-bound and unable to travel. We lost 1–0 to Liverpool in a horrible game. They rang me and asked, 'What are we going to do?' I told them, 'We've got Arsenal at home soon.' And they saw a 6–1 massacre. What a difference. It was 5–1 at half-time. Yorkie tore them apart.

Despite our 7–1 win over Roma, our Champions League campaign was ended by a 3–0 defeat in Milan on 2 May. We had been forced to field a full team on the previous Saturday in order to beat Everton 4–2 at Goodison Park, while Milan had rested nine players for their game against us, which was on the Tuesday. We were simply not as well prepared as our Italian opponents. We conceded twice in 15 minutes, it bucketed with rain, and we just couldn't break out of our own half. We simply weren't ready for it. Winning on the Saturday had been a mammoth task because we had been 2–0 down against Everton, yet we won the game to move five points clear in the League.

Along with Tévez and Larsson, other global talents joined us. Carlos, through his Portuguese connections, told us there was a young boy at Porto from Brazil called Anderson. He was 16 or 17. We kept an eye on him. He was in and out of the team. A game here, an appearance from the bench there. Then he played against us in the Amsterdam tournament and I resolved to act, but the following week he broke his leg.

When his recovery was complete, I sent Martin over to watch him in every game for four or five weeks. Martin said: 'Alex, he's better than Rooney.'

'For Christ's sake, don't say that,' I told him. 'He'll need to be good to be better than Rooney.' Martin was adamant. At that stage, Anderson was playing off the striker. At the end of the tournament we moved to buy both him and Nani, who I went to see for myself. What attracted me to Nani was his pace, strength and aerial ability. He had two fine feet. All the individual attributes were there, which brought us round to the old question: what type of boy was he? Answer: a good one, quiet, could speak English reasonably well, never caused any problems at Sporting Lisbon, and was an excellent trainer. My word he's a fit boy. Gymnastic, too. His athletic read-outs were always first-class. So the foundations were there. Carlos went over with David Gill: called into Sporting Lisbon to sign Nani and then drove up to Porto to capture Anderson. All in one day.

Two years on, we were able to say that the reasons for signing them were correct. There were complications with Anderson in the winter of 2009–10. He wasn't playing as much as he would have liked to and wanted to return home. He was Brazilian, and the complication, as ever, was the World Cup, which he was desperate to play in. His scheme was to go to Vasco Da Gama for the rest of the season so he could play in the South Africa World Cup of 2010. 'You're not leaving here. We're not investing millions of pounds in a player so he can shoot off to Brazil,' I told him. Lovely personality, Anderson.

I have always respected Brazilian footballers. Name a Brazilian player who doesn't excel in big games? They were born for the big occasion. They have a special quality: deep pride in themselves. Great belief. There is a myth that Brazilians regard training as an onerous interruption to a life of pleasure. Not true. They train conscientiously. The notion that they hate the cold is another fallacy. The two Da Silva brothers for example: no tracksuit bottoms, no gloves – out they go. No country can apply the rich mix of ingredients you gain from a top Brazilian player. Argentines are deeply patriotic but I found they lack the expressive personalities of Brazilians.

With Nani we were buying pure raw material. He was immature, inconsistent, but with a wonderful instinct for football. He could control the ball with either foot, head the ball and he bristled with physical strength. He could cross, shoot. When you buy a player with all those talents, the trick is to put them in order. He was a bit disorganised and needed to be more consistent. It was inevitable that he would work in Ronaldo's shadow because he was a winger from Portugal with some of the same attributes. Had he been from Serbia, no one would have made the comparison. But both Ronaldo and Nani had come through Sporting Lisbon, so they were always being studied side by side.

Ronaldo was blessed with outrageous talent, and was brave, with two great feet and a wonderful leap. It was perhaps daunting for Nani to assert himself as a Man United starter against that backdrop. To be up against Ronaldo in team selection was a problem in itself. In his first year he was on the bench a lot. Nani picked up the language quickly but Anderson took longer. Because he's Brazilian, though, he brought incredible self-belief to the job. Brazilians think they can play against anybody.

I would say to Anderson: 'Have you seen this Neymar in Brazil?'

'Oh, great player. Fantastic.'

'Have you seen Robinho?'

'Wonderful. Incredible player.'

Every Brazilian name I mentioned would elicit this response. He thought everyone back home was world class. When Brazil battered Portugal in a friendly, Anderson told Ronaldo: 'Next time we'll play our fifth team to give you a chance.' Ronaldo was not amused. That's the kind of country Brazil is. I love that story about the competition in Rio to unearth new No. 10s and thousands turning up. One boy travelled for 22 hours on a bus. It's a massive country, with talent everywhere.

I look back less fondly on our move for Owen Hargreaves, who was phenomenal in the summer of 2006 and was just the type of player we needed to fill the gap left by Keane. We started to put together a bid for him. But I studied his playing record and felt a tinge of doubt. I didn't feel a strong vibe about him. David Gill worked hard on the deal with Bayern. I met Owen's agent at the World Cup final in Berlin. Nice man, a lawyer. I told him we could develop Hargreaves at United. It turned out to be a disaster.

Owen had no confidence in himself whatsoever. He didn't show nearly enough determination to overcome his physical difficulties, for my liking. I saw him opt for the easy choice too often in terms of training. He was one of the most disappointing signings of my career.

He went everywhere in search of cures for his various injuries: Germany, America, Canada. I felt he lacked the confidence to overcome his injuries. It went from bad to worse. He was away in America for the best part of a year. He saw Hans Müller-Wohlfahrt, the club doctor at Bayern Munich, for his calf. In the games he did actually play, I had no qualms about his contribution. He was lightning quick and a great set-piece deliverer. He could play right-back, wide right or central midfield. I played him wide right in the 2008 final against Chelsea, and when we started to struggle against their midfield three, I put him in the middle of the park with Rooney wide right and it worked. He had definite value. But it was all lost in the fog of his lack of games. Yet Hargreaves was fantastic for England at the 2006 World Cup, plugging gaps, racing to the ball.

In September 2011, we took a blast from Hargreaves about how he had been supposedly let down by our medical staff in his time with us. He claimed we had used him like 'a guinea pig' for treatments for his tendonitis and various knee problems. We took legal advice and could have proceeded against him, but the doctor was not sufficiently offended to seek legal redress. We did the best for that lad. No matter what the staff did for him, he created his own agenda.

I would say to him, 'How are you this morning?'

'Great, boss,' he would reply. 'But I think I'll do something on my own. I'm feeling it a bit.'

One of his allegations was that we picked him for the Wolves game in early November 2010 when he had asked not to be selected. Rubbish. Three weeks before that fixture, he had advised us that he would be ready for such and such a date, which happened to be a European tie. I was reluctant to bring him back in a European game after he had been out for so long. There was a reserve game that week, which he was meant to play in, but he withdrew.

In the week of the Wolves game, to my knowledge, he said nothing to our staff to indicate he had a problem. My concern, which I expressed to Mick Phelan, was that he would pick up an injury in the warm-up. My understanding was that he told one of the players he was feeling his hamstring a bit. When he came in from the warm-up, I specifically asked him: 'Are you all right?' I said it to reassure him. My message was: enjoy it. Well, he lasted five minutes. His hamstring went. But it was no surprise.

When I signed him, there was something about him I didn't like. The thing every good leader should have is an instinct. Mine said to me: 'I don't fancy this.' When he came over to Old Trafford for the medical, I still had some indefinable doubt. He was very hail-fellow-well-met. Almost too nice. Kléberson also left me with doubts, but only because he was so timid, and could barely look you in the eye. He had good ability, Kléberson, but he paid too much attention to what his father-in-law and wife wanted.

I read later that the FA were going to fast-track Hargreaves into coaching. That's one of the things that's wrong with our game. That wouldn't happen in France or Germany or Holland, where you would spend three years earning your stripes.

Bébé is the only player I ever signed without first seeing him in action. We have a good scout in Portugal who had flagged him up. This boy had been playing homeless football and became a triallist for a second division team. He did really well. Our scout told us, 'We need to watch him.' Then Real Madrid were on his tail. I know that's true because José Mourinho told me Real were ready to sign him and that United had jumped in front of them. We took a wee gamble on it, for about 7 million euros.

Bébé came with limitations but there was a talent there. He had fantastic feet. He struck the ball with venom, off either foot, with no drawback. He was not the complete player, but we were coaching him to be better. We farmed him out to Turkey and he injured his cruciate knee ligament after two weeks. We brought him home and put him on remedial work, then in the reserves. He did all right. He trained well in the short games, eight v. eight, goal to goal. On the big pitch his concept of team play needed work. With feet like his he was capable of scoring 20 goals a season. He was a quiet boy, spoke reasonable English, and had obviously had a hard upbringing wandering the streets of Lisbon.

With so many players coming in, I was proud of the work we did on those who were to end up with other clubs. In the spring of 2010, for instance, there were 72 players throughout Scotland, Europe and England who had been through an apprenticeship at Man Utd. Seventy-two.

Fabio Capello told a good friend of mine that if you put gowns and masks on Man Utd players, he could spot them a mile away, which was quite a compliment. Their behaviour and training stand out. We had three in Denmark, one in Germany, two in Belgium, and others all over the place in England. We had seven goalkeepers out there, none of whom had made the first team: Kevin Pilkington, Michael Pollitt, Ben Williams and Luke Steele among them.

We were adept at identifying the players who would become first-team regulars. There is something visible in a top-grade Manchester United player that forces you to promote him to the first team. Darron Gibson was an example of one who brings you to that crossroads where a decision needs to be made about whether he is going to be a first-team player.

In 2009–10 he was at the stage where we were in danger of not being fair to him. He had different qualities to most of my other midfielders. His main attribute was that he could score from outside the box. Scholes was the only other player who could do that, but he was coming to the end. So the judgment was a tough one, as it was with Tom Cleverley, who was at Watford, where he had scored 11 times from midfield. Cleverley had no physique, was wiry as hell, but he was as brave as a lion, had good feet and could score a goal. David Gill said one day, 'What are you going to do with Cleverley next year? He's scoring a lot of goals at Watford.' My answer was, 'I'll tell you what I'm going to do, I'm going to play him, to find out whether he can score goals for me as well as Watford.'

Could he score six for me? Nobody else was getting half a dozen from midfield. Michael Carrick had struck a high note of five. If Cleverley could score six goals in the Premier League from midfield, he would become a consideration. The demarcation line was always: what can they do and what can they not do? The can-do question was: can they win me the game? If they could score six goals, I could ignore some of the negatives.

At 20 or 21, players would sometimes stagnate. If they were not in the first team by then they could become disheartened. I reached that moment in my own playing career. At 21 I was fed up at St Johnstone and took papers out to emigrate to Canada. I was disillusioned. Football's not for me, I was saying. I'm not getting anywhere. At the United reserve level, we encountered this dilemma all the time. We would send players out on loan in the hope they would come back better, but often sent them to a level that would suit them more in the long term anyway, so they could find careers. We were proud to have relocated the 72 players I talked about elsewhere in the game.

The ones who make it have a way of telling you they are certainties to reach the grade. Welbeck is an example. At one point I tipped him to make Fabio Capello's 2010 World Cup squad, but he had issues to do with the pace he was growing at. At 19 he was still shooting up and encountering problems with his knees. I told him to go carefully in training sessions and save his best for matches. He was on course to end up 6 feet 2 inches or 6 feet 3 inches tall. But what a good player. Such a confident boy. I said to him: 'One of these days I'm going to kill you,' because he was such a cocky so-and-so, and he replied, 'I'll probably deserve it.' Touché. He had an answer for everything.

A constant in our discussions about young players was whether they could handle the demands of the Old Trafford crowd and the short patience span of the media. Would they grow or shrink in a United shirt? We knew the make-up of every young homegrown player who came into the United starting XI, from the training ground, from reserve team football. By the time a player graduated from youth or reserve team football, we aimed to be sure about their temperaments, sure about their characters and sure of their abilities.

But plainly, when we bought players in from abroad, we knew less about them, however hard we investigated their backgrounds, and the peculiar swirl of playing for United could undo some of these imported names. In 2009–10, we were researching Javier Hernández – nicknamed Chicharito (it means 'little pea'). He was 21 years of age. We sent a scout out to live in Mexico for a month. The information we received was that he was a family boy who was reluctant to leave Mexico. Our contact out there helped us research his background down to every detail.

United's support is odd in some respects. We would sign a player for £2 million and some fans would consider it a sign of weakness and believe we had lowered our standards. Gabriel Obertan was in that price range. He was greased lightning. But in the final third of the field, his feet were sometimes all over the place. His task was to coordinate his speed with his brain and deliver the hurt in the final third of the pitch.

Mame Biram Diouf was recommended by Ole Gunnar Solskjaer through his contacts at Molde in Norway. Hannover 96 and Eintracht Frankfurt were starting to sniff around him when we stepped up our interest. So we sent Ole and a club official over and acquired him for 4 million euros. Again, the background was right, though he never established himself with us.

Chris Smalling was bought from Fulham in January 2010 with the idea that he would join us for the start of the 2010–11 campaign. He had been playing with non-league Maidstone until 2008, but Roy Hodgson developed a high regard for him at Fulham. He cost us around £10 million. We moved for him when Rio Ferdinand started having problems with his back and other parts. We were on to centre-backs everywhere, all over. We watched them all through 2009–10 and thought Smalling was a young guy who would mature into his frame. Long-term, I could imagine a central defence forming around Chris Smalling and Jonny Evans.

There was no resting on the status quo, even in the best times. The longer I stayed, the further I looked ahead. Regeneration was an everyday duty.

:ing helped me escape the pressures of
:nagement. Fellow owner Ged Mason and I
:ebrate What A Friend's big win at Aintree.

Ruby Walsh tells me how he guided What A
Friend to victory. I always enjoy the company
of jockeys.

:t in front. What A Friend leads them home in The Betfred Bowl Chase.

Vidić and Ferdinand were a rock to build a team on. Nemanja has just scored against Inter Mila in the Champions League and Rio is hitching a ride.

Left-backs are like rare birds. But we had one of the best in Patrice Evra, a born winner.

he greatest goal in my time at United was this bicycle kick by Wayne Rooney against Man City
February 2011.

We prepared meticulously for the 2011 Champions League final against Barcelona at Wembl[...] Plans don't always work.

The best team I ever faced. The great Barcelona side of 2011.

at better man could you have beside you than Bobby Charlton? He was a loyal and wise friend
ie.

not an old bus stop, it's The Cliff, our training ground until 1999. Scholes and Giggs travel
k in time with me.

Lyn Laffin, my indispensable P.A., helps me with the daily mountain of admin.

David Gill was the best chief executive I worked with. Straight-talker; knew the game; always loya

Read all about it. Phil Townsend, our communications director, talks me through the day's pap

f numbers increased enormously in my
2 years at the club. I valued them all. Here I
with the laundry team.

Albert Morgan, kit man, friend and
wisecracker, in the Old Trafford changing
room, August 2011.

vin van der Sar was one of the great
lkeepers of the last 30 years. I should have
ed him earlier.

David de Gea, a magnificently athletic young
goalkeeper, who grew in stature after joining us
from Spain.

The tunnel of love. Making my way to the pitch, Old Trafford, August 2011.

The one-time King of Old Trafford, Eric Cantona, returns for Paul Scholes's testimonial in the summer of 2011.

Mick Phelan and René Meulensteen were my trusted assistants at the end. I owe all my coaches great debt.

seventeen

ONE NIGHT IN MOSCOW

BEFORE the Moscow Champions League final of 2008, I was the reluctant holder of possibly the worst record in penalty shoot-outs. I had lost two semi-finals at Aberdeen, a European tie at Aberdeen, an FA Cup tie at Old Trafford against Southampton, an FA Cup final against Arsenal and a European tie in Moscow through penalty shoot-outs. Six defeats and one victory was the inauspicious context to Carlos Tévez placing the ball on the spot at the start of our shoot-out with Chelsea in Roman Abramovich's home town.

With those memories, you would hardly expect me to have been optimistic. All those earlier disappointments were in my head as the game stretched beyond extra time and the match crept into the early hours of the following day after a 10.45 p.m. kick-off. When Van der Sar saved from Nicolas Anelka to win the trophy for us, I hardly made it off my seat, because I could barely believe we had won. I stayed motionless for several moments. Ronaldo was still lying on the turf crying because he had missed his penalty kick.

Our goalkeeping coach had compiled all the video analysis we could possibly need, and was able to pull the data up on a screen to show Van der Sar how each Chelsea player might take his spot kick. For several days we had discussed the order in which our players would step up. They were all good, apart from Ronaldo, who had been scoring them all season. Giggs' execution was the best: hard and low, inside the post. Hargreaves battered his into the top corner. Nani was a touch lucky because the goalkeeper should have saved it and got a hand to it. Carrick's was straightforward. Ronaldo hesitated and stopped.

John Terry had only to knock his in to win the game for Chelsea. At that point I was still and calm, thinking: 'What am I going to say to the players?' I knew I would have to be careful with my words in defeat. It would be unfair to slaughter them after a European final, I told myself, because they had worked so hard to get there, and these are deeply emotional moments for those in the thick of the action. When Terry missed the tenth penalty in the sequence and we headed into sudden death, my optimism returned. Anderson's penalty, the first in the do-or-die stage, had lifted our supporters because he had run to them to celebrate, and they were then buoyant again. The kicks were taken into our end of the ground, which was an advantage.

In no sense was this a conventional European final. The time zone was the first quirk, which meant the game had kicked off at 10.45 p.m. I always remember, too, that the rain had drenched me and ruined my shoes, so I attended the victory party in trainers, for which I took plenty of stick from the players. I knew I should have packed a spare pair of shoes. It was between 4 and 5 a.m. by the time we sat down for the buffet. The food was poor but the players gave Giggs a wonderful gift to commemorate him passing Bobby Charlton's appearance record. This was his 759th game. On the stage they all sang his name.

The game itself was a marvellous drama which drew some terrific performances from our side. I thought Wes Brown had one of his best games for United and set up Ronaldo's opening goal with an excellent cross.

In Chelsea's semi-final, Michael Essien had played right-back, and I decided while watching Avram Grant's team that Ronaldo would play wide left to make life uncomfortable for Essien, a midfielder by trade.

For our goal, Ronaldo out-jumped Essien, so the plan worked. A midfielder playing right-back against an attacker of Ronaldo's brilliance was a big ask, and our man tore him apart. Moving Ronaldo left opened the door for someone to play wide right. I chose Hargreaves, who was quick, had energy and could cross the ball. He did well in that role. In the centre of midfield we had Scholes and Carrick, though Scholes was to come off with a bleeding nose. His breathing was starting to become congested. Giggs went on in his place and prospered.

Despite the culture shock of Moscow and the hotel, our preparation had been smooth. In the semi-finals we had beaten Barcelona, drawing 0–0 over there and winning by a single goal at our place. Scholes' goal was magnificent, a typical thunderbolt from 25 yards. In the first 20 minutes at Camp Nou we played well, as we often did against them, striking the bar and missing a penalty. When they took a grip on the game we just retreated towards the box, which we might have done again in the 2009 and 2011 finals, had I not been determined to win those games our way.

You could call that tactically naive if you wish, but I disagree. We were trying to strengthen our philosophy about winning in the right manner. My thought on two semi-finals was that we endured a lot of heart-stopping moments. We lived on the edge of the box, or inside it, desperate to escape. At Old Trafford, in an even game, we ought to have won by more, with our good counter-attacking. Equally, when they brought on Thierry Henry for the last 15 minutes, they besieged us in our penalty box. It was agony on the touchline, looking at my watch. Later I called it the greatest example of the fans getting behind our men. Every clearance from our box raised a cheer, unusually. Henry missed a sitter. We showed great character. The team absorbed immense pressure and maintained their concentration.

After the game I also said: 'They can't be shrinking violets here. They have to be men, and they were men that night.'

We always fancied our chances of adding to the European Cups of 1968 and 1999, provided we could take control of the ball quickly in Moscow, which we did from the start. Our game was full of thrust and invention and we might have been three or four goals up. I started to think it would be a massacre.

Goals can turn games upside down, however, and Chelsea enjoyed a dash of luck just before half-time, equalising through Frank Lampard, which set us on the back foot. Chelsea progressed from there and were the better side for 25 minutes of the second half. Drogba struck a post. That was my signal to think fast about how we might regain a hold on the game. I sent Rooney wide right and brought Hargreaves into a more central position, which put us on top in the game again. By the end I felt we were the superior group of players.

Caught in the ebb and flow of events at pitch level, you can never be quite sure whether the spectacle in front of you is entertaining. But everyone felt this was a terrific piece of theatre, one of the best European Cup finals. It was satisfying to be part of a show that displayed our League in such a good light. I must give credit to Edwin van der Sar for the intelligence of his shot-stopping. As Anelka jogged towards the penalty spot I was thinking – dive to your left. Edwin kept diving to his right. Except for the penultimate Chelsea kick, which Salomon Kalou took, when Edwin dived to his left. So when Anelka approached his moment of truth, he must have been the first Chelsea player to ask himself: 'I wonder whether he's going to dive to his right or his left?' Van der Sar kept pointing to his left to unnerve the taker. Yes, Anelka's penalty was poor, but Edwin chose the right way to dive.

Avram Grant is a nice man. My fear was always that he might not be strong enough for that group of Chelsea players. Their behaviour in the final was terrible, dragging themselves out for the second half one at a time, giving the referee stick on the way into the dressing room. A team goes out together, they don't amble out one by one. The referee had been urging them to get a move on, but they just ignored him. At the interval they tried every trick in the book. That might have played on the referee's mind when Drogba was sent off.

The red card for Drogba followed a clash with Carlos Tévez, which brought Vidić over to support his team-mate. Up went Drogba's hand to flick Vida's face. If you lift your hands, you've no chance. My understanding was that the referee asked the linesman who the offender had been. And boomph, Drogba was off. By then we had already restored our hold on the game. Drogba's dismissal was not the turning point. Giggs had a shot cleared off the line. We created chances in extra time and should have killed them off. Chelsea, in my view, played for the draw and gambled on winning the shoot-out.

Though he was removed from the fray that night, Drogba was always a handful for us. He was a powerful, big lad, but what marked him out in my book was a talent for spectacular goals, say, on the turn, from 30 yards. I was surprised to see him missing from the team-sheet against us in a game during Carlo Ancelotti's finals weeks in charge. Torres started, but Drogba came on to score and force Chelsea back into the match.

From that Chelsea team, which we found it difficult to play against, the goalkeeper, Petr Čech, was outstanding. I should have signed him at 19 when I had my chance. Instead, Chelsea took him that summer for £8 million.

John Terry was always an influence in their team. Ashley Cole always gave them energy going forward. And Frank Lampard was incredibly reliable and consistent from box to box. He avoided defensive work a bit in his prime, but he was end to end and hardly missed a game. With Drogba, they were the core, the central five. They were a powerful presence in the dressing room.

At no point before the game did I accept that Chelsea would be under more pressure than us by virtue of Abramovich's Moscow background, though he was there in the stands, gazing down on his vast investment. I didn't see that as a factor in the game itself. Security was my main concern. Moscow is a city of great mysteries. I've read books on the Russian Revolution and on Stalin, who was worse than the czars, killing his own people to collectivise agriculture. We took two chefs with us, and the food was mostly fine, unlike in Rome, where it was a joke, a disgrace.

What a season Ronaldo had in that European Cup winning campaign. Forty-two goals for a winger? In some games he played centre-forward, but he was essentially a wide man in our system. In every game he would create three chances for himself. I watched him one night at Real Madrid and he had about 40 shots on goal.

Moscow was a relief, above all, because I always said Manchester United ought to be achieving more in Europe. It was our third European Cup victory and took us closer to Liverpool's five. I always felt we would match Liverpool's total within a reasonable stretch of time, even after the two defeats to Barcelona in 2009 and 2011, because we had earned extra respect in Europe. With a win in either of those Barcelona finals, we would have been on four, equal with Bayern Munich at the time, and with Ajax.

In our moment of triumph there was no champagne to

be found at the Luzhniki Stadium. In the absence of the real stuff, staff were dispatched to a bar to buy some kind of fizzy liquid. Heaven knows what it was. 'I can't even offer you a glass of champagne,' I apologised to Andy Roxburgh, who came into our dressing room to congratulate us. Whatever was in those bottles, we shook it about and made a fuss. There was a lot of hilarity and nonsense, with the players giving each other stick. You're pleased and proud of them. I was soaked to the skin from the rain, and forced to change into my tracksuit. There was no sign of Abramovich and I don't recall any Chelsea players coming in.

The 1999 final in Barcelona, when we beat Bayern Munich, fell on the late Sir Matt Busby's birthday. Sometimes you hope the gods are with you, or that old Matt is looking down. I'm not a great believer in coincidences, but there is such a thing as fate, and I wondered whether it played a hand in both victories. Matt had taken our club into Europe when the English League was firmly set against it. Matt was shown to be right because English football has had some glorious nights in Europe.

With a major trophy in your possession, you should always buy players to refresh the squad and avoid the risk of stagnation. It was in the weeks after Moscow that we added Dimitar Berbatov to our squad. Berbatov had been on our target list before he moved to Spurs. He had talent in abundance: good balance, composure on the ball and a fine scoring record. He was a good age, tall, athletic. I felt we needed a bit more composure in the last third of the field, the attacking third.

But it ended up as a scrap with Daniel Levy, the Tottenham

chairman, which left us reluctant to return to Spurs for players. This was our second trip on the Big Dipper following our move for Michael Carrick. You come off dizzy. You can't discuss both sides of the issue with Daniel. It's about him, and Tottenham, nothing more, which is no bad thing from his club's perspective.

eighteen

PSYCHOLOGY

Fᴵʀsᴛ of all, you must tell them the truth. There is nothing wrong with presenting the hard facts to a player who has lost his form. And what I would say to anyone whose confidence was wavering is that we were Manchester United and we simply could not allow ourselves to drop to the level of other teams.

Faced with the need to confront a player who had performed below our expectation, I might have said: 'That was rubbish, that.' But then I would follow it up with, 'For a player of your ability.' That was for picking them back up from the initial blow. Criticise but balance it out with encouragement. 'Why are you doing that? You're better than that.'

Endless praise sounds false. They see through it. A central component of the manager–player relationship is that you have to make them take responsibility for their own actions, their own mistakes, their performance level, and finally the result. We were all in the results industry. Sometimes a scabby win would mean more to us than a 6–0 victory with a goal featuring 25 passes. The bottom line was always that Manchester United had to be victorious. That winning culture could be maintained only if I told a player what I thought about his performance in a climate of honesty. And yes, sometimes I would be forceful and aggressive. I would tell a player what the club demanded of them.

I tell young managers now: don't seek confrontation. Don't look for it, because you can bet your life it will come your way. If you seek a clash, the player is placed in a counter-attacking role, which gives him an advantage. When the former Aberdeen, United and Scotland captain Martin Buchan went to manage Burnley, he punched the captain on the first Saturday. 'That was a good start, Martin,' I told him.

He was a very principled guy, Martin Buchan. In his playing days, he moved to Oldham and was given a £40,000 signing-on fee, which was a lot of money back then. Struggling for form, he handed the £40,000 back to the board. He couldn't bring himself to keep money he felt he had not earned. Imagine that happening today.

In general, across my career, people always assumed I had elaborate Machiavellian strategies. In reality I didn't set out to master the dark arts. I did try the odd trick. Saying we always finished the campaign at a higher gallop and with heightened resolve could be classified as a mind game, and I was intrigued to see Carlo Ancelotti, the Chelsea manager, twig it, in the winter of 2009. To paraphrase, he said, 'Alex is saying United are stronger in the second half of the season, but we are, too.'

I did it every year. 'Wait till the second half of the season,' I would say. And it always worked. It crept into the minds of our players and became a nagging fear for the opposition. Second half of the season, United would come like an invasion force, hellfire in their eyes. It became a self-fulfilling prophecy.

Tapping my watch was another psychological ploy. I didn't keep track of the time in games. I kept a loose eye on it but it was too hard to work out how long might be added for a stoppage to have an accurate sense of when the game should end. Here's the key: it was the effect it had on the other team, not ours, that counted. Seeing me tap my watch and gesticulate, the opposition would be spooked. They would immediately think another 10 minutes were going to be added. Everyone knew United had a knack of scoring late goals. Seeing me point to my timepiece, our opponents would feel they would have to defend against us through a spell of time that would feel, to them, like infinity.

They would feel besieged. They knew we never gave up and they knew we specialised in late drama. Clive Tyldesley said it, in his ITV commentary on the 1999 Champions League final, at the beginning of stoppage time: 'United always score', which was comparable to Kenneth Wolstenholme in the 1966 World Cup final. That's a mind game.

There is a psychological dimension also to handling individual players. With errant behaviour it helps to look for a moment through their eyes. You were young once, so put yourself in their position. You do something wrong, you're waiting to be punished. 'What's he going to say?' you think. Or, 'What's my dad going to say?' The aim is to make the biggest possible impact. What would have made the deepest imprint on me at that stage of life?

A manager's advantage is that he knows the player wants to play. Fundamentally, they all want to be out there on the park. So when you deprive them of that pleasure you're taking away their life. It becomes the ultimate tool. This is the greatest lever of power at your disposal.

With the incident with Frank McGarvey at St Mirren, I was consistent in telling him, 'You're never going to play again.' He believed that. For three weeks he believed it. He finished up begging me for another chance. In his mind was the idea that all the power was on my side. Freedom of contract wasn't a reality then.

People talked non-stop about my mind games. Every time I made a public utterance, a swarm of analysts would look for the hidden meaning, when 98 per cent of the time there was none. But psychological pressure has its place. Even superstitions, because everyone has one.

A woman said to me at Haydock races one day in 2010: 'I see you on the television and you're so serious, yet here you are laughing and enjoying yourself.'

I told her, 'Well, do you not want me to be serious at work? My job is about concentration. Everything that goes on in my brain has to be beneficial to the players. I cannot make mistakes. I don't take notes, I don't rely on video evidence, and I have to be right. It's a serious business and I don't want to be making mistakes.'

I made plenty, of course. In a Champions League semi-final against Borussia Dortmund, I was convinced Peter Schmeichel had made an error. But at that time I wasn't

wearing my spectacles at games. Peter said: 'It took a deflection.'

'Deflection, my arse,' I shouted. 'No deflection.'

When I saw the replay later, I could see the ball had made
a violent change in direction. So I started wearing my glasses
to games. I couldn't afford to make mistakes like that, to
embarrass myself. If you ask a defender, 'Why did you try
to play him offside?' and his reply is, 'I didn't try to play
him offside,' you need to know you're correct in your assertion.

It makes no sense to offer players an easy chance to tell
themselves, 'The manager's lost it.' If they lose faith in your
knowledge, they lose faith in you. That grasp of the facts
must be kept at a high level, for all time. You have to be
accurate in what you say to the players. Trying to be right
could be fun, too. It wasn't all a quest for the truth. A game
we would play was trying to guess the opposition's starting
XI. One night I made my usual confident prediction about
who would play. When the team came under the door, for
a Champions League game, René announced, 'Boss, they've
made six changes.'

I froze, then saw my opportunity. Indignation would get
me out of this hole. 'See this?' I barked at the players.
'They're taking the piss out of us. They think they can come
here with their reserve team!'

An early experience was playing Coventry in the FA Cup,
at Old Trafford, after we had knocked Man City out in the
third round. The week before, I had been to watch Coventry
play Sheffield Wednesday. You wouldn't believe how bad
Coventry were. Archie Knox and I drove home without a

care. Guess what? Coventry were brilliant against us at Old Trafford. Teams who came to our ground often became a different species. Different tactics, different motivation; everything. From those early lessons, I learned always to prepare in home games for the opposition's best team, best tactics, best performance, and make sure they were not in the game.

The better teams would always come to Old Trafford looking to give us a fright. Arsenal, especially; Chelsea, to an extent, and often Liverpool. City, when the Sheikh Mansour era started, would also arrive with noticeably enhanced ambition. Clubs managed by ex-Manchester United players would also be bold. Steve Bruce's Sunderland, for example, were not shy on our turf.

My longevity rendered me immune in the end to the normal whispering and speculation that would envelop other managers after three defeats in a row. My success insulated me against the media calling for an execution. You saw that with other clubs but not with me. That gave me strength in the dressing room. Those benefits transferred themselves to the players. The manager would not be leaving so nor would the players. The coaches and the backroom staff would not be leaving because the manager was staying. Stability. Continuity. Rare, in the modern game. In a bad run we didn't panic. We didn't like it, but we didn't panic.

I like to think, also, that we were conscious of the spirit of the game. Johan Cruyff said to me one night back in the 1990s, 'You'll never win the European Cup.'

'Why?'

'You don't cheat and you don't buy referees,' he said.

I told him: 'Well if that's to be my epitaph, I'll take it.'

A certain toughness is required in professional football and I learned that early on. Take Dave Mackay – I played against him at 16 years old. At the time I was with Queen's Park and playing in the reserves. Dave was coming back from a broken toe and was turning out for the reserves at Hearts, who had a great team during those years.

I was inside-forward and he was right-half. I looked at him, with his big, bull-like chest, stretching. The first ball came to me and he was right through me. In a reserve game.

I thought: 'I'm not going to take this.'

The next time we came together I wired right into him.

Dave looked at me coldly and said, 'Do you want to last this game?'

'You booted me there,' I stammered.

'I tackled you,' said Dave. 'If I boot you, you'll know all about it.'

I was terrified of him after that. And I wasn't afraid of anyone. He had this incredible aura about him. Fabulous player. I have the picture in my office of him grabbing Billy Bremner. I took a risk one day and asked him, cheekily, 'Did you actually win that fight?' I was there at Hampden Park when they picked the best Scottish team of all time and Dave's name was absent. Everyone was embarrassed.

I could criticise my team publicly, but I could never castigate an individual after the game to the media. The supporters were entitled to know when I was unhappy with a performance. But not an individual. It all went back to Jock Stein; I would question him all the time about everything. At Celtic he was always so humble. It almost became annoying. When

I was quizzing him about Jimmy Johnstone or Bobby Murdoch, I'd expect him to take credit for his team selection or tactics, but Jock would just say, 'Oh, wee Jimmy was in such great form today.' He would never praise himself. I wanted him to announce, just once: 'Well, I decided to play 4–3–3 today and it worked.' But he was just too humble to do it.

Jock missed a Celtic trip to America after a car crash and Sean Fallon had sent three players home for misbehaving. 'No, I wouldn't have done that, and I told Sean so,' Jock told me when I pressed him to tell me how he would have dealt with it. 'When you do that you make a lot of enemies,' he said.

'But the supporters would understand,' I argued.

'Forget the supporters,' Jock said. 'Those players have mothers. Do you think any mother thinks their boy is bad? Their wives, their brothers, their father, their pals: you alienate them.' He added, 'Resolve the dispute in the office.'

Sometimes ice works as well as fire. When Nani was sent off in a game at Villa Park in 2010, I didn't say a word to him. I let him suffer. He kept looking at me for a crumb of comfort. I know he didn't try to do what he did. Asked about it on TV, I called it 'naive'. I said he wasn't a malicious player but that it was a two-footed tackle and he had to go. Straightforward. There was no lasting damage. I merely said he had made a mistake in a tackle, as we all have, because it's an emotional game.

People assumed I was always waging psychological war against Arsène Wenger, always trying to cause detonations in his brain. I don't think I set out to provoke him. But sometimes I did use mind games in the sense that I would plant small inferences, knowing that the press would see them as psychological forays.

I remember Brian Little, who was then managing Aston Villa, calling me about a remark I had made before we played them.

'What did you mean by that?' he asked.

'Nothing,' I said. I was baffled. 'I thought you were up to your mind games again,' Brian said. When he put the phone down, apparently, Brian couldn't stop thinking: 'What's he up to? What was he trying to say?'

Though it served me well to be unnerving rival teams, quite often I unsettled opponents without even meaning to, or realising that I had.

nineteen

BARCELONA (2009–11) – SMALL IS BEAUTIFUL

B ARCELONA were the best team ever to line up against my Manchester United sides. Easily the best. They brought the right mentality to the contest. We had midfield players in our country – Patrick Vieira, Roy Keane, Bryan Robson – who were strong men, warriors; winners. At Barcelona they had these wonderful mites, 5 feet 6 inches tall, with the courage of lions, to take the ball all the time and never allow themselves to be bullied. The accomplishments of Lionel Messi, Xavi and Andrés Iniesta were amazing to me.

The Barcelona side that beat us at Wembley in the 2011 Champions League final were superior to the team that conquered us in Rome two years earlier. The 2011 bunch were at the height of their powers and brought tremendous maturity to the job. In both instances I had to wrestle with the knowledge that we were a really good team but had encountered one that had handled those two finals better than us.

I wish we could have played the Rome final again the next day. The very next day. There was a wonderful atmosphere in Rome's Stadio Olimpico, on a beautiful night, and it was my first defeat in a European final, in five outings. To collect a runners-up medal is a painful act when you know you could have performed much better.

Bravery was a prerequisite for confronting those Barcelona sides. They were the team of their generation, just as Real Madrid were the team of theirs in the 1950s and 1960s, and AC Milan were in the early 1990s. The group of world-beaters who formed around Messi were formidable. I felt no envy towards these great sides. Regrets, yes, when we lost to them, but jealousy, no.

In each of those two European Cup finals, we might have been closer to Spain's finest by playing more defensively, but by then I had reached the stage with Manchester United where it was no good us trying to win that way. I used those tactics to beat Barcelona in the 2008 semi-final: defended really deep; put myself through torture, put the fans through hell. I wanted a more positive outlook against them subsequently, and we were beaten partly because of that change in emphasis. If we had retreated to our box and kept the defending tight, we might have achieved the results we craved. I'm not blaming myself; I just wish our positive approach could have produced better outcomes.

Beating us in Rome accelerated Barcelona's development into the dominant team of their era. It drove them on. A single victory can have that catalytic effect. It was their second Champions League win in four seasons and Pep Guardiola's team were the first Spanish side to win the League, Copa del Rey and Champions League in the same campaign. We were the reigning European champions but were unable to become the first in the history of the modern competition to defend that title.

Yet we shouldn't have lost that game in the Eternal City. There was a way to play against Barcelona, as we proved the year before. There is a way to stop them, even Messi. What we did, 12 months previously in the away leg, was to deploy Tévez off the front and Ronaldo at centre-forward, so we could have two areas of attack. We had the penetration of Ronaldo and Tévez to help us get hold of the ball.

We still found it hard, of course, because Barcelona monopolised possession for such long periods and in those circumstances your own players tend to lose interest. They start watching the game: they are drawn into watching the ball weave its patterns.

Our idea was that when we had any semblance of possession, Ronaldo would go looking for space and Tévez would come short to get on the ball. But they were busy spectating. I made that point to them at half-time. 'You're watching the game,' I said. 'We're not counter-attacking at all.' Our method was not that of Inter Milan; they defended deep and played on the counter-attack throughout. We were in attack mode in the second half.

A major inhibiting factor in Rome, I will now say, was the

choice of hotel. It was a shambles. For meals we were in a room with no light; the food was late, it was cold. I took a chef there and they dismissed him, ignored him. On the morning of the game, two or three of our team were feeling a bit seedy, particularly Giggs. A few were feeling under the weather and one or two played that way. The role Giggs was assigned came with a high workload that was incompatible with the slight bug in his system. It was too big a task for him to operate on top of Sergio Busquets, Barcelona's defensive midfielder, and then advance as a striker and come back in to cover again.

You would never think about criticising Ryan Giggs, not in any shape or form, after what he achieved at our club. It was just a pity he was below his normal energy level that night in Rome.

We started the game really well, however, with Ronaldo threatening the Barcelona defence three times: first, from a dipping free kick, then two shots from distance, which heaped pressure on Victor Valdés, their goalkeeper. But ten minutes in, we conceded a really awful goal on account of our midfield's failure to retreat in time to stop Iniesta making a pass to Samuel Eto'o. Eto'o struck the shot and Edwin van der Sar didn't quite deal with it as the ball slipped inside the near post.

Barcelona began with Messi wide right, Eto'o through the middle and Thierry Henry wide left. Just prior to the goal, they pushed Eto'o wider right and Messi into midfield, as a deep central striker. They changed Eto'o to the right-hand side because Evra had been breaking away from Messi, early on. Evra was racing forward persistently and they changed their shape to stop him. Afterwards Guardiola acknowledged that point. Messi had been moved to save him from having to deal with Evra.

By making that alteration, Barcelona created a position for Messi he enjoys, in the centre of the park. That's where he played from then on, in that hole, which made life hard for the back four because they were unsure whether to push in against him or stay back and play safe.

After Eto'o's goal, and with Messi central, Barcelona had an extra man in midfield. Iniesta and Xavi just went boomp-boomp-boomp, kept possession all night. They were superior to us at ball-circulation. I won't waste time contesting that fact.

Conceding the ball to Guardiola's men came at an awful price because their numerical superiority in midfield reduced you to a spectating role again. To counteract their passing game, I sent on Tévez for Anderson at half-time and watched him miss a fine chance when he went round a defender but decided to beat him a second time, pulling the ball back in and losing it. Barcelona's clinching goal came an hour after their first: a header, unusually, by Messi, from a cross by Xavi.

Later I discussed Barcelona's evolution with Louis van Gaal, their former Dutch coach. The basis of their philosophy was laid down by Johan Cruyff, a terrific coach who conceived their ideas about width and ball-circulation, always with an extra man in midfield. After Bobby Robson, they went back to the Dutch way, with Van Gaal and Frank Rijkaard. What Guardiola added was a method of pressing the ball. Under Pep they had this three-second drill, apparently, where the defending team would be allowed no more than three seconds on the ball.

After the win in Rome, Guardiola said: 'We're fortunate to have the legacy of Johan Cruyff and Charly Rexach. They were the fathers and we've followed them.'

What I could never quite understand is how their players were able to play that number of games. They fielded almost the same side every time. Success is often cyclical, with doldrums. Barcelona emerged from theirs and went in hot pursuit of Real Madrid. I don't like admitting, we were beaten by a great team, because we never wanted to say those words. The biggest concession we ever wanted to make was: two great teams contested this final, but we just missed out. Our aim was to attain that level where people said we were always on a par with Europe's best.

To beat Barcelona in that cycle you needed centre-backs who could be really positive. Rio and Vidić were at an age where their preference was to defend the space. Nothing wrong with that. Quite correct. But against Barcelona it's a limited approach. You need centre-backs who are prepared to drop right on top of Messi and not worry about what is happening behind them. OK, he'll drift away to the side. That's fine. He's less of a threat on the side than he is through the centre.

They had four world-class players: Piqué, the two centre-midfield players and Messi. Piqué was without doubt the most underrated player in their team. He is a great player. We knew that when he was a youngster player with us. At a European conference, Guardiola told me he was the best signing they had made. He created the tempo, the accuracy, the confidence and the penetration from that deep position. That's what we tried to nullify by shoving our strikers on top of them and being first to the ball or forcing them to offload it. For the first 20 or 30 minutes it worked really well, but then they score. They wriggle out.

They had this wonderful talent for escapology. You put the bait in the river and a fish goes for it. Sometimes it doesn't, though. Xavi would pass the ball to Iniesta at a pace that encouraged you to think you were going to win it. And you were not going to win it, because they were away from you. The pace of the pass, the weight of the pass, and the angle, just drew you into territory you shouldn't have been in. They were brilliant at that form of deception.

The Premier League desperately want a more lenient policy on work permits. There would be a danger in such a laissez-faire approach. You could flood the game with bad players. But the big clubs should be granted that freedom, because they have the ability to scout the best players. That's a bit elitist, I know, but if you want to win in Europe, one way round it is to change the work permit status in favour of the clubs. In the EU we could take players at 16.

Two years later, our clubs converged on the final again, this time at Wembley. We had the same intention as in Rome, started well, and were then just overrun in the middle of the pitch in a 3–1 defeat. We started with Edwin van der Sar in goal, Fabio, Ferdinand, Vidić and Evra across the back, Giggs, Park, Carrick and Valencia in midfield and Rooney and Hernández up front.

We didn't handle Messi. Our centre-backs weren't moving forward onto the ball. They were wanting to sit back. Yet the preparation for that game was the best I have seen. For 10 days we practised for it on the training ground. You know the problem? Sometimes players play the occasion, not the game. Wayne Rooney, for example, was disappointing. Our tactic was for him to raid into the spaces behind the full-backs and for Hernández to stretch them back, which he did, but we failed to penetrate those spaces behind the full-backs. For some reason, Antonio Valencia froze on the night. He was nervous as hell. I don't mean to be over-critical.

We never really attacked their left-back, who had just come back from an illness and hadn't played a lot of games. We thought that would be a big plus point for us – either him or Puyol playing there. Valencia's form leading up to the final had been excellent. He tortured Ashley Cole two or three weeks before Wembley and had twisted the blood of the full-back at Schalke. You might be better going back to your box against Barcelona, but we should have been better at pushing on top of Messi. Michael Carrick was below his best too.

The first newsflash that night was that I had left Dimitar Berbatov out of the match-day squad. Instead, Michael Owen took the striker's seat on the bench. He obviously took it badly and I felt rotten. Wembley has a coach's room, nice and private, where I explained the reasons for my decision. Dimitar had gone off the boil a bit and wasn't always the ideal substitute. I told him: 'If we're going for a goal in the last minute, in the penalty box, Michael Owen has been very fresh.' It probably wasn't fair but I had to take those decisions and back myself to be right.

I signed Berbatov in the summer of 2008 because he had

that lovely balance and composure in the attacking areas. I thought it would balance out the other players I had in the team, but by doing so I created an impasse with Tévez, who wasn't having it. He was sub, playing, then sub again. In fairness to Tévez, he always made an impact. He would get about the game. Yet it definitely caused that blockage and gave his camp something to bargain with at other clubs.

Berbatov was surprisingly lacking in self-assurance. He never had the Cantona or Andy Cole peacock quality, or the confidence of Teddy Sheringham. Hernández also had high confidence: he was bright and breezy. Berbatov was not short of belief in his ability, but it was based on his way of playing. Because we functioned at a certain speed, he was not really tuned into it. He was not that type of quick-reflex player. He wants the game to go slow and to work his way into the box in his own time. Or he'll do something outside the area and link the play. His assets were considerable. Although we had a few inquiries for him in the summer of 2011, I was not prepared to let him go at that stage. We had spent £30 million on him and I was not willing to write that off just because he had missed a few big games the previous season. We might as well keep him and use him.

In training he practised getting to the ball faster. But when the play broke down he was inclined to walk. You couldn't do that at our place. We had to regroup quickly or we would be too open, with too many players up the pitch. We needed people to react to us losing the ball so the opposition would be under pressure quickly. But he was capable of great moments. He also had a huge appetite, of

Nicky Butt proportions. Head down at meal-times, and sometimes with food to take home as well.

Berbatov wouldn't have featured in the Wembley game, even if he had been on the bench. I had been forced to take off Fábio and send on Nani, which left me with only two options. I wanted to get Scholes on because I needed an experienced player to orchestrate our passing, so Paul came on for Carrick. We had talked about Scholesy's retirement for many months and I had tried to talk him round, to entice him with one more season, but his view was that 25 games a season were not enough. He also admitted his legs tended to be empty in the last 25–30 minutes. He had survived two knee operations and an eye problem that had kept him out for months at a time, yet he was still playing at that high level. Phenomenal.

The goal he scored at his testimonial that summer was a beauty. He gave Brad Friedel in goal no hope. It was a rocket. Eric Cantona, the visiting manager, was applauding. On Talksport later I heard a presenter say Paul wasn't in the top four of modern English players. His assertion was that Gascoigne, Lampard and Gerrard were all better players. Absolute nonsense.

After our second Champions League final defeat to Barcelona, I had to ask: what is the problem here? Fact No. 1 is that some of our players fell below the level they were capable of. A contributing factor might have been that we were accustomed to having most of the possession in games. When that advantage transferred itself to the opposition it might have damaged our confidence and concentration. There was some credence in the theory that our players were unsettled by having to play a subservient role: even a player such as Giggs, or Ji-Sung Park, who, in the quarter-final against Chelsea, tackled everybody and was up and down the pitch all day. We never saw him, in that way, against Barcelona, whose starting XI was: Valdés; Alves, Piqué, Abidal, Mascherano; Busquets, Xavi, Iniesta; Messi, Villa and Pedro.

They took the lead through Pedro from one of Xavi's countless clever passes but Rooney equalised for us after a quick exchange with Giggs. But then the Barcelona carousel really started spinning, with Messi at the controls. He and Villa scored the goals that finished us off in Van der Sar's last game for the club.

I made an error at half-time. I was still focusing on winning the game and told Rooney he needed to keep running into those gaps behind the full-backs. 'We'll win the game if you keep doing that,' I urged him. I forgot the big issue with playing Barcelona. So many of their games were effectively won in the first 15 minutes of the second half. I should have mentioned that to my players. I might have been better assigning Park to mark Messi for the first 15 minutes and pushing Rooney wide left. If we had employed those tactics, we might just have sneaked it. We would still have been able to counter-attack. Those changes would have left Busquets free, so maybe we would have been driven back towards our box, but we'd have posed more of a threat, with Rooney attacking from a wide left position.

I had intended to replace Valencia after 10 minutes of the second half, but then Fábio was attacked by cramps again and I was forced to re-jig around his injury. My luck in finals was generally good. Favour deserted me in this one. On the balance of all those big games and the success I had enjoyed, I could hardly start pitying myself at Wembley, the scene of United's win over Benfica in 1968.

We thought we might have a chance at corner kicks but they never came our way. As our defeat was confirmed, there was no smugness about Barcelona. Not once did they flaunt their superiority. Xavi's first move after the final whistle was to make a move for Scholes' jersey. Footballers should have a role model. They should be saying to themselves: 'He's where I want to get to.' I had it with Denis Law. Denis was a year and a half older than me and I looked at him and said, 'That's what I want to be.'

In the days after that loss I began taking a serious look at the coaching in our academy. Gary Neville, Paul Scholes and I exchanged a lot of opinions. I looked at appointing another technical coach to the academy. Our club was always capable of producing great players and Barcelona's next wave were not better than ours. No way. Thiago was on a par with Welbeck and Cleverley but there was no fear about the rest of theirs coming through.

Looking ahead is vital. We were on to Phil Jones long before that Champions League final. I tried to buy him in 2010 but Blackburn would not sell. Ashley Young was bought to replace Giggs. The goalkeeping situation was all settled in December. Granted, David de Gea had a torrid start to his United career, but he would develop. Smalling and Evans were outstanding prospects. We had Fábio and Rafael, and Welbeck and Cleverley were coming through; Nani was 24, Rooney 25. We had a nucleus of young talent.

We shed five that summer because with Jones joining it wasn't going to be easy for Wes Brown or John O'Shea to make the starting XI. They were good servants to me. The horrible part of management is telling people who have given their all for you that there is no longer a place for them in your plans. After the Premier League title parade, in the rain, we returned to the school from where we had started the procession. I spoke to Darron Gibson and asked him how he saw his future. Perhaps it wasn't the perfect place to begin that discussion, but he got the gist of what I was thinking. He was off on holiday that night so we needed to start the conversation. Wes Brown, I struggled to reach by telephone. It was horrible to let players of that experience and loyalty to me go.

I lost five players aged 30 and above and let Owen Hargreaves go. We were bringing back Welbeck, Cleverley, Mame Diouf and Macheda from loan spells, and signing three new players. The average age of the squad was reduced to around 24.

With Scholes and Neville, my plan was to let them roam about the place, with the youth team, academy and reserves, then the three of us would sit down for an assessment of how strong we were. I was going to place a big burden on them to shape the future, because they knew better than anyone what it took to be one of our players. It's something I'd wanted to do for years and years: feed my top players into the stream.

Scholes was a man of excellent opinions. His assessments were brilliant. Always in one line. There were no maybes. When we had a problem with Van Nistelrooy, Paul was instantly clear that Ruud could not be allowed to cause disruption. His language was blunt. Gary asked him, 'Are you sure, Scholesy?' – just winding him up.

At that point, on the coaching side, we had Brian McClair, Mick Phelan, Paul McGuinness, Jim Ryan and Tony Whelan. They were all United players or academy graduates. I wanted to strengthen those areas. Clayton Blackmore and Quinton Fortune did a few bits on the development side.

After the inquest, I told myself: 'When we play Barcelona next time in a Champions League final, I would have Jones and Smalling, or Smalling and Evans, right on top of Messi.' I wasn't going to let him torture us again.

twenty

THE MEDIA

THE best piece of advice I ever received on the media
front was from a friend called Paul Doherty, who was
then at Granada TV. Great lad, Paul. He sought me out one
day and said: 'I've been watching your press conferences
and I'm going to point something out to you. You're giving
the game away. You're showing your worries. Look in that
mirror and put the Alex Ferguson face on.'

Appearing beleaguered is no way to handle the press.
Showing your torments to them is no way to help the team
or improve your chances of winning on a Saturday. Paul was
right. When he gave me that advice I was displaying the
strains of the job. I couldn't allow a press conference to
become a torture chamber. It was my duty to protect the
dignity of the club and all that we were doing. It was important to be on the front foot and control the conversation
as much as possible.

Before I went through that door to face the world, I trained myself, prepared myself mentally. Experience helped. I reached the point in my Friday press conferences where I could see the line a journalist was pursuing. Sometimes they agreed a party line, telling one another: 'Right, you start that, I'll go the other way.' I could read them all. Experience gave me that. Plus, the internal mechanism starts to work faster. I loved it when a journalist asked a big long question because it allowed me time to prepare my answer. The hard ones were the short questions: 'Why were you so bad?'

That kind of pithy inquiry can cause you to elongate your response. You stretch it out while you're trying to think, and end up justifying your whole world to them. There's an art to not exposing the weaknesses of your team, which is always your first priority. Always. You might have a game three days later and that, too, should be at the forefront of your thoughts when being interrogated. Winning that game is what counts, not scoring intellectual points in a news conference.

The third objective is not to make a fool of yourself by answering stupidly. Those were the considerations working away in my brain as I was being grilled. The skills, that greater awareness, took years to acquire. I remember being on television as a young player and blubbing about a six-game suspension I had received from the Scottish Football Association. I said on air: 'Aye, that's the Star Chamber justice they operate in Scotland.'

Right away, a letter from the SFA came flying in to the club. Thinking you have a duty to be interesting, you can say something you regret. I was right that day in Scotland but I finished up having to write a letter to explain myself.

The manager asked me: 'Where the hell did you get that one from – the Star Chamber justice line?'

I couldn't hide the origins of my speech. 'I was reading a book and just thought it sounded good,' I told him.

Of course my longest and biggest media bust-up was with the BBC, which lasted seven years until I decided enough was enough in August 2011. There were many annoyances from my perspective, including an article in *Match of the Day* magazine, but the step too far was a documentary called *Fergie and Son*, broadcast on 27 May 2004, on BBC3, which featured a horrible attack on my son Jason. They looked at the transfers of Jaap Stam to Roma and Massimo Taibi to Reggina in relation to Jason's involvement with the Elite Sports Agency. Before the broadcast went out, the United board cleared me, Jason and Elite of any wrongdoing in transfers, but decided that Jason could no longer act for the club on transfer dealings.

The BBC would not apologise and the allegations they made were not true.

In the aftermath, Peter Salmon of the BBC came up to see me and I told him, 'You watch that programme and tell me whether it does the BBC credit.' I wanted to sue them, but my solicitor and Jason both opposed the idea. Salmon assumed his old friendship with me from Granada TV would end the standoff.

'The BBC's a Manchester firm now,' he said.

'Great,' I said. 'And you need to apologise.' No answer. His plan was to get me to address the *Fergie and Son* programme in an interview with Clare Balding. Why would I do that? But we did agree to differ in the end and I resumed my interviews with BBC staff. By then I had made my point.

More generally Sky television changed the whole media climate by making it more competitive and adding to the hype. Take the coverage of the Suárez biting incident in the spring of 2013. I was asked about it in a press conference. The headline on my answer was: 'Ferguson feels sympathy for Liverpool'. They asked me a question about Suárez and I said, 'I know how they feel because Cantona received a nine-month ban for kung-fu kicking a fan.' My point was – never mind ten games, try nine months. Yet they ran a headline suggesting I felt sorry for Suárez.

Another headline was: 'Ferguson says José Mourinho is going to Chelsea'. The question they had asked me was: 'Who will be your main challenger next year?' I replied that Chelsea would be there next season and added that if the papers were right and Mourinho was going back, it would give them a boost. The headline became: Ferguson says Mourinho's going back to Chelsea.

I had to text Mourinho to explain. He texted back and said, 'It's OK, I know, I saw it.' That headline ran every ten minutes. Mourinho did end up back at Chelsea but that's not the point.

So there was an intensity and volatility about the modern media I found difficult. I felt that by the end it was hard to have relationships with the press. They were under so much pressure it was not easy to confide in them. When I first came to Manchester, I was wary of some but wasn't guarded in the way I was in my final years. Characters like John Bean and Peter Fitton were decent lads. Bill Thornton. David

Walker. Steve Millar. Decent guys. And I had my old friends from Scotland.

On tours we used to have a night out with the press lads. One evening we ended up back in my room and Beano was in striking form, tap-dancing on my table. Another night I was in bed, at about 11 o'clock, when the phone rang and a voice said: 'Alex! Can you confirm or deny that you were seen in a taxi with Mark Hughes tonight?'

It was John Bean. I told him, 'It would be very difficult, John, because he was playing for Bayern Munich tonight in a European tie.'

John said: 'Oh yes, I watched that game.'

I banged down the phone.

John then turns up on the Friday. 'A million apologies, Alex. I know you'll accept my apology.' And sat down.

Latterly we had a lot of young reporters who dressed more casually than the men I had known in my early years. Maybe it was a generational thing, but it just didn't sit well with me. It's a difficult job for those young reporters because they are under so much pressure from their editors. Forget off the record. It doesn't exist any more. I banned a couple of reporters in 2012–13 for using off-the-record remarks. I banned another for saying Rooney and I never spoke in training sessions – and that everyone at the club could see it. Not true.

I didn't read all the papers, but from time to time our media staff would point things out that were inaccurate. The process can drain you. Years ago I used to take action, but it ends up costing you money. As for an apology, 40 words tucked away on page 11 was a long way from a story with banner headlines on the back page. So what was the point?

In banning reporters I would be saying: I'm not accepting your version of events. Again, I was in a strong position, because I had been at Man United a long time and had been successful. If I had been some poor guy struggling on a bad run of results, the scenario would have been different. In most cases I felt an underlying sympathy because I knew that extrapolation or exaggeration was a product of the competitive nature of the business. Newspapers are up against Sky television, websites and other social media channels.

Any Premier League manager should have an experienced press officer, someone who knows the media and can act quickly on stories. You can't stop them all but you can warn the author when the facts are wrong and seek corrections. As a backup, a good press officer can extricate you from trouble. Every day, for 24 hours, Sky News is rolling. A story will be repeated over and over again. Dealing with the press is becoming more and more problematic for managers.

Say Paul Lambert is having a bad time at Aston Villa. The press conference is bound to be dominated by negativity. Only someone who knows the press can train a manager for that. When I had my bad spell at United, Paul Doherty told me: 'You're tense, you're bait for them. Before you get in that press conference, look in the mirror, rub your face, get your smile on, get your act together. Be sure they can't eat you up.'

That was marvellous advice. And that is what you have to do. Most times you have to go with the flow and make the best of it. A standard question is: do you feel pressure? Well, of course you do. But don't give them a headline. I held my press conferences before training. A lot of managers hold theirs afterwards. In that scenario, you are concentrating on your training session and not thinking about the press. For a 9 a.m. press conference I would have been briefed by Phil Townsend, our director of communications, on what might come up.

He would tell me, for example, that I might be asked about the Luis Suárez biting incident, say, or the Godolphin doping scandal in racing, or a possible move for a player such as Lewandowski. I always started by talking about players who would be available for that particular game. Then the emphasis would usually switch to issues around the game, personalities. The Sundays would often look to build a piece around one subject. Michael Carrick's good form, for instance.

I was generally fine in press conferences. The most difficult challenge was how to address the problem of bad refereeing. I was penalised for making remarks about referees because my reference point was the standards I set for football, not match officials. I wasn't interested in the standards referees set themselves. As a manager I felt entitled to expect refereeing levels to match those of the game they were controlling. And as a group, referees aren't doing their job as well as they should be. They talk of refereeing now as a full-time job, but that's codswallop.

Most start at 16 or so, when they are kids. I admire the impulse to want to referee. The game needs that. I wanted to see men such as the Italian Roberto Rosetti referee here. He's 6 feet 2 inches tall, a commanding figure, built like a boxer, and he flies over the pitch, calms players down. He's in control. I liked to see the top referees in action. I enjoyed observing proper authority, properly applied.

It would have been hard to get rid of a Premier League referee on grounds of incompetence or weight. They all have lawyers. The union is very strong. Plus, young referees are not coming through, so they cling to the ones they have.

Refereeing was the one area of the game where maybe I should have walked away from interviews without expressing my opinions. The following week, I might be the beneficiary of a decision in our favour; so to go overboard after one bad decision could be interpreted as selective outrage.

I support The Referees' Association. At Aberdeen I would bring them into training to help them get fit. I like standards. I like to see a fit referee. And I don't think that levels of fitness are high enough currently in the English game. How far they run is not the correct standard of measurement. It's how quickly they cover the ground. If there's a counter-attack on, can they reach the right end of the pitch in time? In fairness, if you look at our 2009 Champions League semi-final against Arsenal, when Rosetti was the referee, he was still 20 yards behind the play when we put the ball in the net. It took us nine seconds to score. So you're asking the referee to run 100 yards in nine seconds. Only Usain Bolt could manage that.

As a rule, I felt that the Football Association tend to go after the high-profile targets because they know it will bring favourable publicity. If you look at the Wayne Rooney incident against West Ham, when he swore into the camera, we felt they pressurised the referee, and Rooney ended up with a three-match suspension. The justification was that it's not nice for children to see a player swear into a TV camera. I can see that, but how often have you seen players swear over the years?

It was never really possible to work out who was running English football's governing body. You would get Exeter schools having a say. Greg Dyke, the new chairman, has to reduce the numbers involved in decision-making. A committee of 100 people can't produce sensible management. These committees are set up to honour people's 'contribution to the game' rather than make the organisation run smoothly. It's an institutional problem. Reformers go in there 6 feet 2 inches tall and come out 5 feet 4 inches.

Our behaviour in big games was generally excellent. One newspaper cited the case of the referee Andy D'Urso being harassed by Roy Keane and Jaap Stam, which we stamped on. Me saying, 'It's none of their business,' evidently irked the FA. I also pointed out that this was the League Cup, not the FA Cup. I was never much impressed with the work of the FA's compliance unit.

When I criticised Alan Wiley for his physique in the autumn of 2009, I was making a wider point about the fitness of referees. In my opinion Alan Wiley was overweight when I made that point after a 2–2 draw with Sunderland at Old Trafford. The comment that landed me in hot water was: 'The pace of the game demanded a referee who was fit. He was not fit. You see referees abroad who are as fit as butchers' dogs. He was taking thirty seconds to book a player. He was needing a rest. It was ridiculous.'

Later I apologised for any personal embarrassment caused to Alan Wiley and said my intention had been to 'highlight a serious and important issue in the game'. But, 16 days after the Sunderland game, I was charged by the FA with improper conduct. I had twice been banned from the touch-line, in 2003, and again in 2007 for having my say about referee Mark Clattenburg. Later I was fined £30,000 and banned from the touchline for five matches for my comments about referee Martin Atkinson in the wake of our 2–1 defeat at Chelsea. After my comments about Alan Wiley, former referee Jeff Winter suggested a 'FIFA-style stadium ban' might be appropriate.

By the end, I felt we hadn't had a really top Premier League referee for a long time. I know Graham Poll had that arrogant streak, but he was the best decision-maker. He had such an ego that it detracted from his performances, and when he entered one of his stroppy moods he could be difficult for you. He was the best judge of an incident over my time at Manchester United.

When a referee is working in front of 44,000 at Anfield, or 76,000 at Old Trafford, and he gives a goal that goes against the home team, and the crowd scream, it does affect a lot of them. That's another distinction: the ability to make decisions against the tide, against the roar of the crowd. The old saying that a referee was 'a homer' does apply. It's not to say a ref is cheating, more that they are influenced by the force of emotion in the crowd.

Anfield was probably the hardest place for a match official to be objective, because it was such a closed-in, volatile environment. There is an intimidation factor, from fans to referees, not just at Liverpool but across the game.

Forty years ago, crowds were not frenzied the way they are

today. So perhaps it would serve a higher purpose for the referee to attend a press conference with his supervisor alongside him and explain how he saw it. For instance, I would have found it interesting to hear from the Turkish referee who handled our Champions League tie against Real Madrid at Old Trafford in March 2013, and listen to what he had to say about Nani's sending-off, which was appalling.

A brief referee's press conference might have been a step forward. You can't stop progress. Take football boots: I was totally against the modern boot, yet manufacturers were pouring money into football and therefore could not be challenged. The level of gimmickry is now very high, to get young kids to buy pink boots, orange boots. A lot of clubs use the kit manufacturers as part of the deal to sign a player: we can get you a deal with Nike or adidas, and so on. They have to get their money back, and it's through boots.

As an audience we are never ever going to be satisfied with referees, because we are all biased towards our own teams. But full-time referees have not been successful, except in terms of man-management. It's impossible for a person to do his normal job and still follow the kind of training programme referees are assigned. So the system is flawed. There should be full-time referees who report to St George's Park every day. You may say – how are they going to travel from Newcastle to Burton-upon-Trent every day? Well, if we signed a player from London, we found him a house in Manchester. Robin van Persie, for example. If they want the best refereeing system, they should be as professional as the Premier League clubs, with the money the game now has.

Mike Riley, the head of the Professional Game Match

Officials Board, once claimed they lacked the finance to take such steps. If he is right, it is incredible that football lacks the resources for proper professional refereeing, with £5 billion in revenues from television. That is ridiculous. Think of the sums available in parachute payments to clubs relegated to the Championship. If referees are going to be full-time, the system should reflect that. It should be done properly.

In Europe, Champions League referees have an arrogance about them because they know they won't see you again the following weekend. I was in four finals and there was only one where the referee could be recognised as a top official: Pierluigi Collina, in the Barcelona final of 1999.

I've lost two important European ties to José Mourinho, not because of the performance of the players but because of the referee. The Porto game in 2004 was unbelievable. The worst decision he made that night was not the disallowed Scholes goal that would have put us 2–0 in front. When Ronaldo broke away with a few minutes to go, he was brought down by the left-back. The linesman flagged for a free kick but the referee chose to play on. Porto went up the park, got a free kick, Tim Howard parried it out and they scored in injury time. So we had plenty of experience of bad decisions against us in Europe.

I was at an AC Milan–Inter game and a senior Inter official said to me: 'Do you know the difference between the English and the Italians? In England they don't think a game can ever be corrupt. In Italy they don't think a game can *not* be corrupt.'

In England, on the plus side, there was an improvement

in man-management. That was good. The communication between match officials and players was much more constructive. People in authority have to be able to make decisions, and a lot of them lacked the ability to reach them quickly. The human element tells you a referee can be wrong. But the good ones will make the correct decisions more often than not. The ones who make the wrong ones are not necessarily bad referees. They just lack that talent for making the right calls in a tight time frame.

It was the same with players. What makes the difference in the last third? It's your decision-making. We were on to players about it all the time. If I were starting again, I would force every player to learn chess to give them the ability to concentrate. When you first learn chess you can be three or four hours finishing a game. But when you've mastered it and start playing 30-second chess, that's the ultimate. Quick decisions, under pressure. What football is all about.

twenty-one

UNITED'S 19TH TITLE

In the build-up to us winning our 19th English League title, there was this constant question about us beating Liverpool's record. My view was that we would pass their haul of 18 championships at some point anyway, so there was no need to make a fuss about it in that particular season. I wanted our attention focused on the campaign itself. But it was something I always felt we needed to achieve.

The Souness–Dalglish Liverpool teams were the benchmark for English football in the 1980s, when I made my first foray into management south of the border. Those Liverpool sides were formidable. I had suffered against them with Aberdeen and brought those memories with me to Manchester. In one European tie we had lost 1–0 at Pittodrie, played really well for the first 20 minutes at Anfield, but still ended up 2–0 down at half-time. I did my usual thing in the dressing room and, as the players were leaving, one,

Drew Jarvie, said, 'Come on, lads, two quick goals and we're back in it.'

We were 3–0 down on aggregate, at Anfield, and he was talking about two quick goals as if they were ours to take. I looked at Drew and said: 'God bless you, son.' Later the players would hammer Drew with the quote. They would say, 'We weren't playing Forfar, you know.'

When that great Liverpool side were 1–0 up against you, it was impossible to get the ball off them. It would be boomp-boomp around the park. Souness would spread the play. Hansen, Lawrenson, Thompson: whatever the combination at the back, they were comfortable on the ball. When I moved to United, they still had Ian Rush, John Aldridge, that calibre of player. Buying John Barnes and Peter Beardsley just elevated them again.

I said at the time: 'I want to knock them off their perch.' I can't actually remember saying that, but the line is attributed to me. Anyway, it was a representation of how I felt, so I have no objection to it being in the newspaper cuttings. Manchester United's greatest rival, though it changed towards the end, was Liverpool – historically, industrially and football-wise. The games were always emotionally intense events.

Our League success in 1993 opened the door, and by the turn of the century we had added a further five champion-ships. In 2000 I looked at Liverpool and knew there was no easy way back for them. They were in for a long haul. Youth development was spasmodic. You had no feeling that Liverpool were a threat again. The impetus was all with us. On the day we reached 18 titles to match their record, I knew fine well we were going to pass them, the way our club was operating.

The weekend of our 19th coronation was an extraordinary one for the city of Manchester. City won their first trophy since the 1976 League Cup, with a 1–0 win over Stoke in the FA Cup final, and we drew 1–1 at Blackburn with a 73rd-minute penalty by Rooney. In 1986, when I arrived, Liverpool led United 16–7 in League titles won. This was the season in which Chelsea had spent £50 million on Fernando Torres and City had invested £27 million in Edin Džeko while Javier Hernández turned out to be a bargain for us at £6 million.

We went 24 games unbeaten before losing at Wolves on 5 February 2011, and finished with only four defeats. A turning point in the race was the 4–2 win at West Ham in early April, after we had been 2–0 down at the interval. I made the point that several of our players had sampled success for the first time and would want more, Valencia, Smalling and Hernández among them.

Winning the title was the most important aim that season, with the 19 as a bonus. By the time I finished we had moved on to 20, which was a number that the fans chanted with great relish. There was no evidence in my final season that Liverpool, despite some excellent performances, possessed a team who might win the League. I was coming out of the Grand National meeting with Cathy in April 2013 and two Liverpool fans came up alongside to say, 'Hey Fergie, we'll hammer you next season.' They were good lads.

'Well, you'll need to buy nine players,' I said.

They looked crestfallen. 'Nine?'

One said: 'Wait till I tell the boys in the pub that.' I think he must have been an Everton fan. 'I don't think we need nine,' said the other as he traipsed away. I nearly shouted, 'Well, seven, then.' Everyone was laughing.

That summer we knew Manchester City were emerging as the team we would have to beat. The danger no longer emanated from London or Merseyside. It was so close you could smell it. An owner with the means to make this a serious municipal contest stood between us and control of the city. We continued down our path of building up strength for the future and hoped it would see us through.

The big player we needed to replace was Edwin van der Sar. Although most people assumed Manuel Neuer was going to be our target (he was on our agenda), we had scouted David de Gea for a long time, right through from when he was a boy. We always thought he was going to be a top goalkeeper.

In the summer of 2011, also, Ashley Young had a year to run on his contract at Aston Villa. He was a solid buy: English, versatile, could work either side of the pitch, could play off the front, and had a decent goal-scoring record. Given that Ji-Sung Park was coming up to 31, and with Ryan Giggs' advancing age, I thought it was a good time to move for Young. Giggs was never going to be a thrusting outside-left any more in the way he had been in the past.

We picked up Young for £16 million, which was a reasonable fee, maybe a pound or two more than we expected to pay, with him in the final year of his contract. But we concluded the deal quickly.

Ashley ran into trouble against QPR in the 2011–12 season, when Shaun Derry was sent off and our player was accused of diving. I left him out for the next game, and told him that the last thing he needed as a Manchester United player was a reputation for going down easily. It wasn't a penalty kick against QPR and Shaun Derry's sending-off was not rescinded. Ashley did it two weeks in a row but we stopped it. Going to ground too willingly was not something I tolerated.

Ronaldo had issues with the same tendency early in his career, but the other players would give him stick for it on the training ground. The speed he was travelling at, you had only to nudge Cristiano to knock him over. We spoke to him many times about it. 'He fouled me,' he would say. 'Yes, but you're overdoing it, you're exaggerating it,' we would tell him. He eradicated it from his game and became a really mature player.

Luka Modrić was an example of a player in the modern game who would never dive. Stays on his feet. Giggs and Scholes would never dive. Drogba was a prominent offender. A Barcelona game at Stamford Bridge in 2012 was the worst example. The press were never hard on him, except in that Champions League fixture. If the media had been tougher on him five years earlier, it would have been better for the game.

The purchase of Phil Jones was a long-term plan from when Sam Allardyce was Blackburn manager. When Rovers beat us in the FA Youth Cup, I called Sam the next day and said, 'What about the boy Jones?'

Sam laughed and said, 'No, he'll be in the first team on Saturday,' which he was. And he stayed there. Sam was a big fan of Jones. Blackburn wouldn't sell him in the 2011 January transfer window because they were in a relegation battle. By the end of the season, every club was on his tail:

Liverpool, Arsenal, Chelsea. He spoke to all four clubs but we managed to coax him to United, at 19 years of age.

At the point we signed Phil, I was unsure what his best position would be. Later I came to feel it would be at centre-back. He gave us versatility. He could play almost anywhere. In the 2011 Community Shield I took Ferdinand and Vidić off at half-time and assigned Jones and Evans to push right on top of the opposition. Evans is good at that too: breaking into the middle of the pitch. Vidić and Ferdinand were more old school. They have got good heads, understand the game well, don't get caught out. They were a great partnership. Increasingly, though, I could apply variations at centre-back, and Jones was a major part of my thinking.

Evans, I think, needed a shake. He didn't appreciate me signing Jones and Smalling. It caused him to question my opinion of him. But he proved himself in his own right and did increasingly well for us. It's always gratifying when a player responds to new arrivals by redoubling his own efforts.

Tom Cleverley, another young hopeful, was the victim of a shocking tackle against Bolton early in that season, which killed his year in many ways. He came back after about a month and we played him right away against Everton. A recurrence of the injury then kept him out for about three months. The plan was to send him off for an operation, which he didn't want. It would have kept him out for nine months. He wanted to carry on, and it worked, but by that time I had Scholes and Carrick back. I was never able to place Tom in the side regularly.

He's a very clever player, the boy. Very intelligent. He's mobile and a good finisher. He was in the London Olympic squad, which pleased me because he needed a challenge to lift his self-belief right up. Darren Fletcher, meanwhile, was battling a colonic illness. In the summer of 2012, it was possible he might have an operation, but he needed to be well to go under the knife. With a setback he had, he was going to be out until December. The previous season I had him with the reserves to do some coaching. He enjoyed that. Scholesy had gone back to the first team. Darren delivered a couple of half-time talks in reserves games and was impressive.

De Gea, who was 20 when we signed him for 24 million euros from Atlético Madrid, had a torrid time to begin with. It was obvious he lacked the physique of Van der Sar or Schmeichel. That part of his body needed to be developed and we devised a programme to help him add muscle mass. A complication for him was that we lost Ferdinand and Vidić in our first game of the 2011–12 League campaign: a 2–1 win at West Bromwich Albion, in which he allowed a weak shot from Shane Long to slip through. I described the battering he received in our penalty box at West Brom as his 'welcome to England'.

Vidić was out for six weeks and Rio for three. De Gea then had Smalling and Jones playing in front of him. Young players. He did all right but was a few degrees short of infallible. There were issues with his handling of the players in front of him. By the time we played Liverpool in October, he conceded the first goal from a corner kick. He should have dealt with that better: not just him but Evans and Smalling, the centre-backs on that occasion.

Their positioning was bad, which locked De Gea in to his six-yard area, but it's the goalkeeper who takes the blame for those rocky moments. In the decisive Premier League game against City at the Etihad Stadium the following April, Jones blocked him in and stopped him getting out to deal with the corner kick that led to Kompany's goal. There was progress to be made on that front. As the season wore on, though, he was more and more effective and self-assured. Some of his saves were miraculous. Our instincts were correct all along. He was one of the world's best young keepers and we were proud to have him with us, where he could develop as so many others had before. At Real Madrid, in the first leg of our Champions League round of 16 tie in February 2013, he saved brilliantly from Ronaldo, Fábio Coentrão and Sami Khedira.

David couldn't speak the language and he had to learn to drive, another illustration of how young he was. It could never be easy for a goalkeeper coming to England from Continental Europe at 20 years of age. If you recall the big goalkeeping moves of the last two decades or so, Buffon was outstanding from the moment he arrived at Juventus as a teenager. But very few who have made a move on the scale of De Gea going to United have clicked straight away. We always looked to invest in the future, though. He will be one of the very best and I was delighted when he was named in the PFA team of the year in my last season.

Jones was unfortunate in that 2011–12 season in sustaining a succession of niggling injuries. Young could look back on an encouraging season in which he scored eight goals. For a winger, that's not bad. He can draw on a good under-standing of the game and a high stamina level. With an extra half-yard of pace, his arsenal would have been complete, but his speed was hardly deficient, and he developed a knack of slipping inside on to his right foot – his strongest foot – and delivering from there. He was excellent through the middle as well, but we were blessed with many options in that area of that field. I was very pleased with Ashley, though. He was a quiet boy and a good trainer. The three of them – Jones, Young and De Gea – were good sorts.

Briefly the idea was mooted of an England comeback for Paul Scholes, but it was never a serious possibility. Paul would tire at the end of games in his later years because he was not born with the genes of Ryan Giggs, and he had little interest in playing international football again. Scholesy still offered us a tempo and a platform for our game when he returned in January 2012. There was nobody better in the rhythm section of our team. In fairness, the FA came to accept Paul's aversion to being recalled. Fabio Capello's assistant approached him before the 2010 World Cup but there was no approach ahead of Euro 2012 in Poland and Ukraine.

Michael Carrick was another interesting case study. No England manager appeared to regard him as a starting midfield player. Michael grew up sitting on the England bench and he had no desire to spend all summer in that observer's role at Euro 2012. As it turned out, he took the opportunity to clear out his Achilles.

Michael's handicap was, I feel, that he lacked the bravado of Frank Lampard and Steven Gerrard. Lampard, for me, was a marvellous servant for Chelsea, but I didn't think of him as an elite international footballer. And I am one of the few who felt Gerrard was not a top,

top player. When Scholes and Keane were in our team, Gerrard seldom had a kick against us. With England, Michael Carrick suffered in the shadow of those two big personalities.

Playing Lampard and Gerrard was a nightmare for England managers because they were incompatible in a 4–4–2 formation. The team functioned better with Hargreaves in central midfield, in 2006. By the bye, in the World Cup quarter-final against Portugal in 2006, which England lost, I told Steve McClaren that he and Eriksson should have had the players celebrating and buoyant after getting to penalties with 10 men, following Rooney's dismissal. A sense of achievement against the odds should have taken hold among Eriksson's penalty takers. Little things like that count. It would have lifted England's players.

I had some strange dealings on the England front. After Capello resigned, the FA wrote to me to ask me not to talk about the England manager's job. At the time, everyone was touting Harry Redknapp as the probable successor, and all I did was endorse the popular view that Harry would be ideally suited to the role. I don't know why they jumped on me that way. Clearly they had it in mind that Harry was not going to be the next England manager, even though everyone assumed he would.

I was offered the England job on two occasions. Adam Crozier, chief executive of the FA from 2000 to 2002, came to see me before Eriksson was appointed in 2001. The first time was before that, when Martin Edwards was chairman, around the time Kevin Keegan took the reins in 1999.

There was no way I could contemplate taking the England

job. Can you imagine me doing that? A Scotsman? I always joked that I would take the position and relegate them: make them the 150th rated country in the world, with Scotland 149.

The England job requires a particular talent – and that skill is the ability to handle the press. Steve McClaren made the mistake of trying to be pally with one or two. If you cut 90 per cent out, the others are after your body. If one person gives you favourable coverage, the others will hound you. No, it wasn't a bed of nails I was ever tempted to lie on.

twenty-two

MAN CITY – CHAMPIONS

Back in the sanctuary of our home, Cathy said, 'That was the worst day of my life. I can't take much more of this.' The afternoon of Sunday 13 May 2012 was crushing. To neutrals it was the most thrilling end to a Premier League title race in history. For us there was only the painful knowledge that we had thrown away a commanding lead. We had broken the Man United rule of not surrendering a position of power. Manchester City were England's champions.

I felt pretty ragged myself, but I could see the distress in my wife. 'Cathy,' I began, 'we have a great life, and we've had a fantastic period of success.'

'I know,' she said, 'but I'm not going out. There are too many City fans in the village.'

Sometimes you forget that setbacks can affect your family more than you. My three sons grew used to the cycle of triumph and disaster. The grandchildren were too young to understand it. Naturally it was worse this time because Man City were the ones celebrating at our expense. And worse, because we'd had the League in our grasp and thrown it away. Of all the setbacks I endured, nothing compared to losing the League to City.

I had faced 14 Man City managers since 1986, starting with Jimmy Frizzell. Finally a manager from across town had beaten me to the line in a title race. A year later, Roberto Mancini became the 14th City manager to lose or leave the job before I stood down. Roberto went after the FA Cup final defeat by Wigan Athletic in May 2013. By then we were League champions again, for the 20th time. We had turned the tables on City. But I would not be taking them on again.

At the start of the 2011–12 campaign, I felt it was between us, City and Chelsea. After a really good start, one of our best, I found myself having to change the team a lot to accommodate injuries. Our 8–2 victory over Arsenal was their heaviest defeat since 1896, when they lost 8–0 to Loughborough Town. It could have been 20. It actually reached the point where I felt – please, no more goals. It was a humiliation for Arsène. The climate at Arsenal was hardly serene to begin with. But we played some fantastic football that day. With the missed chances on either side, it might have been 12–4 or 12–5.

Arsenal played a young boy in midfield; I had hardly heard of him – Francis Coquelin – and he barely played again. He was completely out of his depth. The player who really disappointed me that day was Arshavin, who could have been sent off for two terrible tackles, over the top of the ball. There had been a change in Arshavin. You make a mental note when a player who usually gets whacked by everybody else turns it round and starts hunting down opponents. His behaviour shocked me. Arshavin contributed nothing to that game. It's disappointing, even as an opposing manager, to see this. Eventually Arsène took him off and sent on a younger replacement. They had players missing, obviously, and were not the same without Fàbregas and Nasri.

For that reason I had discounted Arsenal as title challengers. For me, Per Mertesacker, the centre-back, wasn't a major signing. We've seen plenty of that type of player in Germany over the years. I didn't think he would be a handicap, but nor did I believe he would lift Arsenal to a higher tier. They needed players who could directly influence their performances and results.

I saw this theme developing in Arsenal's transfer trading. We watched Marouane Chamakh, the Arsenal striker, at Bordeaux. We had good scouts in France but they never rated him. Olivier Giroud was another purchase. Arsène seemed willing to buy French players of that standard and I felt he might be overestimating French football.

After the 8–2 win over Arsenal came the farce of a 6–1 home defeat to City. We battered them for 40 minutes in that game. Absolutely battered them. We should have been three or four up. The referee allowed Micah Richards to boot lumps out of Ashley Young, overlooking five fouls in a row. At half-time we were really controlling the game. Then we had a man sent off just after the break. If you watch it again, Mario Balotelli pulls Jonny Evans first, but our centre-back then brought him down and was dismissed.

So at 2–0 down I made a change and brought on Phil Jones,

who kept flying forward. We dragged it back to 3–1 and the crowd went crazy. A famous comeback was on the cards. Fletcher had scored a wonderful goal, so we began attacking, and then conceded three goals in the last seven minutes. Suicide.

It looked humiliating but it was actually self-annihilation. There was never a point in the game when City looked a superior side to us. At 3–0 up they were in a comfort zone, that's fair to say, but they were not playing a style of football that was tearing us apart.

The last passage of play was a disgrace. It was comedy. And it led me to lean on Rio Ferdinand not to gamble any longer with his pace, which had declined. At his quickest, Rio would show the attacker where to knock the ball and then take it off him. Now he was trying that with David Silva and wasn't able to beat him in the sprint. That game was a watershed for Rio.

De Gea was shell-shocked. Six goals flew past him and he didn't have a hand in any of them. We also lost Welbeck, who was becoming a useful asset for us.

After the final whistle, I informed the players they had disgraced themselves. Then we set about fixing our attention on the defensive part of the team. There was a leak in there that we needed to correct. That remedial work led us into a period of stability where we were strong at the back. We worked on players coming back into the right positions, on concentration and on taking the defending more seriously.

We fell nine points behind Man City with that 6–1 defeat, but by New Year's Day the gap was down to three points. Losing to Blackburn Rovers at home was a real shocker,

indestructibles: Paul Scholes, Ryan Giggs and Gary Neville.

25th anniversary dinner, in November 2011. Some of our foreign players might have been confused by the kilt.

I felt Roberto Mancini was hassling the fourth official too much in this Manchester derby and told him so. A brief skirmish, soon forgotten.

I respected Mancini's work at City. I saw a City managers off in my time.

The Hillsborough commemoration at Anfield in September 2012 was brilliantly handled by bo clubs. Sir Bobby Charlton and Ian Rush clasp hands.

press gave me a cake with a hairdryer on as ~ting gift. I was fierce in news conferences, ~here were laughs too.

My successor, though I didn't know it then. David Moyes brought Everton to our ground in February 2013.

final ingredient. Robin van Persie's hat-trick against Aston Villa secured our 2012–13 title A great buy.

I still don't know how David Gill persuaded Cathy to unveil a statue of me. She refused to b
its feet.

Success gave me control. With each trophy won my thoughts turned to the next one.

en the statue was unveiled I joked: 'I've out-lived death.' What an honour.

The 2012–13 Premier League trophy is waiting for us out on the pitch at Old Trafford. My wo
is nearly done.

Special fans, and a special day at Old Trafford in May 2013, as my time as manager draws to an e

...y rarely came to games but she was ...ys there for me. We pose with the ...nier League trophy one last time.

Drama to the end. At West Brom, for my final game, waving to my family before a match that finished 5–5.

next wave of Fergusons. My wonderful grandchildren were part of the farewell party.

Still going strong, friends from my Harmony Row days reunite in Manchester, March 2013.

Would you take us on? Harmony Row, at our annual reunion. Football teams go on forever.

especially as it coincided with my 70th birthday, though that was nothing new to me. On my 50th we were beaten 4–1 by Queens Park Rangers. I'd suspended Evans, Gibson and Rooney for having a big night out and turning up for training dishevelled. Carrick and Giggs were injured. All of which forced me to play Rafael and Ji-Sung Park in the middle of the pitch. Blackburn played well that day. We pulled it back to 2–2 and they received a corner kick, which De Gea didn't handle properly, and Grant Hanley grabbed the winner.

In the meantime, United managed to name a stand after me without me knowing anything about it. When I walked onto the pitch, the two teams lined up to mark my 25 years as United manager, which was really nice. The Sunderland players, O'Shea, Brown, Bardsley and Richardson, all former United men, were smiling broadly and very appreciative. I felt proud of that. I was told to walk to the centre circle to meet David Gill, who had an object at his feet. I assumed he was going to make a presentation to me. But as I reached him, David turned me towards the South Stand. Apparently only he and the company who did the work were aware of what was going on. It was all carried out under a cloak of absolute secrecy.

David made a speech and then turned me round to see the lettering. You get some churning moments in your life when you feel, 'I don't deserve this.' This was one. David had worked hard to think of an appropriate acknowledgement of the 25 years. That's what it was about. David threw me off by saying, 'We want to build a statue of you, but do you think we should wait until you've finished the job?' His last words during that conversation were, 'We must do something, but we're not sure what it should be.' The answer he came up with was humbling. I had been United manager for 1,410 games. The moment didn't cause me to think any more deeply about retirement. But after the last game of the season in 2011–12, I said to my boys, 'That may be it. One more season and then that's me,' because it did take a lot out of me. That last minute took it all out of me.

Going out of the Champions League in the group stage was my fault. I took the competition for granted. We had come through previous group stages comfortably and looking at this one I felt it would be straightforward, though of course I never said that publicly.

I rested players: two or three when we played Benfica away. We came away with a draw and played quite well. Then, against Basel, we were 2–0 up and cruising, but ended up drawing 3–3. They had won their first game so it put them two points in front of us already. We won our next two games against Cluj, but Benfica and Basel were still in the chase.

We played well but only drew at home with Benfica, which meant that if we lost in Basel we would be out. The pitch was very soft in Switzerland and we lost Vidić in the first half to a serious injury. They had a couple of good forwards in Frei and Streller and won the game 2–1. Against Basel at home, the players had been complacent defensively, not getting back to the ball.

In the Carling Cup we were eliminated by Crystal Palace, who prepared well against our young players. The League Cup is always regarded now as a bonus tournament. We were also knocked out of the FA Cup in the fourth round after beating Man City earlier in the competition. Because the focus was now on the Premier League, we didn't make much headway in the Europa League, going out to Athletic Bilbao in early March with a 3–2 defeat at home. I wanted to win the Europa League and represent us in the right way. But our home record in Europe was poor: one win from five games.

At that point the malaise hits you. You've been knocked out of the Champions League group stage, you've had a 6–1 defeat to Man City and you're out of the Carling Cup, at home to Crystal Palace. You have a challenge ahead. But we were good at those. We had the energy and wherewithal to concentrate fully on the League. Our form after that, apart from the Blackburn Rovers result, was terrific. Between January and early March, we beat Arsenal and Tottenham away, defeated Liverpool and drew with Chelsea.

In February the Suárez–Evra affair blew up again when Suárez refused to shake Patrice's hand in a game at Old Trafford. I brought the players together on the Tuesday of the game and told them, 'I think you need to be big.' They were not inclined to be nice about it. I stuck to my theme: you need to be bigger than them. Gradually they changed their minds and came round to the idea of a handshake. Ferdinand, the most experienced player, also had the incident with John Terry and Anton Ferdinand in his thoughts. By the Friday they were fine with it. There would be a handshake from Evra's side.

I've watched the footage several times. Suárez seemed to quicken as he passed Patrice. Perhaps he thought no one would notice that. As Suárez passed him, Evra was annoyed and said something to him. It was all over very quickly, but the repercussions lingered.

When Kenny Dalglish gave his initial pre-match TV interview, he gave the impression that Suárez had agreed to shake Evra's hand. A club of Liverpool's stature should have done something about that, but he played in the game all the same. I called Suárez a 'disgrace to Liverpool' and said they would be wise to 'get rid' of him. I also reprimanded Patrice for celebrating too close to Suárez as the players walked off the pitch.

The whole saga had started at Anfield with Patrice sitting in the corner looking aggrieved. 'What's happened?' I asked.

'He called me a black —,' Patrice said.

I told him he would first have to report it to the referee. I went into the referee's room with Patrice and told the match official, 'Look, Patrice Evra says he's been racially abused.'

Phil Dowd, the fourth official, began writing everything down. The referee, Andre Marriner, told me he thought something had happened, but had no idea what it might have been. Patrice said it happened several times. Then they called in Kenny Dalglish. Later, when we were having a drink, John Henry also came in. He was introduced to me but didn't say much. Steve Clarke's son was pouring the drinks. One or two from the old school came in to join us.

But nothing more was said. Then it exploded in the papers. Later, Liverpool wore those T-shirts supporting Suárez, which I thought was the most ridiculous thing for a club of Liverpool's stature. I felt we handled it well, mainly because we knew we were in the right. The FA asked us several times not to discuss it, but Liverpool could not leave the subject alone. David Gill would not have allowed any manager to handle it that way. Nor would Bobby

Charlton. They are experienced people who know about life. There seemed nobody at Liverpool willing to pull Kenny's horns in.

Suárez came to the hearing and said he had called Evra '*Negrito*'. The specialist said yes, you can call your friend *Negrito*, but you can't call a stranger that, in an argument. Then it becomes racist.

I left Evra out of the Europa League game at Ajax five days after the non-handshake at Old Trafford because it was a trying time for him and he needed a break. He's a strong wee guy. I checked on his state of mind regularly and he would say: 'I'm fine, I have nothing to be ashamed of, I feel I've done the right thing. It's disgraceful what he said to me.'

He also said he was doing it purely for himself, on a point of principle, and was not trying to fight a larger political battle on behalf of black players.

I think Kenny was falling back on the old chip on the shoulder. The problem, I felt, was that there was no Peter Robinson at Anfield. Peter Robinson would never have allowed the Suárez situation to be handled the way it was. The young directors there idolised Kenny and there was no one to say, 'Hey, behave yourself, this is out of order, this is Liverpool Football Club.' Equally, no one could ever overstate Kenny's dignified and statesmanlike handling of the Hillsborough tragedy, which earned him a level of respect that no later political difficulty could nullify.

After the grandstand unveiling of the statue, another great honour was the FIFA Presidential Award for 2011. At the ceremony I was sitting beside Pep Guardiola and right in front of Messi, Xavi and Iniesta. The three musketeers. I felt privileged to be in that company. As I sat there on my own, the three made their way towards me to shake my hand. Xavi said: 'How's Scholes?' In his own victory speech, Messi said his Ballon d'Or award should go to Xavi and Iniesta. 'They made me,' he said. Messi is such a humble lad.

It was a really pleasurable night. Sepp Blatter, the FIFA president, had been very kind with his words and there were video messages from Gordon Brown, Tony Blair, José Mourinho, Eric Cantona, Ronaldo and David Beckham. The point of the award was to recognise my 25 years at Manchester United. I said it was an honour in the 'twilight of my life'. If you could have seen me at the end of that season, you'd have thought I was right.

I didn't use mind games with City because I felt we were in control. Patrick Vieira, however, did claim it was a sign of weakness for us to bring Scholes back from retirement in January 2012. In that campaign we had great momentum until we were beaten at Wigan, where we really didn't play well. The one that killed us was the home fixture against Everton on 22 April. With seven minutes to go, we're winning 4–2, Patrice Evra hits the post and Everton go and score. Instead of 5–2, it becomes 4–3. When we drew that game 4–4, I felt we had lost the League. City won comfortably at Wolves to reduce our lead to three points, with the Manchester derby at City's ground to come. It was self-destruction. I knew the City game away was bound to be tough and I thought they would play to kill the game, slow the pace down, give fouls away in our half and move the ball to Nasri and Silva to dribble with. By then, City were versed in such clever tactics.

At the Etihad Stadium we wanted the two wide players to

come in all the time to support Rooney, on his own, and play Ji-Sung Park in Yaya Touré's area to work him all the time. There was nobody better at that than Park. Physically he was not in the same league as Touré, who was in outstanding form, but I needed to try and negate the threat he posed on those marauding runs of his. But I made a mistake. Nani was terrible that night. We brought Valencia on, who did a lot better, but City went 1–0 up and killed the game. Smalling was caught out by a David Silva corner for the Vincent Kompany header just before half-time. It was hard to take.

For the first 20 minutes we were fine. Our possession of the ball was good and we had a couple of half-chances. What we decided to do was keep the channels tight. Zabaleta kept getting to the by-line and winning corner kicks. Nothing came from Clichy's side. It was all Zabaleta. And it was a corner kick that did for us.

If we had made it to half-time at 0–0 we would have won the game. We had a plan for the second half, a way to play, that involved Welbeck coming on for Park. But Nigel de Jong did him straight away through the back, and that was Danny out for the rest of the season until he played for England. De Jong was only booked for the tackle down Welbeck's ankle.

Roberto Mancini was badgering the fourth official through the whole game: it was Mike Jones, who I feel is not one of the stronger officials. When De Jong landed that tackle on Welbeck, Mancini came rushing out to protect his player. I told Mancini where to go. That's what our little clash was about. Roberto tried to dominate the fourth official and I had seen enough. He wanted the referee to come over to him and speak to him so he could get the home crowd going. Andre Marriner left it to Mike Jones to sort out. Yaya Touré was the one who made the difference, no doubt about that. He was the best player against us in the 1–0 game. He was brilliant.

There was no animosity later. Roberto and I had a drink. With the exception of Frank Sinatra, just about everyone was in the office where we tried to talk. The place was mobbed. I said to Mancini, 'This is ridiculous, how can we have a chat with all these people in the room?'

The one surprise about Mancini in his time as City manager was his stance over Carlos Tévez. He had a chance to make a stand over player power and I felt he should have thrown him out. Instead, after their clash at a Champions League game in Germany, Tévez went to Argentina for three months, playing golf, and then came back saying he wanted to fight to win the League for them.

Taking him back showed desperation. Or perhaps Sheikh Mansour intervened to end the standoff. I do remember Mancini saying, 'He'll never play for me again.' Say Edin Džeko or Balotelli were not happy and had disappeared for three months: would they have been treated differently from Tévez? Mancini made a rod for his own back. In terms of his prestige as a manager, he let himself down.

I was told that some of the players and staff didn't like him, but he was not there to be liked. Results backed up his methods. He chose his players well, with a good balance and age range. I believe he wanted to avoid players over 30 and those under 24. His players were mostly in that band of 24 to 28. Most of them were at their peak, which, in theory, gave him two to three years with that squad.

Tactically you saw his Italian instincts. As soon as City went in front, he would often play five at the back. He had that defensive mentality: give nothing away. That costs you some games.

Goal difference was still a factor, though. In our two remaining games, against Swansea and Sunderland, we attempted to close the gap. Against Swansea, Smalling and Giggs missed chances. We could have gone in at half-time five up. We only scored one in the second half, in which Rooney and Cleverley both missed sitters. If we had won 5–0, we would have been five goals adrift. In the Sunderland game, their goalkeeper was out of this world. Simon Mignolet. His saves were incredible. We hit the post twice, Rooney hit the bar; we could have won 8–0. What a way that would have been to win the League: on goal difference.

In the event, Rooney's 34th goal of the season from a Valencia cross was our only mark on the scoreboard. Our fans were wonderful. I kept looking at the young boy from Sky, and he was saying it was still 2–1 at City. How long to go? Five minutes added time. But I knew. City scored twice in 125 seconds, through Džeko and Agüero. Džeko's was timed at 91 minutes 15 seconds, then Agüero went right through QPR's defence, exchanging passes with Mario Balotelli, and struck the shot that won them the title for the first time in 44 years. The clock showed 93 minutes 20 seconds.

We were champions for 30 seconds. When our whistle blew we were champions. In fairness to our players, they knew they had ballsed it up. There were no excuses.

I told them, 'You walk out of that door with your heads up. You've got nothing to be ashamed of. Don't show any weakness.' They understood that message. Their interviews were all positive. I did what I had to do: congratulate City. I had no problem with that.

There is no point torturing yourself over what might have been in the City–QPR game. In my career at Manchester United we came back time and time again and we would do it again. The question in my mind that summer was: would City get better? They had the confidence from winning the League; there were no boys in their team and they were a very experienced side, in that mid-twenties range. Money was not an object, but the size of the playing staff and the wage bill were, in the context of the Financial Fair Play regulations. I asked of us: could we get through the following campaign with a better injury record?

There was a young Paul Scholes missing from our team. We needed that kind of playmaking influence. People spoke about Modrić but we were reluctant to deal with Spurs after the Berbatov carry-on.

Rafael was developing into a really, really good player, but he made mistakes. Some players can never stop making mistakes, it's hereditary, but others learn by them. Rafael was sent off against Bayern Munich and then improved his disciplinary record dramatically. He's such a competitive boy, quick and aggressive, and he believes in himself. He has a really positive attitude to the game. One thing we lacked was cover at left-back, where Patrice Evra had been averaging 48–50 games a season. We needed to fill that breach.

I said in a press conference, to our fans: you'd better get used to this, because we're going to be seeing a lot of this new Man City. There will be a lot of games between us and they will all be like this. I would love to have been in their Champions League group the following term, because it would have made us alive to it. For the 2012–13 campaign, I resolved to leave no man behind and take the group stage much more seriously, to win the group.

Before the final round of Premier League games, Mick Phelan and I had been to Germany to see the German cup final, to watch Shinji Kagawa, Robert Lewandowski and Mats Hummels and I had told him: 'Mick, the only way City will beat us tomorrow is if they score late on. They'll have a hard game against Queens Park Rangers. I wouldn't be surprised if QPR get a result, but if City score late on, we'll lose the League.'

We finished with 89 points: the highest total ever for a runner-up. The general feeling was that we lacked a bit of stability in the defensive positions, particularly with the injury to Vidić, but once Evans and Ferdinand formed a partnership, we shot up the table. Our goal difference was good and 89 points was a healthy return. But those early departures from League Cup, FA Cup and Champions League obliged us to mark it down as a bad season.

I was sad but not demoralised. I felt I had a core of players who were sure to improve. Rafael, Jones, Smalling, De Gea, Cleverley, Welbeck, Hernández. I had a nucleus who would be good for the long haul. The challenge was replacing Scholes. I don't know where you find those players. A fit Anderson would make up part of the gap. We were planning to sign Kagawa and the young boy, Nick Powell, from Crewe. We had five natural centre-backs. Plus Valencia and Nani. Young would give us plenty of options wide. We knew where the challenge was: the noisy neighbours. It would suit us, I decided, if they fared better in Europe and grew distracted.

On the Tuesday we were down to go to Belfast to play in Harry Gregg's testimonial. It was hard to lift the players, but it turned out to be quite inspiring, because Harry Gregg has been a great servant and the support was wonderful. It helped us push the disappointment through the system.

A postscript to that painful denouement was a medical scare. I travelled to Berlin to see the Dortmund–Bayern German Cup final, then to Sunderland, then back to Manchester, then to Belfast for Harry Gregg's testimonial and then back home, and on to Glasgow, where I was supposed to speak at a Rangers function, with a flight booked to New York on the Saturday.

Shaving in Glasgow, I noticed a drip of blood. Then another and another. I just couldn't stop the flow and ended up in hospital, where they cauterised it. The doctor thought I would be all right to fly, but it didn't stop bleeding for two days, so we cancelled the New York trip. The doctor came round on the Friday, Saturday and Sunday. It was painful but eventually settled down.

I used to get nosebleeds as a player, mainly from knocks. But this was an especially bad one. The cause was diagnosed as too many flights, too much cabin pressure.

It was a wee warning. If you do too much, you're inviting trouble.

twenty-three

FAMILY

SHE always waited up for me. Even if I came through the door at two or three in the morning, Cathy would be there to greet me. 'Why don't you go to bed?' I would say to her over the phone as we travelled home. 'No, no,' she would say, 'I'll wait till you get back.' For 47 years she maintained this line.

I could go about my work in football knowing family life was completely taken care of. Cathy is a remarkable person. David Gill was a genius to persuade her to unveil a statue of me at Old Trafford. There is no way I could have coaxed her into the light like that.

The truth about Cathy is that she has never changed. She's a mother, a grandmother and a housewife. That is her life. She doesn't court friendships. It's not that she discourages them, more that she prefers the company of family and a few close friends. She almost never went to the football. When I married her we would go to dances at weekends, with friends from Glasgow. She was always comfortable in Glaswegian company. But after our move to United, she wasn't a social animal at all. She displayed no inclination to go out on the circuit and I would go to most functions and dinners on my own.

A house with gates is useful for when Tory politicians come canvassing. Cathy would hear the local Conservatives announce themselves through the Tannoy and say, 'Sorry, Mrs Ferguson is out, I'm the cleaner.' In all respects she is faithful to her roots.

When I stopped playing at 32 and had pubs in Glasgow and managed St Mirren, my day started at Love Street, where I would be until 11 o'clock, and then to the pub, until 2.30 p.m. Sometimes I would go home and sometimes directly to Love Street for training. Then it was back to the pub, then home.

So the children seldom saw me at that very early age. Cathy brought them up. By the time they reached manhood, they were closer to me, but have always had the utmost love and respect for their mum.

Going to Aberdeen was a blessing because I didn't have the pubs and there was more of a family life for the five of us. I was there all the time unless we had a game. Darren was a ball boy and Mark would go to the games with his pals. Cathy would take Jason, who wasn't hugely interested in football at this stage.

But at 13 or 14 he took up playing and ended up representing Scotland Boys Club against Wales. He wasn't a bad player. He was a late developer who was interested in books.

He's a very clever boy. When we moved to Old Trafford he stayed in Aberdeen to continue his studies. Then he joined us in Manchester, where he played for our B team a few times.

Darren was always a natural, with a left foot of great quality. Mark was a very good player who appeared for Aberdeen reserves a few times. He went to college and polytechnic in Sheffield for a land economy degree. Mark became a great success in the City. All my sons have done well. They are all driven people, as is Cathy, who is clever and has a determination about her.

People used to say I was like my dad. But people who really knew me said I was more like my mother, who was a very determined woman. My father was too, but was much quieter. My mother, like all good mothers, was the boss. She ran the family. Cathy made all the family decisions in our house, too, which was fine by both of us.

When Darren was 14, Brian Clough called and said he wanted to sign him for Nottingham Forest. Brian was full of contradictions. He would never answer the phone to me. It was always Ron Fenton, Clough's assistant, who picked up the receiver. At Aberdeen I went south to see Forest play Celtic in the UEFA Cup on rock-hard frosty ground. I knew Ron Fenton reasonably well. As I entered the directors' lounge, Ron said, 'Alex, have you met the boss?' I hadn't, and was quite looking forward to making his acquaintance.

Ron introduced me and Brian said, 'What did you think of the game?'

My opinion was that Celtic had deserved to win. I then told him Forest would beat them at Celtic Park. 'Well young man, I've heard enough,' said Brian. And walked out. Archie Knox burst out laughing.

In the event, Darren stayed with us at United. The problem was keeping him in the first team. Cathy never forgave me for selling him. He started the first 15 games in the year we won the League for the first time. But, in a Scotland U-21s game, he sustained a really bad hamstring tear that kept him on the sidelines for three months. That was him out until February, and by that time Bryan Robson was back fit. Neil Webb, Mick Phelan and Paul Ince were also on the scene. Then Roy Keane became available for £3.75 million. That killed Darren as a first-team player.

He came to see me and said it wasn't working for him. He said he would need to move. He was also sensitive to the difficulties for me. So we sold him to Wolves, a club in turmoil, with big expectations and a large fan base.

I watched Darren play there a lot. He was easily the best footballer, but they changed manager so many times after Graham Turner was sacked. Graham Taylor, Mark McGhee, Colin Lee. When McGhee came in, his appearances started to dwindle.

He then moved to Sparta Rotterdam and once more did well. They changed the coach while he was away on holiday and the new man didn't want him. He then came back to Wrexham and became settled there. As his playing career wound down, Barry Fry called from Peterborough and asked what Darren was doing. He ended up as manager there and got them promoted to the Championship, where they punched well above their weight. Tensions crept in with the chairman and he resigned and went to Preston, which was a disaster, before a second stint at Peterborough displayed his qualities again.

Darren's approach is to play penetrating football with players who pass the ball and move. That's hard when you're bottom of the League because teams down there tend to be desperate. It was poignant for me to see Darren face the struggles I encountered in my early years, with budgets and chairmen and players. I reminded him all the time about that motto of ours: 'Sweeter after difficulties'. My advice to any young coach is to be prepared. Start early. Don't leave it until you are 40 to acquire your coaching badges.

I was totally opposed to fast-tracking coaches. It is a disgrace. In Holland and Italy it might take four or five years for you to receive your badges. The reason they need to go through that intense, prolonged scrutiny is to protect them from what's to come in management. It cost Darren £8,000 to earn his badges at the Warwick Business School. By fast-tracking big names, the FA rode roughshod over all the people who scraped together to get their qualifications the proper way.

I didn't torture myself about being away a lot or consumed with work during the boys' childhoods. The reason was that we were all very close, regardless, and the boys themselves were very tight-knit. They are in constant contact with us. They are all busy lads. Even I couldn't always get hold of Mark, who was in a business where you have to keep your eye on the ball. His is a world of tiny fractions, where you could miss a buy or a sell in seconds, the way the markets move.

All my sons are a credit to Cathy, who was always there for them, and for me, whatever time I turned the key in the door.

twenty-four

ROONEY

IT was August 2004 and we had just played Everton. Bill Kenwright was crying. Sitting in my office, crying. Present were David Moyes, David Gill, Bill and me. As we studied the Everton chairman in his sorrow, he announced that he would like to make a call. Through his tears, Bill said: 'I'll need to phone my mother.'

'They're stealing our boy, they're stealing our boy,' he said down the line. Then he passed the phone to me. 'Don't you dare think you're getting that boy for nothing. That boy's worth fifty million pounds,' said a female voice. Wonderful. 'This is a trick, this,' I laughed. 'Is this a game?' But it was real. You had only to mention Everton to Bill to turn his taps on. He was a very likeable guy and unapologetically emotional.

David Moyes was giving me the eyes. For a minute I thought it was a get-up, a performance. Bill's background was in theatre, after all. It occurred to me while all this was going on that I ought to check Wayne's medical records. Was there something physically wrong we had missed? Was this a ruse to push the price up? My God, it was funny. Did the boy have one leg? Was I being lured into a gigantic sting?

The negotiations to buy England's most promising young talent were protracted, to say the least. Bill knew the value of the boy. David Moyes was the more combative party – as I would have been, in his position. David was realistic. He knew the club were about to receive a healthy fee and that Everton were hardly awash with money. The official price was just over £25 million with add-ons. Everton needed that injection. When the tears had dried and the talking was over, Wayne signed on the line seven hours short of the deadline on 31 August 2004.

By the time he joined us, he hadn't played for 40-odd days and had trained for only a couple of sessions. We thought the Champions League tie at home to Fenerbahçe would be a suitable introduction, 28 days after he had become a Manchester United player. This tentative approach yielded a spectacular return: a Rooney hat-trick in a 6–2 victory.

After that dramatic introduction his fitness level dropped a bit and we had some work to do to bring him to the level of the other players. Understandably there was no repeat of the Fenerbahçe performance for several weeks.

None of this stifled my enthusiasm for him. Wayne possessed a marvellous natural talent and was entitled to be given time to make the transition from boy to man. He was a serious, committed footballer with a hunger for the game. At that point in his development, Wayne needed to train all the time, and did so willingly. He was never the sort who could take days off. He needed to train intensively to be on the sharp edge of his game. Whenever he was out for a few weeks with an injury, Wayne's fitness would drop quite quickly. He has a big, solid frame, and broad feet, which may partly explain his metatarsal injuries in that period.

I knew straight away that he was the player our intuition said he would be. Courageous, reasonably two-footed – though he uses his left foot less than he could. We signed players at 24 thinking they would peak at 26, and Wayne's progress with us from a much earlier age supported my conviction that he would be at his best around that age. With the kind of physique he had it was always hard to imagine him playing into his mid-thirties, like Scholes or Giggs, but I developed an expectation when he re-signed for us, in October 2010, that he might end up as a midfielder.

All our intelligence about Wayne Rooney as an Evertonian schoolboy could be condensed into a single phrase. This was a man playing in under-age football.

The reports at our academy were always glowing and the club tried to acquire him at 14, when there is a loophole in the last week of May that allows you to sign a boy from another academy. But Wayne wanted to stay at Everton. We tried again at 16 before he signed his academy forms and again he wasn't interested. Everton were in his blood.

Geoff Watson and Jim Ryan were our two academy men who had monitored Rooney's progress and been so impressed with him in games between the clubs. He played in the FA Youth Cup final at 16 against Aston Villa.

When Walter Smith joined me as assistant he said: 'Get

that Rooney signed.' Walter was unequivocal. He described him as the best he had ever seen. That confirmed everything we knew of him. Then came Wayne's debut, at 16, and his wonder goal against Arsenal.

At Everton he also became the youngest player to win a full England cap, in a game against Australia, and was then picked by Sven-Göran Eriksson for the vital World Cup qualifier against Turkey. He scored his first international goal at 17 years and 317 days. So he was already on the national map by the time he came to us.

My first meeting with him contradicted my expectation that he would have an assertive personality. He was a shy boy. But I think there was an awe about him that reflected the large transfer fee and all the attention it was bringing. He soon stopped being shy. On our training ground he gave everybody hell. Everybody. The referee, the other players. The poor refs – Tony Strudwick, or Mick or René – would all say to me, 'You're the only one with the authority – you should ref these games.'

My reply was: 'There's no way I'm refereeing these matches.'

I remember Jim blowing his whistle mildly for a foul on a day when Roy Keane was in one of his dark moods, giving everyone stick. His team, our team, the ref, any living creature he could find. Jim turned to me with his whistle and said: 'I hope Roy's team wins.'

'That's ridiculous, that,' I said, trying not to laugh.

'Yeah, but the grief I'll get in that dressing room,' Jim said. At one point we even discussed hiring referees.

I admit I gave Wayne a few rollickings. And he would rage

in the dressing room when I picked him out for criticism. His eyes would burn, as if he wanted to knock my lights out. The next day he would be apologetic. When the anger subsided, he knew I was right – because I was always right, as I liked to tease him. He would say: 'Am I playing next week, boss?'

'I don't know,' I would say.

In my opinion, he was not the quickest learner but what he had was a natural instinct to play the game, an intuitive awareness of how football worked. A remarkable raw talent. Plus, natural courage and energy, which is a blessing for any footballer. The ability to run all day is not to be undervalued. In a training ground exercise he wouldn't absorb new ideas or methods quickly. His instinct was to revert to type, to trust what he already knew. He was comfortable in himself.

In those early years I seldom had to be dictatorial with him. He made some daft tackles in games and there were flashpoints on the pitch. Off the field, though, he caused me no anxiety. My problem was that, being a centre-forward myself, I was always harder on the strikers than anyone in the team. They were never as good as me, of course. I'm sorry, but none was as good as I was in my playing days. Managers are allowed such conceits and often inflict them on players. Equally, the players think they are better managers than the men in charge – until they try it, that is.

If I saw attackers not doing the things I believe I used to do, it would set me off. They were my hope. I looked at them and thought: you are me. You see yourself in people.

I could see myself in Roy Keane, see myself in Bryan Robson, see bits of me in Paul Scholes and Nicky Butt and the two Nevilles, Gary and Phil. Teams reflect the character of their manager. Never give in: that's a great religion, a great philosophy to have. I never gave in. I always thought I could rescue something from any situation.

Something was always happening at Man United. There was always a drama. It was routine to me. When Wayne Rooney's personal life was exposed in the *News of the World,* and a sense of crisis was brewing in his world in the late summer of 2010, there was no council of war in my office, no pacing of the room.

I didn't phone him the morning after the story broke. I know he would have wanted me to. That's where my control was strong. He would have been looking for a phone call from me, an arm round his shoulder. To me that wasn't the way to deal with it.

When these sorts of allegations surfaced the first time, he was 17 years old, and allowances were made for his youth, but this time we were seven years on. Coleen, his wife, had her head screwed on. She always struck me as a stabilising force.

I certainly felt under pressure in relation to him during that World Cup in South Africa. I knew there was something bugging him at the 2010 World Cup. I could see it. Although he had been named PFA Player of the Year and Football Writers' Association Footballer of the Year that season he was in a strange mood in South Africa. 'Nice to see your home fans boo you,' he said into a TV camera after England's goalless draw with Algeria in Cape Town. England went out in the second round and there were no goals in four matches for Wayne.

I needed to get his attention. Yet the best way to achieve that was by not saying anything to him – not offering consolation – to force him to think. When I left him out away to Everton in September, to protect him from abuse by the crowd, he was relieved, because he knew I was doing the right thing by him. Your job is to make an impact on each personality with the best possible output in terms of performance.

We can all moralise but everyone will commit indiscretions. I was never going to moralise with Rooney. On 14 August 2010 Wayne informed us that he would not be signing a new contract at United. This was a shock, as the plan had always been to sit down after the World Cup to discuss a new contract.

As the drama gathered pace, David Gill called me to say that Wayne's agent, Paul Stretford, had been to see him to say that Wayne wanted away. The phrase he had used was that he didn't think the club were ambitious enough. We had won the League Cup and the League the year before and reached the final of the Champions League.

David said that Wayne would be coming to see me. At that meeting, which was in October, he was hugely sheepish. I felt he'd been programmed in what he was trying to say. The basis of his complaint was that we were not sufficiently ambitious.

My response was to ask Wayne: 'When have we not challenged for the League in the last 20 years? How many European finals have we been to in the last three or four years?'

I told him that to say we weren't ambitious was nonsense. Wayne said that we should have pursued Mesut Özil, who had joined Real Madrid from Werder Bremen. My reply was that it was none of his business who we should have gone for. I told him it was his job to play and perform. My job was to pick the correct teams. And so far I had been getting it right.

We had a European tie the following day. Two hours before we played Bursaspor, on 20 October, Wayne issued the following statement: 'I met with David Gill last week and he did not give me any of the assurances I was seeking about the future squad. I then told him that I would not be signing a new contract. I was interested to hear what Sir Alex had to say yesterday and surprised by some of it.

'It is absolutely true, as he said, that my agent and I have had a number of meetings with the club about a new contract. During those meetings in August I asked for assurances about the continued ability of the club to attract the top players in the world.

'I have never had anything but complete respect for MUFC. How could I not have done, given its fantastic history and especially the last six years in which I have been lucky to play a part?

'For me its all about winning trophies – as the club has always done under Sir Alex. Because of that I think the questions I was asking were justified.

'Despite recent difficulties, I know I will always owe Sir Alex Ferguson a huge debt. He is a great manager and mentor who has helped and supported me from the day he signed me from Everton when I was only 18.

'For Manchester United's sake I wish he could go on forever because he's a one-off and a genius.'

I wasn't sure what he meant by this statement but I assumed he was trying to build some bridges with me and the fans. I hoped it meant he'd changed his mind and was happy to stay with us.

The press conference after that game, when all the media were there, gave me an opportunity to say what I wanted to say, which was that Wayne was out of order.

I told the press: 'As I said, three Premier League titles in a row is fantastic and we were within one point off a record fourth. It didn't happen for us and we didn't like that and we want to do something about it. We'll be OK – I've got every confidence in that. We have a structure at the club which is good, we have the right staff, the right manager, the right chief executive, he's a brilliant man. There's nothing wrong with Manchester United, not a thing wrong with it. So we'll carry on.'

And I said on television: 'I had a meeting with the boy and he reiterated what his agent had said. He wanted to go. I said to him, "Just remember one thing: respect this club. I don't want any nonsense from you, respect your club." What we're seeing now in the media is disappointing because we've done everything we can for Wayne Rooney, since the minute he's come to the club. We've always been there as a harbour for him. Any time he's had a problem, we've given advice. But you do that for all your players, not just Wayne Rooney. That's Manchester United. This is a club which bases all its history and its tradition on the loyalty and trust between managers and players and the club. That goes back to the days of Sir Matt Busby. That's what it's founded on. Wayne's been a beneficiary of this help, just as Ryan Giggs, Paul Scholes and all the players have been. That's what we're there for.'

In a conference call with the Glazers, the future ambitions of the club were discussed and Wayne was made one of the highest-paid players in the country, I would imagine. The next day he came in to apologise. I told him: 'It's the fans you should be apologising to.'

There was a mixed reaction from the players. Some were put out; others were not bothered by him. It was a sorry episode for Wayne because it portrayed him as a money man who had dropped his grievance the minute his salary was raised. That's the way it was presented, but I don't think it was Wayne's intention to make it a financial issue. It blew over quickly. With the fans, however, there was a residue of mistrust.

He was fine so long as he was scoring, but in fallow times there was perhaps a stirring of the old resentment. Players can underestimate the depth of feeling for a club among fans. In the most extreme cases it leads supporters to think they own the club. Some of them have stood behind the club for 50 years. They're there for life. So when a player is deemed to have shown disloyalty to a club, there is no messing about with them.

Very few players want away from Manchester United. We had a generation of players who had pledged their whole careers to our club – Giggs, Scholes, and so on – and it was alien to our supporters to see a player agitating for a move or to hear him criticising transfer policy.

In the winter of 2011, I did have to take disciplinary action after Wayne, Jonny Evans and Darron Gibson had a night out. They went across to Southport to a hotel to celebrate our 5–0 Boxing Day win against Wigan. They came into training the next day weary. I went into the gymnasium where they were doing their exercises and told them they would be fined a week's wages and not considered for selection against Blackburn on the Saturday.

Wayne needed to be careful. He has great qualities about him but they could be swallowed up by a lack of fitness. Look at the way Ronaldo or Giggs looked after themselves. Wayne needed to grasp the nettle. It was not wise for England to give him a week's holiday before Euro 2012 because he might lose his edge. If he missed a couple of weeks for United, it could take him four or five games to get his sharpness back. The Ukraine game was over a month after his last game for us.

He would receive no leniency from me. I would hammer him for any drop in condition. It was quite simple – he wouldn't play. That's the way I always dealt with fitness issues, regardless of the player involved, and I saw no reason to change in the final years of my career.

Wayne had a gift for producing great moments in games. In my final year, when he was left out a few times, and replaced in games, I felt he was struggling to get by people and had lost some of his old thrust. But he was capable of making extraordinary contributions. That pass to Van Persie in the win over Aston Villa that secured the title for us was marvellous, as was his overhead kick against Man City. Those flashes guaranteed his profile. But as time wore on, I felt he struggled more and more to do it for 90 minutes, and he seemed to tire in games.

I took him off in that Aston Villa game because Villa were

a very fast young side, full of running, and their substitute was running past Wayne. He came into my office the day after we won the League and asked away. He wasn't happy with being left out for some games and subbed in others. His agent Paul Stretford phoned David Gill with the same message.

All players are different. Some are happy to stay at the same club their whole careers; others need fresh challenges, as Van Persie felt when he joined us from Arsenal. The urge to fight and flourish would not be extinguished in Wayne. I left him to discuss his future with David Moyes, hoping to see many more great performances from him at Old Trafford.

twenty-five

THE LAST CAMPAIGN

WE were hardly strangers to majestic individual talent, but it took us a while to understand just how good Robin van Persie is. The quality of his runs was not immediately apparent to even our cleverest players. Even Paul Scholes and Michael Carrick, two of the best passers I ever had, had trouble at first picking up the speed of his movements.

Robin was the leading light of my final season as Manchester United manager, in which we were the first team to win 25 of their first 30 top-flight fixtures. The prize at the end of it was the club's 20th League title. We regained the Premier League trophy from Manchester City with four matches still to play. Van Persie was my final major transfer buy and his goals, some of them spectacular, brought an extra Cantona-esque quality to an already very good side.

If we had a bad habit going into the 2012–13 season, it was overpassing in the middle of the pitch: players circulating the ball to acquire a feel of it. With Van Persie, we learned in time, you needed to look for that early pass to split the opposition defence. Until we grasped those possibilities, we could not make the most of Robin's marvellous mobility and killer instinct.

But we learned the lesson in time to make it pay. If Wayne Rooney received possession in an attacking midfield position, he could be sure Van Persie would be on the move, hunting, spearing into gaps. Robin was exactly what I wanted him to be. His pre-season with Arsenal had consisted of 21 minutes' playing time against Cologne, in Germany, so his match fitness was slightly lacking. The right type of conditioning was already there but we needed to get him into a match-fit state. I was deeply impressed with him from the start.

I said to Robin quite early: 'Don't be afraid to instruct the other players. You were the leader at Arsenal and if you don't get fed, get into them.' He was quieter than I expected, but with a vicious left foot that would freeze goalkeepers with its force. People asked why I allowed him to take corners as a centre-forward. He would take them from the right-hand side, not the left, when he would be in the penalty box. The answer is that his corner-taking from the right was terrific. Howard Wilkinson remarked to me that season that a study he had overseen had showed a decrease in the number of goals from set pieces. Yet we had scored ten from corners in the first half of 2011–12.

The existing squad didn't see Robin as any kind of outsider: an Arsenal player creeping onto their territory. Mine were a very welcoming bunch who asked only that the new arrival commit himself to the cause and respect the traditions of our dressing room. I always remember Verón arriving at the club and all the players leaving the training session to shake his hand. They were always good like that. Perhaps the greeting is always warmest for the player who might win you a tight game, an indispensable asset at the very highest level.

Like everyone in the business, I had been reading that Van Persie's contract was about to expire, but I felt sure Arsenal would reach a deal to stop him leaving. Towards the end of the 2011–12 season, however, I sensed increasingly that he would not be staying in north London.

His agent contacted us. By then he had already been talking to Man City, but the message was that Robin would be very, very interested in having a discussion with us. Eventually City were advised that he would not be joining them, so it appeared to be between us and Juventus; the club had, I gathered, offered him an immense salary to move to Turin.

My thinking was: there are two reasons why a player wants to move. 1. For the glory, and 2. For the money. I could see why he might have wanted to join Juventus – a fine team – for an astronomical reward. The package we could offer was good enough to show him how much we respected him. Our invitation was backed up with great enthusiasm.

Next, we began talking to Arsenal about a possible transfer fee. David Gill phoned Ivan Gazidis, the Arsenal chief executive, a number of times, starting in April, but was told that Arsenal believed they could persuade him to sign a new deal. This carried on for a while until David suggested I should call Arsène directly as he would clearly have the final say on any transfer. By then it had become apparent the boy was leaving.

Arsène's attitude, understandably, was: why should we sell to Manchester United when we could get £30 million off Man City or Juventus? My response was to point out that the player had no desire to go to our Manchester rivals. Arsène's counter-argument was that Robin's view of it might change if City made him a further offer he could not refuse.

It was certainly possible.

These discussions, I should say, were amicable. There was no hint of hostility. We were two experienced managers confronting reality. The sticking point was that Arsène hoped to receive £30 million or more for his best player. It continued to drag on for several weeks, during which time I phoned Arsène two or three more times.

In time we all arrived at the point where Arsenal knew Robin was not going to re-sign and accepted that. Their options were Juventus or United. Arsenal were trying to sell him abroad, but the player only wanted to join us. My understanding is that Van Persie sat down with Arsène and told him United was his preferred destination. Our offer, from David Gill to Gazidis, was £20 million. I warned Arsène that we would never get to £25 million.

Arsène was incredulous. He could not believe that Manchester United would refuse to stretch to £25 million for such a player.

I told him again: I wouldn't go to £25 million. Arsène asked what my best offer would be. Answer: £22 million. The reply was that Arsenal would take £22.5 million and a further £1.5 million if we won the Champions League or Premier League during the period of his contract.

Deal done.

My intuition was that Arsène was relieved not to be selling Van Persie to Man City, who had already taken Kolo Touré, Gaël Clichy, Emmanuel Adebayor and Samir Nasri from his team. Perhaps he is not a fan of City's ownership model. And although we had many battles over the years, I think he respected the way Manchester United was run. He said that to me on occasions. I always remember Arsène saying to me about Van Persie: 'You don't realise what a good player you're getting.'

I thought of Cantona and Ronaldo and Giggs. But Arsène was right. Robin's movement and the timing of runs were mesmerising. He was also blessed with a formidable physique.

Van Persie took a lower, but still fantastic, wage from us to come to a place where he believed he could be most successful. At his unveiling he said his inner child had been 'screaming for United'. He told me later that in Holland every kid dreams of playing for Man United.

He knew I had been to see him when he was 16. Arsenal beat us to him when he was emerging as a star at Feyenoord but he stressed what a dream it was for Dutch kids to wear the United crest. He was impressed with the youth of our team. We had Giggs and Scholes but we also had Chicharito and the two Da Silvas, Evans, Jones and Smalling, Welbeck. Carrick, at 31, was having his best-ever season for us. It dawns on some players, when they perform at their best, just how important they are to the team, and in turn it makes them grow, as it did with Carrick.

Robin knew he was coming to a settled club. City had been terrific the previous season, but you would not call them a settled organisation. There was always an issue, with someone setting off fireworks or falling out with the manager; Tévez wanting to play golf in Argentina. City had won the League largely through the efforts of four top performers: Yaya Touré, Sergio Agüero, Vincent Kompany and Joe Hart. Plus David Silva for the first half of the season, though he trailed away somewhat after Christmas.

I say this all the time about strikers. Cantona, Andy Cole: if they are not scoring they think they are never going to score again. In his brief dry spell in the March of that season, Van Persie wasn't playing as well and it affected him. But from the minute he scored against Stoke on 14 April, he was on fire again.

Over the years I witnessed some immortal Manchester United goals. Cantona treated the crowd to two or three wonderful chipped finishes. Rooney's bicycle kick against City took some beating. The execution was incredible. It's not as if that unforgettable overhead finish was delivered from the six-yard line. He was 14 yards from goal. It also took a deflection as he was running in. Nani's cross veered off a City player, so Wayne was forced to make an amazing mid-air adjustment. That was the best one, for my money.

But Van Persie's against Aston Villa in the 3–0 win that secured us the title on 22 April was special too: an over-the-shoulder volley from a long drilled ball by Rooney. A normal player would try that trick a hundred times in training and score once. Van Persie could do it regularly. Shoulder down, head down, eyes down, through the ball. The same mastery of technique brought him a goal of similar quality for Arsenal against Everton. He was a wonderful signing who finished the season with 26 League goals: 12 at home and 14 away.

He struck 17 times with his left foot and eight with his right, plus once from a header. Those figures earned him the Golden Boot, awarded to the Premier League's top scorer, for the second consecutive year.

At the other end of the age scale, we continued to place our faith in youth. Nick Powell, who joined in July 2012, had been in our sights since November 2011. Crewe brought him into their team at outside-left when he was 17 and still a bit gangly. Our academy staff had drawn a ring round his name and we scouted for him regularly. Jim Lawlor went to look at him and said he was interesting, though he was not sure what his best position would be and thought he might be a wee bit laidback.

So I sent out Martin to watch him twice. Martin's view was that he definitely had something but was not the full package yet. Then Mick Phelan went to examine him in a couple of fixtures. Finally it was my turn. Crewe v. Aldershot. After five minutes in the stands, I told Mick, 'He's a player. Mick, he's a player.' It was his touch on the ball and his vision.

At one point in the game I saw he got a half-run on the opposition's defence, had a wee look over his shoulder and just lofted the ball to the centre-forward to have a shot on goal. Then he showed us a header, then a turn of pace. Coming away I said to Mick: 'I'm going to phone Dario Gradi,' now director of football at Crewe.

'I see you were at the game yesterday,' said Dario.

'The boy Powell,' I said. 'Now don't get carried away. What's your ballpark figure?'

Dario said: 'Six million.'

Laughing, I told him where to go. But we constructed a potential deal in that direction with add-ons for first-team and England appearances. Powell was not told until after that season's play-offs. He is an absolute certainty to be in the England team one day. He could play anywhere: off the front, even through. He's quick as hell, has two good feet and shoots from outside the box. In the winter of 2012 he picked up a virus and his girlfriend had a nasty car accident. He's quite a detached figure – good at switching off – but he's a player, believe me.

Shinji Kagawa was another good catch that summer. We elected not to move for him after his first season in German football, because sometimes a player rises a notch and you want to be sure he can sustain it. He played in a very good Dortmund team, which I considered capable of winning the 2013 Champions League. In the event they reached the final but lost to Bayern Munich. The first thing I noticed was Shinji's sharp football brain. Mick and I flew to Berlin for the German cup final in the summer of 2012 and I found myself sitting next to the Mayor of Dortmund and his wife. He was wearing trainers. Angela Merkel was nearby, along with Joachim Löw, the German coach. Introduced to Mrs Merkel, the German chancellor, I thought to myself: 'My word, I've come a long way.'

There was no way I could hide in that seat – but everyone knew I was going anyway.

That summer the Glazers were perfectly happy to go for Van Persie or Robert Lewandowski and Kagawa. In many of our greatest phases we could call on four fantastic strikers. Making sure they all felt valued could be problematic. It required a range of diplomatic skills. Dortmund, however, refused to sell Lewandowski, who has a wonderful physique and has good lines of running.

The other signing was Alexander Büttner, from Dutch club Vitesse Arnhem. We had allowed Fábio to go to Queens Park Rangers on loan and we had a couple of young left-backs with potential. But we needed experience in that area and backup for Evra. Büttner was flagged up. He was always taking the ball, having shots, taking on defenders: a bargain at 2.5 million euros. He was an aggressive boy, determined, quickish and a good crosser of the ball.

There were times in the first half of that season when we couldn't have defended a sandcastle. We conceded way too many times for my liking before tightening up from January onwards. The goalkeeping position was complicated. De Gea developed a tooth infection and needed an operation to remove his two rear molars. He missed a couple of games on that account and Anders Lindegaard didn't do anything wrong in the No. 1 spot. He had a good game at Galatasary and against West Ham. My message to De Gea was that I needed to be fair to Anders. But after our narrow 4–3 win at Reading on 1 December, De Gea came back in and did well throughout the second half of the season, especially in the 1–1 draw at Real Madrid in February, where he was brilliant.

I still had high hopes for Javier Hernández. The issue with Chicharito was freshness. For three seasons in a row he played all summer with his country. Despite that we cooperated well with Mexico. The presidents of their FA and Olympic association came over, with their coaches, for a meeting with me. I showed them the medical file. Under discussion was whether he could play in two World Cup qualifiers as well as the Olympics.

Chicharito said, 'I'd rather miss the other two games and play in the Olympics because I think we'll win it.' I thought he was joking.

He went on, 'If we don't get Brazil in the quarter-finals, we'll win it.'

Meanwhile we had invested heavily in a marvellous new medical centre for Carrington. We can now do everything on site, apart from operations. We had a chiropodist, dentist, scanners, everything. The benefit was that, apart from having it all on site, injuries would not become instant public knowledge. In the past we might send a player to hospital and rumours would flash round the city. This told you we weren't standing still. It might have been one of our best buys.

A major incident from that season requires a mention: the allegation, later dismissed by the authorities, that referee Mark Clattenburg had used racist language against Chelsea players in our 3–2 victory at Stamford Bridge on 28 October. A word about the game, first: against Di Matteo's Chelsea we needed to work out how we would operate against Juan Mata, Oscar and Eden Hazard. Those three were hammering teams and turning on the style. The two sitting midfielders, Ramires and Mikel, were bombing on. We elected to load the right side to attack the areas they had vacated by attacking us, and squeeze Mata's space.

It was a thrilling game until the shenanigans at the end of the match. When Fernando Torres was sent off, Steve Holland, one of Di Matteo's assistants, blamed me. I looked at him, bemused. Mike Dean, the fourth official, could make no sense of Holland's accusation. Torres should already have been sent off in the first half for a tackle on Cleverley.

When Hernández scored the winning goal, half a seat came on and hit Carrick on the foot, along with lighters and coins.

I still wonder whether the Clattenburg allegation was a smokescreen to obscure the crowd trouble.

Twenty minutes after the game, I went in with my staff for a drink, and in that wee room were Bruce Buck, the Chelsea chairman, Ron Gourlay, the chief executive, Di Matteo and his wife. You could sense an atmosphere. Something wasn't right. We stood in the doorway and thought it wise to leave them to it.

The food was covered and the wine was uncorked. They said, 'Help yourselves,' and left the room.

My own staff had seen Mikel fly into the referee's room with John Terry and Di Matteo. Whoever told Mikel that Clattenburg had said something inflammatory was making a big call. It was also a big move by Chelsea to inform the press pretty much straight away that an alleged incident had been reported. A lawyer might have sat back and said, 'Let's wait until tomorrow.'

The Branislav Ivanović sending-off in that game was perfectly straightforward. Torres went down easily but Evans did catch him. When you see where Clattenburg was, you can why he sent him off for simulation. He took one step, then went down. A toe is enough to fell a player moving at speed, but Torres did go over softly. I've no idea why Holland thought I had forced Clattenburg to send him off. A few days later, Di Matteo announced that I had too much power with referees.

I had run-ins with match officials all my life. I was sent off eight times as a player. I was sent to the stands three or four times as a manager in Scotland. I was fined so many times in England. I always had disputes of one sort or another. But I called it as I saw it. I never went out of my way to drop a referee in the soup.

There is no way, in my mind, that a top referee would be racist to a player. I called Mark Clattenburg and said, 'I'm just sorry we are the other team involved in this.' I was poised for someone in authority to bring us into the inquiry, which fortunately never happened. I had no knowledge of it until we boarded the plane back to Manchester. The FA took a hell of a long time to reach the decision that Mark was innocent. It could have been concluded in two days.

From January 2013 we really motored on in the League, piling pressure on Man City all the way. For me, knowing I was standing down, the sense of release and relief was delayed until the night we beat Aston Villa to win the title. We were going to win it anyway, but to finish the job in April, on our own ground, was immensely comforting. I would go out with a bang. I continued to make my team talks and prepare for games properly. The professionalism of Manchester United remained intact.

The only disappointment, of course, was losing our Champions League round of 16 tie to Real Madrid, in a game that featured a ludicrous sending-off for Nani by Cüneyt Çakir, the Turkish referee, for an innocuous challenge. In Spain in the first leg we had been terrific, weathering a 20-minute storm at the start of the match. We could have won by six. I held no fear of facing José Mourinho's team again at home. Our preparation was perfect. We devised a good plan for the game, our energy was terrific and we forced three or four great saves from their goalkeeper. David de Gea barely made a stop.

Nani was sent off in the 56th minute for leaping to meet the ball and making slight contact with Álvaro Arbeloa, and for ten minutes we were up against it. We were in shock. On came Modrić for Real to equalise Sergio Ramos's own goal and then Ronaldo finished us in the 69th minute. But we might have scored five in the last ten minutes. It was an absolute disaster.

I was particularly upset that night and gave the post-match press conference a miss. If we had beaten Real Madrid, there would have been every reason to imagine we could win the competition. I left Wayne out of that second leg because we needed someone to get on top of Alonso and play off him. The Ji-Sung Park of earlier years would have been perfect for that job. Andrea Pirlo's passing rate for Milan had been 75 per cent. When we played them with Ji-Sung Park in the hounding role we reduced Pirlo's strike rate to 25 per cent. There was no better player in our squad to keep on top of Alonso than Danny Welbeck. Yes, we sacrificed Wayne's possible goal-scoring, but we knew we had to choke Alonso and exploit that gain.

Ronaldo was wonderful in those two games. In the Madrid leg he made his way into our dressing room to sit with our players. You could tell he missed them. After the Old Trafford game, as I was watching the video of the sending-off, he came in to sympathise. The Real players knew the sending-off had been absurd. Mesut Özil confessed to one of our players that José's team felt they had got out of jail. Cristiano declined to celebrate his goal, which is just as well, because I would have strangled him. There were no issues with him at all. He's a very nice boy.

My final thought on Man City losing the title to us was that they couldn't call on enough players who understood the significance of what they had achieved by winning the League for the first time for 44 years. Evidently it was enough for some of them to have beaten Manchester United in a title race. They settled down into a sense of relief. Retaining a title is the next hard step and City were not in the right state of mind to defend what they had won on the most dramatic closing day in Premier League history.

When I won the League for the first time in 1993, I didn't want my team to slacken off. The thought appalled me. I was determined to keep advancing, to strengthen our hold on power. I told that 1993 side: 'Some people, when they have a holiday, just want to go to Saltcoats, twenty-five miles along the coast from Glasgow. Some people don't even want to do that. They're happy to stay at home or watch the birds and the ducks float by in the park. And some want to go to the moon.

'It's about people's ambitions.'

CAREER RECORD

SENIOR PLAYING CAREER

1958-60 Queen's Park
Games 31
Goals: 15

1960-64 St Johnstone
Games: 47
Goals: 21

1964-67 Dunfermline Athletic
Games: 131
Goals: 88

Played for Scottish League (0) v. Football League (3) at Hampden Park, 15 March 1967.

Scottish FA XI summer tour 13 May–15 June 1967: scored 10 goals in seven appearances against Israel, Hong Kong Select, Australia (three matches), Auckland XI, Vancouver All Stars.

1967-69 Rangers
Games: 66
Goals: 35

Played for Scottish League (2) v. Irish League (0) in Belfast, 6 September 1967. Scored one goal.

1969-73 Falkirk
Games: 122
Goals: 49

1973-74 Ayr United
Games: 22
Goals: 10

Total
Games: 415
Goals: 218
(Scottish League, Scottish Cup, Scottish League Cup and European competitions only)

MANAGERIAL CAREER

JUNE-OCTOBER 1974 East Stirlingshire

OCTOBER 1974-MAY 1978 St Mirren
Finished fourth in Division One in 1975–76; Division One champions 1976–77; finished eighth in Premier Division 1977–78.

1978-86 Aberdeen

Season 1978–79
SCOTTISH PREMIER DIVISION

	P	W	D	L	F	A	Pts
Home	18	9	4	5	38	16	22
Away	18	4	10	4	21	20	18
Total	36	13	14	9	59	36	40

Final position: fourth
Scottish Cup: semi-final
Scottish League Cup: finalists
European Cup Winners' Cup: second round

Season 1979–80
SCOTTISH PREMIER DIVISION

	P	W	D	L	F	A	Pts
Home	18	10	4	4	30	18	24
Away	18	9	6	3	38	18	24
Total	36	19	10	7	68	36	48

Final position: champions
Scottish Cup: semi-final
Scottish League Cup: finalists
UEFA Cup: first round

Season 1980–81
SCOTTISH PREMIER DIVISION

	P	W	D	L	F	A	Pts
Home	18	11	4	3	39	16	26
Away	18	8	7	3	22	10	23
Total	36	19	11	6	61	26	49

Final position: runners-up
Scottish Cup: fourth round
Scottish League Cup: fourth round
European Champion Clubs' Cup: second round
Drybrough Cup: winners

Season 1981–82
SCOTTISH PREMIER DIVISION

	P	W	D	L	F	A	Pts
Home	18	12	4	2	36	15	28
Away	18	11	3	4	35	14	25
Total	36	23	7	6	71	29	53

Final position: runners-up
Scottish Cup: winners
Scottish League Cup: semi-final
UEFA Cup: quarter-final

Season 1982–83
SCOTTISH PREMIER DIVISION

	P	W	D	L	F	A	Pts
Home	18	14	0	4	46	12	28
Away	18	11	5	2	30	12	27
Total	36	25	5	6	76	24	55

Final position: third
Scottish Cup: winners
Scottish League Cup: quarter-final
European Cup Winners' Cup: winners

Season 1983–84
SCOTTISH PREMIER DIVISION

	P	W	D	L	F	A	Pts
Home	18	14	3	1	46	12	31
Away	18	11	4	3	32	9	26
Total	36	25	7	4	78	21	57

Final position: champions
Scottish Cup: winners
Scottish League Cup: semi-final
European Cup Winners' Cup: semi-final
European Super Cup: winners

Season 1984–85
SCOTTISH PREMIER DIVISION

	P	W	D	L	F	A	Pts
Home	18	13	4	1	49	13	30
Away	18	14	1	3	40	13	29
Total	36	27	5	4	89	26	59

Final position: champions
Scottish Cup: semi-final
Scottish League Cup: second round
European Champion Clubs' Cup: first round

Season 1985–86
SCOTTISH PREMIER DIVISION

	P	W	D	L	F	A	Pts
Home	18	11	4	3	38	15	26
Away	18	5	8	5	24	16	18
Total	36	16	12	8	62	31	44

Final position: fourth
Scottish Cup: winners
Scottish League Cup: winners
European Champion Clubs' Cup: quarter-final

Season 1986–87 (August–1 November 1986)
SCOTTISH PREMIER DIVISION

	P	W	D	L	F	A
Home	7	4	2	1	12	3
Away	8	3	3	2	13	11
Total	15	7	5	3	25	14

Scottish League Cup: fourth round
European Cup Winners' Cup: first round

SUMMARY

	P	W	D	L	F	A
League	303	174	76	53	589	243
Scottish Cup	42	30	8	4	89	30
League Cup	63	42	9	12	148	45
Europe	47	23	12	12	78	51
Drybrough Cup	4	3	0	1	10	5
Overall total	459	272	105	82	914	374

ABERDEEN'S EUROPEAN CAMPAIGNS DURING ALEX FERGUSON'S MANAGERSHIP

Season 1978–79 Cup Winners' Cup
Round 1 Marek Dupnitsa (Bulgaria) (a) 2–3, (h) 3–0, Agg: 5–3
Round 2 Fortuna Düsseldorf (West Germany) (a) 0–3, (h) 2–0, Agg: 2–3

Season 1979–80 UEFA Cup

Round 1 Eintracht Frankfurt (West Germany) (h) 1–1, (a) 0–1, Agg: 1–2

Season 1980–81 European Cup

Round 1 Austria Memphis (Austria) (h) 1–0, (a) 0–0, Agg: 1–0
Round 2 Liverpool (h) 0–1, (a) 0–4, Agg: 0–5

Season 1981–82 UEFA Cup

Round 1 Ipswich Town (a) 1–1, (h) 3–1, Agg: 4–2
Round 2 Argeş Piteşti (Romania) (h) 3–0, (a) 2–2, Agg: 5–2
Round 3 SV Hamburg (West Germany) (h) 3–2, (a) 1–3, Agg: 4–5

Season 1982–83 Cup Winners' Cup

Preliminary round Sion (Switzerland) (h) 7–0, (a) 4–1, Agg: 11–1
Round 1 Dinamo Tirana (Albania) (h) 1–0, (a) 0–0, Agg: 1–0
Round 2 Lech Poznań (Poland) (h) 2–0, (a) 1–0, Agg: 3–0
Quarter-final Bayern Munich (West Germany) (a) 0–0, (h) 3–2, Agg: 3–2
Semi-final Waterschei (Belgium) (h) 5–1, (a) 0–1, Agg: 5–2
Final (Gothenburg, Sweden) Real Madrid (Spain) 2–1 (aet)

Season 1983–84 Super Cup

SV Hamburg (West Germany) (a) 0–0, (h) 2–0, Agg: 2–0

Cup Winners' Cup

Round 1 Akranes (Iceland) (a) 2–1, (h) 1–1, Agg: 3–2
Round 2 SK Beveren (Belgium) (a) 0–0, (h) 4–1, Agg: 4–1
Quarter-final Újpest Dózsa (Hungary) (a) 0–2, (h) 3–0 (aet), Agg: 3–2
Semi-final Porto (Portugal) (a) 0–1, (h) 0–1, Agg: 0–2

Season 1984–85 European Cup

Round 1 Dinamo Berlin (East Germany) (h) 2–1, (a) 1–2, Agg: 3–3 (Lost 5–4 on penalties)

Season 1985–86 European Cup

Round 1 Akranes (Iceland) (a) 3–1, (h) 4–1, Agg: 7–2

Round 2 Servette (Switzerland) (a) 0–0, (h) 1–0, Agg: 1–0
Quarter-final IFK Gothenburg (Sweden) (h) 2–2, (a) 0–0, Agg: 2–2
(Lost on away-goals rule)

Season 1986–87 Cup Winners' Cup
Round 1 Sion (Switzerland) (h) 2–1, (a) 0–3, Agg: 2–4

HONOURS

EUROPEAN CUP WINNERS' CUP

Winners: 1983

SCOTTISH PREMIER DIVISION

Champions: 1980, 1984, 1985

SCOTTISH CUP

Winners: 1982, 1983, 1984, 1986

SCOTTISH LEAGUE CUP

Winners: 1985–86

EUROPEAN SUPER CUP

Winners: 1983

DRYBROUGH CUP

Winners: 1980

OCTOBER 1985–JUNE 1986 Scotland

FULL INTERNATIONALS

	P	W	D	L	F	A
Home	3	2	1	0	5	0
Away	7	1	3	3	3	5
Overall	10	3	4	3	8	5

RESULTS

October 1985	East Germany (friendly, home) 0–0
November 1985	Australia (World Cup play-off, home) 2–0
December 1985	Australia (World Cup play-off, away) 0–0
January 1986	Israel (friendly, away) 1–0
March 1986	Romania (friendly, home) 3–0
April 1986	England (Rous Cup, away) 1–2
April 1986	Netherlands (friendly, away) 0–0
June 1986	Denmark (World Cup, Mexico City) 0–1
June 1986	West Germany (World Cup, Querétaro) 1–2
June 1986	Uruguay (World Cup, Mexico City) 0–0

1986–2013 Manchester United

Season 1986–87
THE TODAY LEAGUE DIVISION ONE
United's record up to Alex Ferguson's arrival

	P	W	D	L	F	A	Pts
Home	7	3	1	3	12	8	10
Away	6	0	3	3	4	8	3
Total	13	3	4	6	16	16	13

League Cup: third round

United's record under Alex Ferguson

	P	W	D	L	F	A	Pts
Home	14	10	2	2	26	10	32
Away	15	1	8	6	10	19	11
Total	29	11	10	8	36	29	43
Overall total	42	14	14	14	52	45	56

Final position: 11th
FA Cup: fourth round

Season 1987–88
BARCLAYS LEAGUE DIVISION ONE

	P	W	D	L	F	A	Pts
Home	20	14	5	1	41	17	47
Away	20	9	7	4	30	21	34
Total	40	23	12	5	71	38	81

Final position: runners-up
FA Cup: fifth round
League Cup: fifth round

Season 1988–89
BARCLAYS LEAGUE DIVISION ONE

	P	W	D	L	F	A	Pts
Home	19	10	5	4	27	13	35
Away	19	3	7	9	18	22	16
Total	38	13	12	13	45	35	51

Final position: 11th
FA Cup: sixth round
League Cup: third round

Season 1989–90
BARCLAYS LEAGUE DIVISION ONE

	P	W	D	L	F	A	Pts
Home	19	8	6	5	26	14	30
Away	19	5	3	11	20	33	18
Total	38	13	9	16	46	47	48

Final position: 13th
FA Cup: winners
League Cup: third round

Season 1990–91
BARCLAYS LEAGUE DIVISION ONE

	P	W	D	L	F	A	Pts
Home	19	11	4	4	34	17	37
Away	19	5	8	6	24	28	23
Total	38	16	12	10	58	45	59*

*One point deducted

Final position: sixth
FA Cup: fifth round
League Cup: finalists
European Cup Winners' Cup: winners
FA Charity Shield: joint winners

Season 1991–92
BARCLAYS LEAGUE DIVISION ONE

	P	W	D	L	F	A	Pts
Home	21	12	7	2	34	13	43
Away	21	9	8	4	29	20	35
Total	42	21	15	6	63	33	78

Final position: runners-up
FA Cup: fourth round
League Cup: winners
European Cup Winners' Cup: second round
European Super Cup: winners

Season 1992–93
FA PREMIER LEAGUE

	P	W	D	L	F	A	Pts
Home	21	14	5	2	39	14	47
Away	21	10	7	4	28	17	37
Total	42	24	12	6	67	31	84

Final position: champions
FA Cup: fifth round
League Cup: third round
UEFA Cup: first round

1992–93 FA PREMIER LEAGUE

| | P | Home | | | | | | Away | | | | | Pts |
		W	D	L	F	A	W	D	L	F	A	
1. **Manchester United**	42	14	5	2	39	14	10	7	4	28	17	84
2. Aston Villa	42	13	5	3	36	16	8	6	7	21	24	74
3. Norwich City	42	13	6	2	31	19	8	3	10	30	46	72
4. Blackburn Rovers	42	13	4	4	38	18	7	7	7	30	28	71
5. Queens Park Rangers	42	11	5	5	41	32	6	7	8	22	23	63
6. Liverpool	42	13	4	4	41	18	3	7	11	21	37	59
7. Sheffield Wednesday	42	9	8	4	34	26	6	6	9	21	25	59
8. Tottenham Hotspur	42	11	5	5	40	25	5	6	10	20	41	59
9. Manchester City	42	7	8	6	30	25	8	4	9	26	26	57
10. Arsenal	42	8	6	7	25	20	7	5	9	15	18	56
11. Chelsea	42	9	7	5	29	22	5	7	9	22	32	56
12. Wimbledon	42	9	4	8	32	23	5	8	8	24	32	54
13. Everton	42	7	6	8	26	27	8	2	11	27	28	53
14. Sheffield United	42	10	6	5	33	19	4	4	13	21	34	52
15. Coventry City	42	7	4	10	29	28	6	9	6	23	29	52
16. Ipswich Town	42	8	9	4	29	22	4	7	10	21	33	52
17. Leeds United	42	12	8	1	40	17	0	7	14	17	45	51
18. Southampton	42	10	6	5	30	21	3	5	13	24	40	50
19. Oldham Athletic	42	10	6	5	43	30	3	4	14	20	44	49
20. Crystal Palace	42	6	9	6	27	25	5	7	9	21	36	49
21. Middlesbrough	42	8	5	8	33	27	3	6	12	21	48	44
22. Nottingham Forest	42	6	4	11	17	25	4	6	11	24	37	40

Season 1993–94
FA CARLING PREMIERSHIP

	P	W	D	L	F	A	Pts
Home	21	14	6	1	39	13	48
Away	21	13	5	3	41	25	44
Total	42	27	11	4	80	38	92

Final position: champions
FA Cup: winners
League Cup: finalists
European Champion Clubs' Cup: second round
FA Charity Shield: winners

1993–94 FA CARLING PREMIERSHIP

		Home					Away					
	P	W	D	L	F	A	W	D	L	F	A	Pts
1. **Manchester United**	42	14	6	1	39	13	13	5	3	41	25	92
2. Blackburn Rovers	42	14	5	2	31	11	11	4	6	32	25	84
3. Newcastle United	42	14	4	3	51	14	9	4	8	31	27	77
4. Arsenal	42	10	8	3	25	15	8	9	4	28	13	71
5. Leeds United	42	13	6	2	37	18	5	10	6	28	21	70
6. Wimbledon	42	12	5	4	35	21	6	6	9	21	32	65
7. Sheffield Wednesday	42	10	7	4	48	24	6	9	6	28	30	64
8. Liverpool	42	12	4	5	33	23	5	5	11	26	32	60
9. Queens Park Rangers	42	8	7	6	32	29	8	5	8	30	32	60
10. Aston Villa	42	8	5	8	23	18	7	7	7	23	32	57
11. Coventry City	42	9	7	5	23	17	5	7	9	20	28	56
12. Norwich City	42	4	9	8	26	29	8	8	5	39	32	53
13. West Ham United	42	6	7	8	26	31	7	6	8	21	27	52
14. Chelsea	42	11	5	5	31	20	2	7	12	18	33	51
15. Tottenham Hotspur	42	4	8	9	29	33	7	4	10	25	26	45
16. Manchester City	42	6	10	5	24	22	3	8	10	14	27	45
17. Everton	42	8	4	9	26	30	4	4	13	16	33	44
18. Southampton	42	9	2	10	30	31	3	5	13	19	35	43
19. Ipswich Town	42	5	8	8	21	32	4	8	9	14	26	43
20. Sheffield United	42	6	10	5	24	23	2	8	11	18	37	42
21. Oldham Athletic	42	5	8	8	24	33	4	5	12	18	35	40
22. Swindon Town	42	4	7	10	25	45	1	8	12	22	55	30

Season 1994–95
FA CARLING PREMIERSHIP

	P	W	D	L	F	A	Pts
Home	21	16	4	1	42	4	52
Away	21	10	6	5	35	24	36
Total	42	26	10	6	77	28	88

Final position: runners-up
FA Cup: finalists
League Cup: third round
UEFA Champions League: first group phase
FA Charity Shield: winners

Season 1995–96
FA CARLING PREMIERSHIP

	P	W	D	L	F	A	Pts
Home	19	15	4	0	36	9	49
Away	19	10	3	6	37	26	33
Total	38	25	7	6	73	35	82

Final position: champions
FA Cup: winners
League Cup: second round
UEFA Cup: first round

1995–96 FA CARLING PREMIERSHIP

	P		Home					Away				Pts
		W	D	L	F	A	W	D	L	F	A	
1. Manchester United	38	15	4	0	36	9	10	3	6	37	26	82
2. Newcastle United	38	17	1	1	38	9	7	5	7	28	28	78
3. Liverpool	38	14	4	1	46	13	6	7	6	24	21	71
4. Aston Villa	38	11	5	3	32	15	7	4	8	20	20	63
5. Arsenal	38	10	7	2	30	16	7	5	7	19	16	63
6. Everton	38	10	5	4	35	19	7	5	7	29	25	61
7. Blackburn Rovers	38	14	2	3	44	19	4	5	10	17	28	61
8. Tottenham Hotspur	38	9	5	5	26	19	7	8	4	24	19	61
9. Nottingham Forest	38	11	6	2	29	17	4	7	8	21	37	58
10. West Ham United	38	9	5	5	25	21	5	4	10	18	31	51
11. Chelsea	38	7	7	5	30	22	5	7	7	16	22	50
12. Middlesbrough	38	8	3	8	27	27	3	7	9	8	23	43
13. Leeds United	38	8	3	8	21	21	4	4	11	19	36	43
14. Wimbledon	38	5	6	8	27	33	5	5	9	28	37	41
15. Sheffield Wednesday	38	7	5	7	30	31	3	5	11	18	30	40
16. Coventry City	38	6	7	6	21	23	2	7	10	21	37	38
17. Southampton	38	7	7	5	21	18	2	4	13	13	34	38
18. Manchester City	38	7	7	5	21	19	2	4	13	12	39	38
19. Queens Park Rangers	38	6	5	8	25	26	3	1	15	13	31	33
20. Bolton Wanderers	38	5	4	10	16	31	3	1	15	23	40	29

Season 1996–97
FA CARLING PREMIERSHIP

	P	W	D	L	F	A	Pts
Home	19	12	5	2	38	17	41
Away	19	9	7	3	38	27	34
Total	38	21	12	5	76	44	75

Final position: champions
FA Cup: fourth round
League Cup: fourth round
UEFA Champions League: semi-final
FA Charity Shield: winners

1996–97 FA CARLING PREMIERSHIP

		Home					Away					
	P	W	D	L	F	A	W	D	L	F	A	Pts
1. **Manchester United**	38	12	5	2	38	17	9	7	3	38	27	75
2. Newcastle United	38	13	3	3	54	20	6	8	5	19	20	68
3. Arsenal	38	10	5	4	36	18	9	6	4	26	14	68
4. Liverpool	38	10	6	3	38	19	9	5	5	24	18	68
5. Aston Villa	38	11	5	3	27	13	6	5	8	20	21	61
6. Chelsea	38	9	8	2	33	22	7	3	9	25	33	59
7. Sheffield Wednesday	38	8	10	1	25	16	6	5	8	25	35	57
8. Wimbledon	38	9	6	4	28	21	6	5	8	21	25	56
9. Leicester City	38	7	5	7	22	26	5	6	8	24	28	47
10. Tottenham Hotspur	38	8	4	7	19	17	5	3	11	25	34	46
11. Leeds United	38	7	7	5	15	13	4	6	9	13	25	46
12. Derby County	38	8	6	5	25	22	3	7	9	20	36	46
13. Blackburn Rovers	38	8	4	7	28	23	1	11	7	14	20	42
14. West Ham United	38	7	6	6	27	25	3	6	10	12	23	42
15. Everton	38	7	4	8	24	22	3	8	8	20	35	42
16. Southampton	38	6	7	6	32	24	4	4	11	18	32	41
17. Coventry City	38	4	8	7	19	23	5	6	8	19	31	41
18. Sunderland	38	7	6	6	20	18	3	4	12	15	35	40
19. Middlesbrough*	38	8	5	6	34	25	2	7	10	17	35	39
20. Nottingham Forest	38	3	9	7	15	27	3	7	9	16	32	34

* three points deducted

Season 1997–98
FA CARLING PREMIERSHIP

	P	W	D	L	F	A	Pts
Home	19	13	4	2	42	9	43
Away	19	10	4	5	31	17	34
Total	38	23	8	7	73	26	77

Final position: runners-up

FA Cup: fifth round

League Cup: third round

UEFA Champions League: quarter-final

FA Charity Shield: winners

Season 1998–99
FA CARLING PREMIERSHIP

	P	W	D	L	F	A	Pts
Home	19	14	4	1	45	18	46
Away	19	8	9	2	35	19	33
Total	38	22	13	3	80	37	79

Final position: champions
FA Cup: winners
League Cup: fifth round
UEFA Champions League: winners

1998–99 FA CARLING PREMIERSHIP

			Home					Away				
	P	W	D	L	F	A	W	D	L	F	A	Pts
1. **Manchester United**	38	14	4	1	45	18	8	9	2	35	19	79
2. Arsenal	38	14	5	0	34	5	8	7	4	25	12	78
3. Chelsea	38	12	6	1	29	13	8	9	2	28	17	75
4. Leeds United	38	12	5	2	32	9	6	8	5	30	25	67
5. West Ham United	38	11	3	5	32	26	5	6	8	14	27	57
6. Aston Villa	38	10	3	6	33	28	5	7	7	18	18	55
7. Liverpool	38	10	5	4	44	24	5	4	10	24	25	54
8. Derby County	38	8	7	4	22	19	5	6	8	18	26	52
9. Middlesbrough	38	7	9	3	25	18	5	6	8	23	36	51
10. Leicester City	38	7	6	6	25	25	5	7	7	15	21	49
11. Tottenham Hotspur	38	7	7	5	28	26	4	7	8	19	24	47
12. Sheffield Wednesday	38	7	5	7	20	15	6	2	11	21	27	46
13. Newcastle United	38	7	6	6	26	25	4	7	8	22	29	46
14. Everton	38	6	8	5	22	12	5	2	12	20	35	43
15. Coventry City	38	8	6	5	26	21	3	3	13	13	30	42
16. Wimbledon	38	7	7	5	22	21	3	5	11	18	42	42
17. Southampton	38	9	4	6	29	26	2	4	13	8	38	41
18. Charlton Athletic	38	4	7	8	20	20	4	5	10	21	36	36
19. Blackburn Rovers	38	6	5	8	21	24	1	9	9	17	28	35
20. Nottingham Forest	38	3	7	9	18	31	4	2	13	17	38	30

Season 1999–2000
FA CARLING PREMIERSHIP

	P	W	D	L	F	A	Pts
Home	19	15	4	0	59	16	49
Away	19	13	3	3	38	29	42
Total	38	28	7	3	97	45	91

Final position: champions
FA Cup: did not enter
League Cup: third round
UEFA Champions League: quarter-final
Intercontinental Cup: winners
FIFA Club World Cup: third in first-round group

1999–2000 FA CARLING PREMIERSHIP

		Home					Away					
	P	W	D	L	F	A	W	D	L	F	A	Pts
1. **Manchester United**	38	15	4	0	59	16	13	3	3	38	29	91
2. Arsenal	38	14	3	2	42	17	8	4	7	31	26	73
3. Leeds United	38	12	2	5	29	18	9	4	6	29	25	69
4. Liverpool	38	11	4	4	28	13	8	6	5	23	17	67
5. Chelsea	38	12	5	2	35	12	6	6	7	18	22	65
6. Aston Villa	38	8	8	3	23	12	7	5	7	23	23	58
7. Sunderland	38	10	6	3	28	17	6	4	9	29	39	58
8. Leicester City	38	10	3	6	31	24	6	4	9	24	31	55
9. West Ham United	38	11	5	3	32	23	4	5	10	20	30	55
10. Tottenham Hotspur	38	10	3	6	40	26	5	5	9	17	23	53
11. Newcastle United	38	10	5	4	42	20	4	5	10	21	34	52
12. Middlesbrough	38	8	5	6	23	26	6	5	8	23	26	52
13. Everton	38	7	9	3	36	21	5	5	9	23	28	50
14. Coventry City	38	12	1	6	38	22	0	7	12	9	32	44
15. Southampton	38	8	4	7	26	22	4	4	11	19	40	44
16. Derby County	38	6	3	10	22	25	3	8	8	22	32	38
17. Bradford City	38	6	8	5	26	29	3	1	15	12	39	36
18. Wimbledon	38	6	7	6	30	28	1	5	13	16	46	33
19. Sheffield Wednesday	38	6	3	10	21	23	2	4	13	17	47	31
20. Watford	38	5	4	10	24	31	1	2	16	11	46	24

Season 2000–01
FA CARLING PREMIERSHIP

	P	W	D	L	F	A	Pts
Home	19	15	2	2	49	12	47
Away	19	9	6	4	30	19	33
Total	38	24	8	6	79	31	80

Final position: champions
FA Cup: fourth round
League Cup: fourth round
UEFA Champions League: quarter-final

2000–01 FA CARLING PREMIERSHIP

		Home					Away					
	P	W	D	L	F	A	W	D	L	F	A	Pts
1. **Manchester United**	38	15	2	2	49	12	9	6	4	30	19	80
2. Arsenal	38	15	3	1	45	13	5	7	7	18	25	70
3. Liverpool	38	13	4	2	40	14	7	5	7	31	25	69
4. Leeds United	38	11	3	5	36	21	9	5	5	28	22	68
5. Ipswich Town	38	11	5	3	31	15	9	1	9	26	27	66
6. Chelsea	38	13	3	3	44	20	4	7	8	24	25	61
7. Sunderland	38	9	7	3	24	16	6	5	8	22	25	57
8. Aston Villa	38	8	8	3	27	20	5	7	7	19	23	54
9. Charlton Athletic	38	11	5	3	31	19	3	5	11	19	38	52
10. Southampton	38	11	2	6	27	22	3	8	8	13	26	52
11. Newcastle United	38	10	4	5	26	17	4	5	10	18	33	51
12. Tottenham Hotspur	38	11	6	2	31	16	2	4	13	16	38	49
13. Leicester City	38	10	4	5	28	23	4	2	13	11	28	48
14. Middlesbrough	38	4	7	8	18	23	5	8	6	26	21	42
15. West Ham United	38	6	6	7	24	20	4	6	9	21	30	42
16. Everton	38	6	8	5	29	27	5	1	13	16	32	42
17. Derby County	38	8	7	4	23	24	2	5	12	14	35	42
18. Manchester City	38	4	3	12	20	31	4	7	8	21	34	34
19. Coventry City	38	4	7	8	14	23	4	3	12	22	40	34
20. Bradford City	38	4	7	8	20	29	1	4	14	10	41	26

Season 2001–02
BARCLAYCARD PREMIERSHIP

	P	W	D	L	F	A	Pts
Home	19	11	2	6	40	17	35
Away	19	13	3	3	47	28	42
Total	38	24	5	9	87	45	77

Final position: third
FA Cup: fourth round
League Cup: third round
UEFA Champions League: semi-final

Season 2002–03
BARCLAYCARD PREMIERSHIP

	P	W	D	L	F	A	Pts
Home	19	16	2	1	42	12	50
Away	19	9	6	4	32	22	33
Total	38	25	8	5	74	34	83

Final position: champions
FA Cup: fifth round
League Cup: finalists
UEFA Champions League: quarter-final

2002–03 BARCLAYCARD PREMIERSHIP

	P	W	D	L	F	A	W	D	L	F	A	Pts
		Home					Away					
1. **Manchester United**	38	16	2	1	42	12	9	6	4	32	22	83
2. Arsenal	38	15	2	2	47	20	8	7	4	38	22	78
3. Newcastle United	38	15	2	2	36	17	6	4	9	27	31	69
4. Chelsea	38	12	5	2	41	15	7	5	7	27	23	67
5. Liverpool	38	9	8	2	30	16	9	2	8	31	25	64
6. Blackburn Rovers	38	9	7	3	24	15	7	5	7	28	28	60
7. Everton	38	11	5	3	28	19	6	3	10	20	30	59
8. Southampton	38	9	8	2	25	16	4	5	10	18	30	52
9. Manchester City	38	9	2	8	28	26	6	4	9	19	28	51
10. Tottenham Hotspur	38	9	4	6	30	29	5	4	10	21	33	50
11. Middlesbrough	38	10	7	2	36	21	3	3	13	12	23	49
12. Charlton Athletic	38	8	3	8	26	30	6	4	9	19	26	49
13. Birmingham City	38	8	5	6	25	23	5	4	10	16	26	48
14. Fulham	38	11	3	5	26	18	2	6	11	15	32	48
15. Leeds United	38	7	3	9	25	26	7	2	10	33	31	47
16. Aston Villa	38	11	2	6	25	14	1	7	11	17	33	45
17. Bolton Wanderers	38	7	8	4	27	24	3	6	10	14	27	44
18. West Ham United	38	5	7	7	21	24	5	5	9	21	35	42
19. West Bromwich Albion	38	3	5	11	17	34	3	3	13	12	31	26
20. Sunderland	38	3	2	14	11	31	1	5	13	10	34	19

Season 2003–04
BARCLAYCARD PREMIERSHIP

	P	W	D	L	F	A	Pts
Home	19	12	4	3	37	15	40
Away	19	11	2	6	27	20	35
Total	38	23	6	9	64	35	75

Final position: third
FA Cup: winners
League Cup: fourth round
UEFA Champions League: first knock-out phase
FA Community Shield: winners

Season 2004–05
BARCLAYS PREMIERSHIP

	P	W	D	L	F	A	Pts
Home	19	12	6	1	31	12	42
Away	19	10	5	4	27	14	35
Total	38	22	11	5	58	26	77

Final position: third
FA Cup: finalists
League Cup: semi-final
UEFA Champions League: first knock-out phase

Season 2005–06
BARCLAYS PREMIERSHIP

	P	W	D	L	F	A	Pts
Home	19	13	5	1	37	8	44
Away	19	12	3	4	35	26	39
Total	38	25	8	5	72	34	83

Final position: runners-up
FA Cup: fifth round
League Cup: winners
UEFA Champions League: first group phase

Season 2006–07
BARCLAYS PREMIERSHIP

	P	W	D	L	F	A	Pts
Home	19	15	2	2	46	12	47
Away	19	13	3	3	37	15	42
Total	38	28	5	5	83	27	89

Final position: champions
FA Cup: finalists
League Cup: fourth round
UEFA Champions League: semi-final

2006-07 BARCLAYS PREMIERSHIP

		Home					Away					
	P	W	D	L	F	A	W	D	L	F	A	Pts
1. **Manchester United**	38	15	2	2	46	12	13	3	3	37	15	89
2. Chelsea	38	12	7	0	37	11	12	4	3	27	13	83
3. Liverpool	38	14	4	1	39	7	6	4	9	18	20	68
4. Arsenal	38	12	6	1	43	16	7	5	7	20	19	68
5. Tottenham Hotspur	38	12	3	4	34	22	5	6	8	23	32	60
6. Everton	38	11	4	4	33	17	4	9	6	19	19	58
7. Bolton Wanderers	38	9	5	5	26	20	7	3	9	21	32	56
8. Reading	38	11	2	6	29	20	5	5	9	23	27	55
9. Portsmouth	38	11	5	3	28	15	3	7	9	17	27	54
10. Blackburn Rovers	38	9	3	7	31	25	6	4	9	21	29	52
11. Aston Villa	38	7	8	4	20	14	4	9	6	23	27	50
12. Middlesbrough	38	10	3	6	31	24	2	7	10	13	25	46
13. Newcastle United	38	7	7	5	23	20	4	3	12	15	27	43
14. Manchester City	38	5	6	8	10	16	6	3	10	19	28	42
15. West Ham United	38	8	2	9	24	26	4	3	12	11	33	41
16. Fulham	38	7	7	5	18	18	1	8	10	20	42	39
17. Wigan Athletic	38	5	4	10	18	30	5	4	10	19	29	38
18. Sheffield United	38	7	6	6	24	21	3	2	14	8	34	38
19. Charlton Athletic	38	7	5	7	19	20	1	5	13	15	40	34
20. Watford	38	3	9	7	19	25	2	4	13	10	34	28

Season 2007–08
BARCLAYS PREMIER LEAGUE

	P	W	D	L	F	A	Pts
Home	19	17	1	1	47	7	52
Away	19	10	5	4	33	15	35
Total	38	27	6	5	80	22	87

Final position: champions

FA Cup: sixth round

League Cup: third round

UEFA Champions League: winners

FA Community Shield: winners

2007–08 BARCLAYS PREMIER LEAGUE

		Home					Away					
	P	W	D	L	F	A	W	D	L	F	A	Pts
1. **Manchester United**	38	17	1	1	47	7	10	5	4	33	15	87
2. Chelsea	38	12	7	0	36	13	13	3	3	29	13	85
3. Arsenal	38	14	5	0	37	11	10	6	3	37	20	83
4. Liverpool	38	12	6	1	43	13	9	7	3	24	15	76
5. Everton	38	11	4	4	34	17	8	4	7	21	16	65
6. Aston Villa	38	10	3	6	34	22	6	9	4	37	29	60
7. Blackburn Rovers	38	8	7	4	26	19	7	6	6	24	29	58
8. Portsmouth	38	7	8	4	24	14	9	1	9	24	26	57
9. Manchester City	38	11	4	4	28	20	4	6	9	17	33	55
10. West Ham United	38	7	7	5	24	24	6	3	10	18	26	49
11. Tottenham Hotspur	38	8	5	6	46	34	3	8	8	20	27	46
12. Newcastle United	38	8	5	6	25	26	3	5	11	20	39	43
13. Middlesbrough	38	7	5	7	27	23	3	7	9	16	30	42
14. Wigan Athletic	38	8	5	6	21	17	2	5	12	13	34	40
15. Sunderland	38	9	3	7	23	21	2	3	14	13	38	39
16. Bolton Wanderers	38	7	5	7	23	18	2	5	12	13	36	37
17. Fulham	38	5	5	9	22	31	3	7	9	16	29	36
18. Reading	38	8	2	9	19	25	2	4	13	22	41	36
19. Birmingham City	38	6	8	5	30	23	2	3	14	16	39	35
20. Derby County	38	1	5	13	12	43	0	3	16	8	46	11

Season 2008–09
BARCLAYS PREMIER LEAGUE

	P	W	D	L	F	A	Pts
Home	19	16	2	1	43	13	50
Away	19	12	4	3	25	11	40
Total	38	28	6	4	68	24	90

Final position: champions
FA Cup: semi-final
League Cup: winners
UEFA Champions League: finalists
FIFA Club World Cup: winners
FA Community Shield: winners

2008–09 BARCLAYS PREMIER LEAGUE

		Home					Away					
	P	W	D	L	F	A	W	D	L	F	A	Pts
1. **Manchester United**	38	16	2	1	43	13	12	4	3	25	11	90
2. Liverpool	38	12	7	0	41	13	13	4	2	36	14	86
3. Chelsea	38	11	6	2	33	12	14	2	3	35	12	83
4. Arsenal	38	11	5	3	31	16	9	7	3	37	21	72
5. Everton	38	8	6	5	31	20	9	6	4	24	17	63
6. Aston Villa	38	7	9	3	27	21	10	2	7	27	27	62
7. Fulham	38	11	3	5	28	16	3	8	8	11	18	53
8. Tottenham Hotspur	38	10	5	4	21	10	4	4	11	24	35	51
9. West Ham United	38	9	2	8	23	22	5	7	7	19	23	51
10. Manchester City	38	13	0	6	40	18	2	5	12	18	32	50
11. Wigan Athletic	38	8	5	6	17	18	4	4	11	17	27	45
12. Stoke City	38	10	5	4	22	15	2	4	13	16	40	45
13. Bolton Wanderers	38	7	5	7	21	21	4	3	12	20	32	41
14. Portsmouth	38	8	3	8	26	29	2	8	9	12	28	41
15. Blackburn Rovers	38	6	7	6	22	23	4	4	11	18	37	41
16. Sunderland	38	6	3	10	21	25	3	6	10	13	29	36
17. Hull City	38	3	5	11	18	36	5	6	8	21	28	35
18. Newcastle United	38	5	7	7	24	29	2	6	11	16	30	34
19. Middlesbrough	38	5	9	5	17	20	2	2	15	11	37	32
20. West Bromwich Albion	38	7	3	9	26	33	1	5	13	10	34	32

Season 2009–10
BARCLAYS PREMIER LEAGUE

	P	W	D	L	F	A	Pts
Home	19	16	1	2	52	12	49
Away	19	11	3	5	34	16	36
Total	38	27	4	7	86	28	85

Final position: runners-up
FA Cup: third round
League Cup: winners
UEFA Champions League: quarter-final

Season 2010–11
BARCLAYS PREMIER LEAGUE

	P	W	D	L	F	A	Pts
Home	19	18	1	0	49	12	55
Away	19	5	10	4	29	25	25
Total	38	23	11	4	78	37	80

Final position: champions
FA Cup: semi-final
League Cup: fifth round
UEFA Champions League: finalists
FA Community Shield: winners

2010-11 BARCLAYS PREMIER LEAGUE

	P		Home					Away				Pts
		W	D	L	F	A	W	D	L	F	A	
1. **Manchester United**	38	18	1	0	49	12	5	10	4	29	25	80
2. Chelsea	38	14	3	2	39	13	7	5	7	30	20	71
3. Manchester City	38	13	4	2	34	12	8	4	7	26	21	71
4. Arsenal	38	11	4	4	33	15	8	7	4	39	28	68
5. Tottenham Hotspur	38	9	9	1	30	19	7	5	7	25	27	62
6. Liverpool	38	12	4	3	37	14	5	3	11	22	30	58
7. Everton	38	9	7	3	31	23	4	8	7	20	22	54
8. Fulham	38	8	7	4	30	23	3	9	7	19	20	49
9. Aston Villa	38	8	7	4	26	19	4	5	10	22	40	48
10. Sunderland	38	7	5	7	25	27	5	6	8	20	29	47
11. West Bromwich Albion	38	8	6	5	30	30	4	5	10	26	41	47
12. Newcastle United	38	6	8	5	41	27	5	5	9	15	30	46
13. Stoke City	38	10	4	5	31	18	3	3	13	15	30	46
14. Bolton Wanderers	38	10	5	4	34	24	2	5	12	18	32	46
15. Blackburn Rovers	38	7	7	5	22	16	4	3	12	24	43	43
16. Wigan Athletic	38	5	8	6	22	34	4	7	8	18	27	42
17. Wolverhampton Wand.	38	8	4	7	30	30	3	3	13	16	36	40
18. Birmingham City	38	6	8	5	19	22	2	7	10	18	36	39
19. Blackpool	38	5	5	9	30	37	5	4	10	25	41	39
20. West Ham United	38	5	5	9	24	31	2	7	10	19	39	33

Season 2011-12
BARCLAYS PREMIER LEAGUE

	P	W	D	L	F	A	Pts
Home	19	15	2	2	52	19	47
Away	19	13	3	3	37	14	42
Total	38	28	5	5	89	33	89

Final position: runners-up

FA Cup: fourth round

League Cup: fifth round

UEFA Champions League: first group phase

UEFA Europa League: second knock-out phase

FA Community Shield: winners

Season 2012–13
BARCLAYS PREMIER LEAGUE

	P	W	D	L	F	A	Pts
Home	19	16	0	3	45	19	48
Away	19	12	5	2	41	24	41
Total	38	28	5	5	86	43	89

Final position: champions

FA Cup: sixth round

League Cup: fourth round

UEFA Champions League: first knock-out phase

2012–13 BARCLAYS PREMIER LEAGUE

		Home					Away					
	P	W	D	L	F	A	W	D	L	F	A	Pts
1. **Manchester United**	38	16	0	3	45	19	12	5	2	41	24	89
2. Manchester City	38	14	3	2	41	15	9	6	4	25	19	78
3. Chelsea	38	12	5	2	41	16	10	4	5	34	23	75
4. Arsenal	38	11	5	3	47	23	10	5	4	25	14	73
5. Tottenham Hotspur	38	11	5	3	29	18	10	4	5	37	28	72
6. Everton	38	12	6	1	33	17	4	9	6	22	23	63
7. Liverpool	38	9	6	4	33	16	7	7	5	38	27	61
8. West Bromwich Albion	38	9	4	6	32	25	5	3	11	21	32	49
9. Swansea City	38	6	8	5	28	26	5	5	9	19	25	46
10. West Ham United	38	9	6	4	34	22	3	4	12	11	31	46
11. Norwich City	38	8	7	4	25	20	2	7	10	16	38	44
12. Fulham	38	7	3	9	28	30	4	7	8	22	30	43
13. Stoke City	38	7	7	5	21	22	2	8	9	13	23	42
14. Southampton	38	6	7	6	26	24	3	7	9	23	36	41
15. Aston Villa	38	5	5	9	23	28	5	6	8	24	41	41
16. Newcastle United	38	9	1	9	24	31	2	7	10	21	37	41
17. Sunderland	38	5	8	6	20	19	4	4	11	21	35	39
18. Wigan Athletic	38	4	6	9	26	39	5	3	11	21	34	36
19. Reading	38	4	8	7	23	33	2	2	15	20	40	28
20. Queens Park Rangers	38	2	8	9	13	28	2	5	12	17	32	25

SUMMARY

Home	P	W	D	L	F	A	Pts
League	517	370	95	52	1098	354	1205
FA Cup	53	38	9	6	105	35	
Europe	109	70	27	12	238	95	
League Cup	44	36	3	5	95	40	
Super Cup	1	1	0	0	1	0	
Total	724	515	134	75	1537	524	

Away	P	W	D	L	F	A	Pts
League	518	255	143	120	848	576	908
FA Cup	67	42	13	12	125	58	
Europe	114	49	33	32	142	108	
League Cup	53	26	7	20	83	67	
FIFA CWC	5	3	1	1	10	7	
IC	1	1	0	0	1	0	
Super Cup	2	0	0	2	1	3	
C. Shield	16	4	7	5	22	22	
Total	776	380	204	192	1232	841	
Overall total	1500	895	338	267	2769	1365	2113

FIFA CWC – FIFA Club World Cup

IC – Intercontinental Cup

Super Cup – UEFA Super Cup

Matches at neutral venues are included as away games

MANCHESTER UNITED IN GLOBAL TOURNAMENTS DURING ALEX FERGUSON'S MANAGERSHIP

Season 1999–2000 Intercontinental Cup
(Tokyo, Japan) SE Palmeiras (Brazil) 1–0

FIFA Club World Championship
Group stage (Rio de Janeiro, Brazil) Club Necaxa (Mexico) 1–1, CR
Vasco da Gama (Brazil) 1–3, South Melbourne (Australia) 2–0 (Finished third in group)

Season 2008–09 FIFA Club World Cup
Semi-final (Yokohama, Japan) Gamba Osaka (Japan) 5–3
Final (Yokohama) LDU Quito (Ecuador) 1–0

MANCHESTER UNITED'S EUROPEAN CAMPAIGNS DURING ALEX FERGUSON'S MANAGERSHIP

Season 1990–91 Cup Winners' Cup
Round 1 Pécsi Munkás (Hungary) (h) 2–0, (a) 1–0, Agg: 3–0
Round 2 Wrexham (h) 3–0, (a) 2–0, Agg: 5–0
Quarter-final Montpellier (France) (h) 1–1, (a) 2–0, Agg: 3–1
Semi-final Legia Warsaw (Poland) (a) 3–1, (h) 1–1, Agg: 4–2
Final (Rotterdam, Netherlands) Barcelona (Spain) 2–1

Season 1991–92 UEFA Super Cup
Red Star Belgrade (Yugoslavia) (h) 1–0

Cup Winners' Cup
Round 1 Athinaikos (Greece) (a) 0–0, (h) 2–0 (aet), Agg: 2–0
Round 2 Atlético Madrid (Spain) (a) 0–3, (h) 1–1, Agg: 1–4

Season 1992–93 UEFA Cup
Round 1 Torpedo Moscow (Russia) (h) 0–0, (a) 0–0, Agg: 0–0 (Lost 4–3 on penalties)

Season 1993–94 UEFA Champions League
Round 1 Kispest Honvéd (Hungary) (a) 3–2, (h) 2–1, Agg: 5–3
Round 2 Galatasaray (Turkey) (h) 3–3, (a) 0–0, Agg: 3–3 (Lost on away-goals rule)

Season 1994–95 UEFA Champions League
Group phase IFK Gothenburg (Sweden) (h) 4–2, Galatasaray (Turkey) (a) 0–0, Barcelona (Spain) (h) 2–2, Barcelona (a) 0–4, IFK Gothenburg (a) 1–3, Galatasaray (h) 4–0 (Finished third in group)

Season 1995–96 UEFA Cup
Round 2 Rotor Volgograd (Russia) (a) 0–0, (h) 2–2 (Lost on away-goals rule)

Season 1996–97 UEFA Champions League
Group phase Juventus (Italy) (a) 0–1, Rapid Vienna (Austria) (h) 2–0, Fenerbahçe (Turkey) (a) 2–0, Fenerbahçe (h) 0–1, Juventus (h) 0–1, Rapid Vienna (a) 2–0 (Finished second in group)
Quarter-final Porto (Portugal) (h) 4–0, (a) 0–0, Agg: 4–0
Semi-final Borussia Dortmund (Germany) (a) 0–1, (h) 0–1, Agg: 0–2

Season 1997–98 UEFA Champions League
Group phase Košice (Slovakia) (a) 3–0, Juventus (Italy) (h) 3–2, Feyenoord (Netherlands) (h) 2–1, Feyenoord (a) 3–1, Košice (h) 3–0, Juventus (a) 0–1 (Finished second in group)
Quarter-final Monaco (France) (a) 0–0, (h) 1–1 (Lost on away-goals rule)

Season 1998–99 UEFA Champions League
Qualifying round 2 ŁKS Łódź (Poland) (h) 2–0, (a) 0–0, Agg: 2–0
Group phase Barcelona (Spain) (h) 3–3, Bayern Munich (Germany) (a) 2–2, Brøndby (Denmark) (a) 6–2, Brøndby (h) 5–0, Barcelona (a) 3–3, Bayern Munich (h) 1–1 (Finished second in group)
Quarter-final Internazionale (Italy) (h) 2–0, (a) 1–1, Agg: 3–1
Semi-final Juventus (Italy) (h) 1–1, (a) 3–2, Agg: 4–3
Final (Barcelona, Spain) Bayern Munich 2–1

Season 1999–2000 UEFA Super Cup
(Monaco, France) Lazio (Italy) 0–1

UEFA Champions League
First group phase Croatia Zagreb (Croatia) (h) 0–0, Sturm Graz (Austria) (a) 3–0, Marseille (France) (h) 2–1, Marseille (a) 0–1, Croatia Zagreb (a) 2–1, Sturm Graz (h) 2–1 (Finished first in group)
Second group phase Fiorentina (Italy) (a) 0–2, Valencia (Spain) (h) 3–0, Bordeaux (France) (h) 2–0, Bordeaux (a) 2–1, Fiorentina (h) 3–1, Valencia (a) 0–0 (Finished first in group)
Quarter-final Real Madrid (Spain) (a) 0–0, (h) 2–3, Agg: 2–3

Season 2000–01 UEFA Champions League
First group phase Anderlecht (Belgium) (h) 5–1, Dynamo Kiev (Ukraine) (a) 0–0, PSV Eindhoven (Netherlands) (a) 1–3, PSV Eindhoven (h) 3–1, Anderlecht (a) 1–2, Dynamo Kiev (h) 1–0 (Finished second in group)
Second group phase Panathinaikos (Greece) (h) 3–1, Sturm Graz (Austria) (a) 2–0, Valencia (Spain) (a) 0–0, Valencia (h) 1–1, Panathinaikos (a) 1–1, Sturm Graz (h) 3–0 (Finished second in group)
Quarter-final Bayern Munich (Germany) (h) 0–1, (a) 1–2, Agg: 1–3

Season 2001–02 UEFA Champions League
First group phase Lille (France) (h) 1–0, Deportivo La Coruña (Spain) (a) 1–2, Olympiacos (Greece) (a) 2–0, Deportivo La Coruña (h) 2–3, Olympiacos (h) 3–0, Lille (a) 1–1 (Finished second in group)
Second group phase Bayern Munich (Germany) (a) 1–1, Boavista (Portugal) (h) 3–0, Nantes (France) (a) 1–1, Nantes (h) 5–1, Bayern Munich (h) 0–0, Boavista (a) 3–0 (Finished first in group)
Quarter-final Deportivo La Coruña (a) 2–0, (h) 3–2, Agg: 5–2
Semi-final Bayer Leverkusen (Germany) (h) 2–2, (a) 1–1, Agg: 3–3 (Lost on away-goals rule)

Season 2002–03 UEFA Champions League

Qualifying round 3 Zalaegerszegi TE (Hungary) (a) 0–1, (h) 5–0, Agg: 5–1

First group phase Maccabi Haifa (Israel) (h) 5–2, Bayer Leverkusen (Germany) (a) 2–1, Olympiacos (Greece) (h) 4–0, Olympiacos (a) 3–2, Maccabi Haifa (a) 0–3, Bayer Leverkusen (h) 2–0 (Finished first in group)

Second group phase Basel (Switzerland) (a) 3–1, Deportivo La Coruña (Spain) (h) 2–0, Juventus (Italy) (h) 2–1, Juventus (a) 3–0, Basel (h) 1–1, Deportivo La Coruña (a) 0–2 (Finished first in group)

Quarter-final Real Madrid (Spain) (a) 1–3, (h) 4–3, Agg: 5–6

Season 2003–04 UEFA Champions League

Group phase Panathinaikos (Greece) (h) 5–0, VfB Stuttgart (Germany) (a) 1–2, Rangers (a) 1–0, Rangers (h) 3–0, Panathinaikos (a) 1–0, VfB Stuttgart (h) 2–0 (Finished first in group)

Quarter-final Porto (Portugal) (a) 1–2, (h) 1–1, Agg: 2–3

Season 2004–05 UEFA Champions League

Qualifying round 3 Dinamo Bucharest (Romania) (a) 2–1, (h) 3–0, Agg: 5–1

Group phase Lyon (France) (a) 2–2, Fenerbahçe (Turkey) (h) 6–2, Sparta Prague (Czech Republic) (a) 0–0, Sparta Prague (h) 4–1, Lyon (h) 2–1, Fenerbahçe (a) 0–3 (Finished second in group)

First knock-out round AC Milan (Italy) (h) 0–1, (a) 0–1, Agg: 0–2

Season 2005–06 UEFA Champions League

Qualifying round 3 Debrecen (Hungary) (h) 3–0, (a) 3–0, Agg: 6–0

Group phase Villarreal (Spain) (a) 0–0, Benfica (Portugal) (h) 2–1, Lille (France) (h) 0–0, Lille (a) 0–1, Villarreal (h) 0–0, Benfica (a) 1–2 (Finished fourth in group)

Season 2006–07 UEFA Champions League

Group phase Celtic (h) 3–2, Benfica (Portugal) (a) 1–0, FC Copenhagen (Denmark) (h) 3–0, FC Copenhagen (a) 0–1, Celtic (a) 0–1, Benfica

(h) 3–1 (Finished first in group)
First knock-out round Lille (France) (a) 1–0, Lille (h) 1–0, Agg: 2–0
Quarter-final Roma (Italy) (a) 1–2, (h) 7–1, Agg: 8–3
Semi-final AC Milan (Italy) (h) 3–2, (a) 0–3, Agg: 3–5

Season 2007–08 UEFA Champions League
Group phase Sporting Lisbon (Portugal) (a) 1–0, Roma (Italy) (h) 1–0,
Dynamo Kiev (Ukraine) (a) 4–2, Dynamo Kiev (h) 4–0, Sporting Lisbon
(h) 2–1, Roma (Italy) (a) 1–1 (Finished first in group)
First knock-out round Lyon (France) (a) 1–1, (h) 1–0, Agg: 2–1
Quarter-final Roma (Italy) (a) 2–0, (h) 1–0, Agg: 3–0
Semi-final Barcelona (Spain) (a) 0–0, (h) 1–0, Agg: 1–0
Final (Moscow, Russia) Chelsea 1–1 (Won 6–5 on penalties)

Season 2008–09 UEFA Champions League
Group phase Villarreal (Spain) (h) 0–0, Aalborg BK (Denmark) (a)
3–0, Celtic (h) 3–0, Celtic (a) 1–1, Villarreal (a) 0–0, Aalborg BK (h)
2–2 (Finished first in group)
First knock-out round Internazionale (Italy) (a) 0–0, (h) 2–0, Agg: 2–0
Quarter-final Porto (Portugal) (h) 2–2, (a) 1–0, Agg: 3–2
Semi-final Arsenal (h) 1–0, (a) 3–1, Agg: 4–1
Final (Rome, Italy) Barcelona (Spain) 0–2

Season 2009–10 UEFA Champions League
Group phase Beşiktaş (Turkey) (a) 1–0, VfL Wolfsburg (Germany) (h)
2–1, CSKA Moscow (Russia) (a) 1–0, CSKA Moscow (h) 3–3, Beşiktaş
(h) 0–1, VfL Wolfsburg (a) 3–1 (Finished first in group)
First knock-out round AC Milan (Italy) (a) 3–2, (h) 4–0, Agg: 7–2
Quarter-final Bayern Munich (Germany) (a) 1–2, (h) 3–2, Agg: 4–4
(Lost on away-goals rule)

Season 2010–11 UEFA Champions League
Group phase Rangers (h) 0–0, Valencia (Spain) (a) 1–0, Bursaspor
(Turkey) (h) 1–0, Bursaspor (a) 3–0, Rangers (a) 1–0, Valencia (h) 1–1
(Finished first in group)

First knock-out round Marseille (France) (a) 0–0, (h) 2–1, Agg: 2–1
Quarter-final Chelsea (a) 1–0, (h) 2–1, Agg: 3–1
Semi-final Schalke 04 (Germany) (a) 2–0, (h) 4–1, Agg: 6–1
Final (Wembley) Barcelona (Spain) 1–3

Season 2011–12 UEFA Champions League
Group phase Benfica (Portugal) (a) 1–1, Basel (Switzerland) (h) 3–3, Oţelul Galaţi (Romania) (a) 2–0, Oţelul Galaţi (h) 2–0, Benfica (h) 2–2, Basel (a) 1–2 (Finished third in group)

UEFA Europa League
Round of 32 Ajax (Netherlands) (a) 2–0, (h) 1–2, Agg: 3–2
Round of 16 Athletic Bilbao (Spain) (h) 2–3, (a) 1–2, Agg: 3–5

Season 2012–13 UEFA Champions League
Group phase Galatasaray (Turkey) (h) 1–0, CFR Cluj (Romania) (a) 2–1, Braga (Portugal) (h) 3–2, Braga (a) 3–1, Galatasaray (a) 0–1, CFR Cluj (h) 0–1 (Finished first in group)
Round of 16 Real Madrid (Spain) (a) 1–1, (h) 1–2, Agg: 2–3

HONOURS

EUROPEAN CHAMPION CLUBS' CUP/UEFA CHAMPIONS LEAGUE

Winners: 1999, 2008
Finalists: 2009, 2011

EUROPEAN CUP WINNERS' CUP

Winners: 1991

FA PREMIER LEAGUE

Champions: 1993, 1994, 1996, 1997, 1999, 2000, 2001, 2003, 2007, 2008, 2009, 2011, 2013
Runners-up: 1995, 1998, 2006, 2010, 2012

FA CUP

Winners: 1990, 1994, 1996, 1999, 2004
Finalists: 1995, 2005, 2007

FOOTBALL LEAGUE CUP

Winners: 1992, 2006, 2009, 2010
Finalists: 1991, 1994, 2003

INTERCONTINENTAL CUP

Winners: 1999

FIFA CLUB WORLD CUP

Winners: 2008

EUROPEAN SUPER CUP

Winners: 1991

FA CHARITY/COMMUNITY SHIELD

Winners: 1993, 1994, 1996, 1997, 2003, 2007, 2008, 2010, 2011
Joint winners (with Liverpool): 1990.

MANCHESTER UNITED PLAYERS UNDER ALEX FERGUSON

Listed here is the name of every player to appear in a senior competitive fixture for Manchester United during Alex Ferguson's time as manager, up to the end of season 2012–13

Albiston, Arthur
Amos, Ben
Anderson
Anderson, Viv
Appleton, Michael
Bailey, Gary
Bardsley, Phil
Barnes, Michael
Barnes, Peter
Barthez, Fabien
Beardsmore, Russell
Bébé
Beckham, David
Bellion, David
Berbatov, Dimitar
Berg, Henning
Blackmore, Clayton
Blanc, Laurent
Blomqvist, Jesper
Bosnich, Mark
Brady, Robbie
Brazil, Derek
Brown, Wes
Bruce, Steve
Butt, Nicky
Büttner, Alexander
Campbell, Fraizer
Cantona, Eric
Carrick, Michael
Carroll, Roy
Casper, Chris

Chadwick, Luke
Chester, James
Clegg, Michael
Cleverley, Tom
Cole, Andy
Cole, Larnell
Cooke, Terry
Cruyff, Jordi
Culkin, Nick
Curtis, John
Davenport, Peter
Davies, Simon
Davis, Jimmy
Diouf, Mame Biram
Djemba-Djemba, Eric
Djordjic, Bojan
Donaghy, Mal
Dong, Fangzhuo
Dublin, Dion
Duxbury, Mike
Eagles, Chris
Ebanks-Blake, Sylvan
Eckersley, Adam
Eckersley, Richard
Evans, Jonny
Evra, Patrice
Ferdinand, Rio
Ferguson, Darren
Fletcher, Darren
Forlán, Diego
Fortune, Quinton

Foster, Ben
Fryers, Zeki
Garton, Billy
Gea, David de
Gibson, Colin
Gibson, Darron
Gibson, Terry
Giggs, Ryan
Gill, Tony
Gillespie, Keith
Goram, Andy
Gouw, Raimond van der
Graham, Deiniol
Gray, David
Greening, Jonathan
Hargreaves, Owen
Healy, David
Heinze, Gabriel
Hernández, Javier
Higginbotham, Danny
Hogg, Graeme
Howard, Tim
Hughes, Mark
Ince, Paul
Irwin, Denis
Johnsen, Ronny
Johnson, Eddie
Jones, David
Jones, Phil
Jones, Ritchie
Kagawa, Shinji
Kanchelskis, Andrei
Keane, Michael
Keane, Roy
Keane, Will
King, Joshua
Kléberson
Kuszczak, Tomasz

Laet, Ritchie de
Larsson, Henrik
Lee, Kieran
Leighton, Jim
Lindegaard, Anders
Lynch, Mark
McClair, Brian
McGibbon, Patrick
McGrath, Paul
Macheda, Federico
McKee, Colin
Maiorana, Giuliano
Manucho
Marsh, Phil
Martin, Lee A.
Martin, Lee R.
May, David
Miller, Liam
Milne, Ralph
Moran, Kevin
Morrison, Ravel
Moses, Remi
Mulryne, Philip
Nani
Nardiello, Daniel
Neville, Gary
Neville, Phil
Nevland, Erik
Nistelrooy, Ruud van
Notman, Alex
Obertan, Gabriel
O'Brien, Liam
O'Kane, John
Olsen, Jesper
O'Shea, John
Owen, Michael
Pallister, Gary
Park, Ji-Sung

Parker, Paul
Persie, Robin van
Phelan, Mick
Pilkington, Kevin
Piqué, Gérard
Poborský, Karel
Pogba, Paul
Possebon, Rodrigo
Powell, Nick
Prunier, William
Pugh, Danny
Rachubka, Paul
Ricardo
Richardson, Kieran
Robins, Mark
Robson, Bryan
Roche, Lee
Ronaldo, Cristiano
Rooney, Wayne
Rossi, Giuseppe
Saha, Louis
Sar, Edwin van der
Schmeichel, Peter
Scholes, Paul
Sealey, Les
Sharpe, Lee
Shawcross, Ryan
Sheringham, Teddy
Silva, Fábio da
Silva, Rafael da
Silvestre, Mikaël
Simpson, Danny
Sivebaek, John
Smalling, Chris
Smith, Alan
Solskjaer, Ole Gunnar

Spector, Jonathan
Stam, Jaap
Stapleton, Frank
Stewart, Michael
Strachan, Gordon
Taibi, Massimo
Tévez, Carlos
Thornley, Ben
Tierney, Paul
Timm, Mads
Tomlinson, Graeme
Tosic, Zoran
Tunnicliffe, Ryan
Turner, Chris
Twiss, Michael
Valencia, Antonio
Vermijl, Marnick
Verón, Juan Sebastián
Vidić, Nemanja
Wallace, Danny
Wallwork, Ronnie
Walsh, Gary
Webb, Neil
Webber, Danny
Welbeck, Danny
Wellens, Richie
Whiteside, Norman
Whitworth, Neil
Wilkinson, Ian
Wilson, David
Wilson, Mark
Wood, Nicky
Wootton, Scott
Wratten, Paul
Yorke, Dwight
Young, Ashley

INDEX